BETTER THAN NOSTRADAMUS

OR

THE SECRETIVE WORLD TAKEOVER

Commenced Writing 24.4.95
Finished Writing 30.10.96

BY

BARRY R. SMITH

First published by:
INTERNATIONAL SUPPORT MINISTRIES
Pelorus Bridge
Rai Valley R.D.2
Marlborough, New Zealand

Printed by Griffin Press, Australia

ACKNOWLEDGMENTS

With grateful thanks I dedicate this book to two dear friends, Hudson and Joan Salisbury.

Without their assistance at a very critical time in my life, this book would not be in existence as its author would have "gone home".

As one who day by day recognises the fragile nature of life, I encourage you both to keep listening to directions from the "still, small, voice". **There is yet more work to be done!**

My family and I love you and thank you.

To Nic Venter, our friend and South African agent, we thank you for the great art work. It is very much appreciated.

To our eldest daughter, Becky Capell, for her patience with an author who always had "that little bit extra" to add to the manuscript. Love and thanks, Dad.

Hudson and Joan Salisbury

CONTENTS

Chapter One   Now Will You Listen? Suspended U.S.
Constitution 1

Chapter Two   Nostradamus 9

Chapter Three   A Mirror from the Past 13

Chapter Four   The History of the Seals 15

Chapter Five   A Detailed Description of the Meaning of the
Seals 27

Chapter Six   The Palladium 33

Chapter Seven   What is a Freemason? Is Lucifer Satan? 37

Chapter Eight   A Mason Reveals All - the Coup de Grace 47

Chapter Nine   The Mystery Revealed - Secret Teachings 60

Chapter Ten   The Occult Nature of the Seals on the U.S.
$1 Bill 63

Chapter Eleven   A Strange Phenomena 74

Chapter Twelve   The Announcement 77

Chapter Thirteen   Setting Up the New World Order - Operation
Desert Storm 81

Chapter Fourteen   The Task to Hand - Try Out the Plan 87

Chapter Fifteen   The Plan - Remove Politicians' Power and
Authority 90

Chapter Sixteen   The Conditions 95

Chapter Seventeen   Conditionalities - World-wide Illustrations .. 103

Chapter Eighteen   Exporting the Plan 113

Chapter Nineteen   Full Speed Ahead for Continual Change 126

Chapter Twenty   A Matter of Sovereignty 131

Chapter Twenty one   The U.S. Role in the New World Order 143

Chapter Twenty two   Setting the Stage for Strong World Leader .. 151

Chapter Twenty three   Who Is He? 158

Chapter Twenty four   Farewell to Cash - Update 175

Chapter Twenty five   Global 2000 - What Fun 180

Chapter Twenty six   Chaos 2000 181

Chapter Twenty seven   The Report From Iron Mountain 185

Chapter Twenty eight   Hi Mother Earth 202

Chapter Twenty nine   Israel – The Geographical Centre 209

Chapter Thirty   An Interesting Calculation 222

Chapter Thirty one   Health, Healing, and Population Control 224

Chapter Thirty two   Religion Versus Relationship 227

Chapter Thirty three   Wake Up in Heaven 236

Chapter Thirty four   Death – The Ultimate Experience 250

Chapter Thirty five   The Cross – The Invitation 259

Glossary 267

PREFACE

Any investigative reporter attempting to do what this author has done, would of necessity require five or more qualifications.

1. He would need to be either a New Zealand citizen, or one who lived in that country during the 1980's and 1990's.

2. He would need to be a serious news-watcher.

3. He would need to be a world traveller.

4. He would require a detailed knowledge of the ancient prophecies.

5. To pass on this knowledge publicly, he would require a concise and clear lecturing ability and would also need to be able to outline events in a logical, consecutive manner, thus making seemingly obscure events clear, to even a non-intellectual reader.

6. A facetious comment regarding a biography, written by a brilliant New Zealand politician, read like this -

    "This is the sort of book that once you have put it down, you can't pick it up."

    We, who send this book out, guarantee that in this case, the very opposite will apply.

7. Readers from every country will **ultimately** identify with this book. Although **the plan** commenced with New Zealand, this is now a **global problem**.

The author is Barry Smith - **"the man the media try to disprove"**.

"Just because up to this point, you have not heard about it, does not in any way imply that it is not taking place." (P. Aristarchus)

FOREWORD

Date: 19th April 1995
British Airways, flight 999 in conjunction with Qantas.

I stacked a pile of airline pillows and placed my own personal pillow on top. It was a blessing that any frequent airline passenger would relish. A whole central row of seats in the "peasants' class" of the giant 747.400. I lay back chuckling at the thought of those who had paid sometimes more than twice as much to sit with the "tax dodgers" in the forward part of the plane. It was a 12 hour journey from Los Angeles to Auckland, and all I wanted to do was sleep.

Suddenly, the tension in the cabin rose as we encountered turbulence that rocked the plane from front to rear and I was now wide awake for hour after hour as our plane was buffeted with violent shakings which of course was magnified in the tail section where I was lying.

Then, **it happened**! My mind was ablaze with pictures, phrases, and outlines for my fifth book. It was as if it was being dictated to me at high speed, yet, as soon as I arrived home I was able to write it all down, almost without pausing to consider how it was all fitting together.

An **absolutely incredible experience!**

The next morning whilst collecting our luggage and going over to the Domestic Terminal, we met some U.S. citizens from Colorado. One of the first questions they asked was **"Have you heard the news about the Oklahoma bombing?"**

We have now and its repercussions are incredible.

CHAPTER ONE

NOW WILL YOU LISTEN!

This is really strange – believe me.

For the last 33 years we have travelled literally hundreds of thousands of miles, spoken to thousands upon thousands of people in at least 30 countries. Many times we have been denied media exposure which, periodically, has led to frustration. However, at last –

THE CAT IS OUT OF THE PROVERBIAL BAG

An outrageous event took place on the 19th April 1995 in Oklahoma, U.S.A. This event, no doubt only the first in a series, forced the world's media to report information that was previously only discussed by a few.

The persons accused of the Oklahoma bombings i.e. possibly members of the nationwide movement called the **Militia**, many of whom are aware of the Luciferian Global Plan outlined here in this book, obviously believe that the end result of all this global talk is in direct conflict with the American Constitution.

Whilst making statements on these matters, we must bear in mind that we are dealing with a nation, **some** of whose leaders planned for their President – John F. Kennedy, to be murdered, and then told lies as to why and how this took place.

Ten years after the event, the doctor, who first examined John Kennedy's body when it arrived at the hospital, confessed that he was instructed by the authorities to make it appear as if the bullet had entered the head **from the rear**, when in actuality, it entered the head **from the front**. He was also told that unless he obeyed these instructions, he was liable for a very long prison term.

The Courier Mail newspaper, Brisbane, Australia, included the following report April 3 1992 – Doctor breaks silence on JFK.

Dr Charles Crenshaw broke a 29 year silence about the assassination in interviews with two nationally televised programs.

Dr Crenshaw said he had been afraid to speak out before this.

"... And for the rest of my life I will always know that he was shot from the front. If I had gone against all the other people and created this bomb, I'd have been a pariah of our medical community." ...

This explanation makes it more clear as to why Jackie Kennedy tried to escape by jumping out over the rear of the car in which she and the President were travelling.

This doctor, a decade later, admitted that as he was getting older, it no longer mattered any more and he wished to clear his conscience.

Therefore, if the Kennedy murder involved a massive, lying, cover up, we cannot be sure that the Militia were in any way involved in the Oklahoma tragedy, save as a possible 'patsy'.

Back to Oklahoma

[1]The 'New American' magazine, 7th August 1995, quotes a retired Brigadier General as saying that *"the photographs provide undeniable proof that demolition charges had been used on four of the building's columns, and that these, not the truck bomb, caused the massive structural damage on April 19th. This man, a premiere munitions and explosive expert, appealed for action to delay the demolition of the building so that vital evidence would not be destroyed. The building was demolished five days later before he arrived at the scene. He made it very clear that the original charges, laid by persons unknown, caused the columns to collapse straight down, and thus the truck bomb did very little structural damage."*

Further investigations will obviously still be hampered, *"yet a lawyer for McVeigh said that he had hired a London law firm to investigate claims that an international conspiracy was behind the deadly Oklahoma City attack last April.*
McVeigh's defence lawyers have been in touch with forensic experts."
Christchurch 'Press', 6th February 1996.

Do I hear Lee Harvey Oswald and Jack Ruby call from the grave "Hear, hear"?

We, in our lectures, link all this information on the New World Order and related subjects, with the ancient prophecies and use the data to encourage our listeners to seek out a strong spiritual base for their lives.

A careful viewing of the video entitled, "Waco – The Big Lie", will provoke extreme anger in the viewer as he observes, with his own eyes, government federal agents in cooperation with the BATF (Bureau of Alcohol, Tobacco, and Firearms), apparently shooting their own men and then the final indignity is the bringing in of a tank with a flame thrower which sets fire to the deadly C2 gas already placed in the building by the same people.

(For copies of this video – **PLEASE DO NOT WRITE TO US**. Instead, please contact: The American Justice Federation, 3850 South Emerson Ave, Indianapolis, IN 46203, U.S.A. Ph: (317) 780 5206, Fax: (317) 780 5209.)

Can you believe that these people who are apparently answerable to no-one, have so much power over the media, that they then proceeded to tell us that this religious group at Waco, an off-shoot from the Seventh Day Adventist Church, set fire to their own compound, thus committing suicide?

If this is the level of control over what is reported, what chance does the man in the street have, as his mind is likewise subject to manipulation.

Regardless of one's religious beliefs, according to the American Constitution, these people in Waco had every right to live in freedom from persecution, particularly from their own government.

However, whoever was responsible for the Oklahoma bombing, (whether the Militia, the FBI, or some other individual or group), made sure that the attack took place on the exact day of the gassing and burning to death of the Branch Davidian people at Waco, Texas.

It is of no small interest that April 19th is a highly important day in the field of witchcraft.

In the light of the Kennedy murder and the Waco murder, are people to be considered paranoid if they are now calling this 'the Oklahoma murder' **possibly** carried out by the same persons in each case?

Food for thought?

Proof 1

'Weekend Press', 29th April 1995: *"From Apple Pie to Mass Murder.*

McVeigh, who planted the bomb, belongs to a movement that has grown up in recent years, imbued with an irrational hatred of Federal Government.

....The movements' adherents train, either openly or in secret, in preparation for what they loosely define as the enemy – the Federal Government.

*They claim they are acting **in defence of the Constitution.***

The movement includes among its founders, veteran right-wing extremists, one of whom was able to describe the horror at the Alfred B. Muragh Federal Building as "a Rembrandt, a masterpiece of science and art put together." (Author's note – My original thoughts on the

Rembrandt statement was that in the back of their minds was the thought – one original, many copies. Let us hope that this is not the intention.)

"*.....**the militias are organised in 40 of the 50 states**....*

After the demise of the Soviet threat, a new, almost "hip" right-wing movement started....the enemy was not in Moscow, but in Washington....the enemy is fascism in the White House.

*....**the fall of the Berlin Wall heralded the dawn of a New World Order** dominated by secret powers aimed at establishing **a global dictatorship**.*

*The Clinton administration is regarded by all these groups as **a puppet of global forces**. Some of the new literature has a militant Christian gist, and describes these powers as "Luciferian" or* **"Luciferian globalist".**

*.....a......**masonic** group called the **Illuminati** is taken seriously and there is a belief that this occult elite is preparing to coincide a push for **world domination** with the advent of the third millennium.*

*....**It is the essence of the American Constitution, says this movement, that a citizen has the right to bear arms, and to form militias.***

They hark back to the days of the American Revolution as their declared inspiration." End quote. (Emphasis added.)

Author's note

It is to be noted that this article calls McVeigh, 'the bomber', before the court case was held. What type of justice is this? As we have already noted, private investigators have discovered that what was supposed to have happened at the scene of the bombing, is not necessarily what did happen.

Sources from North America have told us that, although the office of the BATF was on the 9th floor of this building, the majority of their staff were absent from the building on that day and the minority, who were left, along with other Federal Agents, were barely touched by the blast.

The 'New American' magazine article that we previously referred to, went on to tell us that the General, who did his own investigations, discovered that the charges were not placed at street level but on the third floor, which means that the bombers had to have had access to the interior of the building.

If the reporting on the Waco murder scene was lies, the point is, can Timothy McVeigh expect a fair trial when he has already been named as the bomber?

Whilst condemning and abhorring the ridiculous, murderous attack on defenceless people, it has to be admitted that in the U.S. Constitution, "**the right to bear arms**" is an important aspect, specifically inserted to prevent the **takeover of personal freedoms** of the individual, which is the **avowed aim of the New World Order.**

Thus, the founding fathers appeared to possess prophetic insight into the future as this right to bear arms was not initially planned as protection against an outside aggressor but against an over-dictatorial Federal or State agency that over-rode its governing powers and became a threat to the privacy and rights of the individual.

Disclaimer

It should be noted at this point, that this author is in no way sympathetic to any of this sort of carrying on in the United States of America, and is interested only in weaving the truth into a logical and understandable expose.

A SUSPENDED AND ALTERED U.S. CONSTITUTION IMPERATIVE

As you continue reading this book, it will gradually become apparent that the name of the exercise is the linking of the USA with Europe and Asia under the heading 'New World Order'. As the U.S. Constitution stands at present (1995), this is impossible.

Therefore, a crisis must soon be 'created', which will give the Federal Government the power to invoke '**FEMA**' – **Federal Emergency Management Act** which would give the incumbent President the power to **suspend the Constitution and emasculate it by introducing strict gun laws.**

The question may now be asked "What about the millions who refuse to hand in their guns?"

Easy – **dry up the sources of ammunition!**

All of this gives relevance to the phrase known to most Americans [1]"*Give me liberty or give me death!*"

Footnotes

1 Order 'New American' magazine from P.O. Box 8040, Appleton, WI 54913, U.S.A. Ph: (414) 749 3784.

    Just prior to this book going to press, the Dunblane massacre in Scotland, and the Port Arthur massacre in Tasmania, have led to further calls for firearms restrictions. The One World Government advocates demand this restriction to apparently safeguard normal citizens but really it is to stop citizens rebelling against any future abuse of power.

Just because a madman drives a car into a group of pedestrians, does not mean that every driver in the country should have their motor car confiscated. Simply deal with the problem i.e. the madman involved is the problem.

Recommended Reading

Set the Trumpet to Thy Mouth by David Wilkerson; David Wilkerson Publishers, World Challenge Inc., P.O. Box 260, Lindale, Texas 75771, U.S.A.

Circle of Intrigue by Texe Marrs; Living Truth Publishers, 1708 Patterson Rd, Austin, Texas 78733-6507, U.S.A.

Dreams and Visions from God by Dimitru Duduman; Hand of Help Inc., P.O. Box 1044, Albany, Oregon 97321-0403, U.S.A. Ph: (503) 928 1142.

Predictions

1. The man chosen to be the President of the U.S.A. from November '96 is already known. His name is Bill Clinton. He is dedicated to following the New Zealand plan already investigated by the Congress and speaker, Newt Gingrich.

    This destructive plan will commence with the abolition of the welfare system.

2. In the year 1982, a new flag was flown alongside and at the same height as the Stars and Stripes over the District of Columbia – the U.S. capital of course is Washington D.C. This flag has three red stars and two red stripes on a white field. The same design appears on license plates and arm bands of police officers. Meaning – the New World Order plans follow the ancient Roman system of leadership called – The Triumvirate or power of three (3 stars on the flag).

    1. London – headquarters of the Crown control economically.
    2. The Vatican – is not part of Rome or Italy and controls spiritually.
    3. Washington D.C. – under the new constitution controls politically.

    In 1982, the State of New Columbia came into existence, along with a new constitution. A new legal system called Lex Fori was also introduced at that stage which was based on the brutal Roman style law of the Forum.

    Revelation 16:19 – "And the great city was divided into three parts and the cities of the nations fell, and the great Babylon came in remembrance before God..."

3. In the year 1990, the "Federal Debt Collection Practices Act" was passed and the United States is now officially the world's largest Corporation called United States Inc. At this time of writing therefore, President Clinton is the first President ever to be elected under the new corporate structure. Note – You cannot easily sell up a country, but you can change directors and then do what you want with the corporation. This will link the U.S.A. with the other countries in the New World Order. Newt Gingrich calls this plan a "Contract with America". (Doesn't that make you smell a rat?)

(For further information, please write to: Last Trumpet Newsletter, P.O. Box 806, Beaver Dam, WI 53916, U.S.A. – September '96 issue.)

From 1996 onwards, watch a Democrat president buckle under to Newt Gringrich and a Republican Congress who have vowed to follow the New Zealand restructuring model. The Clintons must face various scandals during their second term. The Republican Congress will see to this i.e. Whitewater – Filegate – Indogate – Paula Jones – Travelgate etc etc.

Should the New World Order planners decide to say goodbye to Bill and Hillary, Al and Tipper Gore can be called in to continue on with this outrageous plan.
4. The U.S. government will come under the control of the United Nations.
5. The U.S. will be attacked from without and these areas will burn:
   a) California
   b) Las Vegas
   c) New York
   d) Florida

George Washington, Daisy Osborne, Dimitru Duduman and David Wilkerson have all seen this take place in the form of visions.
6. The stockmarket, the government, the buildings and investments will all be burned. Food, transport, and communications will go in a period of 1 hour.
7. Thus, world attention will turn away from the U.S.A. to the E.U. and its future dictator.
8. Take note that when Russia invades Israel, America will no longer be in any state to fly to Israel's defence.

God Himself will do all the fighting necessary on Israel's behalf!

CHAPTER TWO

NOSTRADAMUS

Many people today, disillusioned with the present and not understanding where they are heading, identify in some way with the prophet Jonah. If you feel confused, how do you think he felt when he was swallowed by a great fish. In their desperation, some even turn to the writings of –

Nostradamus

Born into a Jewish family, he later converted to Roman Catholicism and died in France on 2nd July 1566.

Although his name is known world-wide, most people know very little about him or his prophecies.

On 6th November 1991, we were passing through Singapore Airport on our way to another venue where we were to conduct lectures on these subjects. A book title regarding Nostradamus caught my eye. I duly parted with my 14.99 pounds feeling satisfied that I had indeed bought the book at a bargain price. I reasoned that this type of book would normally cost at least 15 pounds.

There have been many other books written about this man and his prophecies, and all seem to agree that Nostradamus was a master **occultist** who studied very old manuscripts and books which clearly outlined certain rituals to be used for discovering the secrets of the future.

His fear of the Inquisition, and its varied tortures applied to any who stepped out of line with orthodox church beliefs, caused him to write his prophecies in a mystical and mainly unintelligible style.

One book in particular was very important to him. It's title, **"De Misteriis Egyptorum"**, published in Lyons in 1547. Nostradamus quoted directly from this book in some of his prophecies. It is of note that he was also very fond of occult Jewish literature – in particular, the **"Kabbalah"**, which book serves as a basis for many of the mysteries in witchcraft and Freemasonry.

This man in his old age, collected all his manuscripts and prophecies together and burnt them as an offering to the Greek god called Vulcan.

Later working on the 'Phoenix principle' i.e. a mystical bird, which is burnt and then at a later time in history, rises again from its own ashes, Nostradamus used gnostic thinking and then rewrote his prophecies in a strange and obscure form, i.e. mystical quatrains, so that future students could delve into them at their leisure.

Only certain individuals, i.e. **the Sages, the Elect, and the Adepts**, would be able to understand these gnostic mysteries at a certain time in history. Others not enlightened, could merely guess and speculate at their meanings.

He began making prophecies about 1547 which he published in 1555 in a book entitled "Centuries" (this word had nothing to do with a hundred years). The work consisted of rhymed quatrains grouped in hundreds called a 'century'. Some of his prophecies, co-mingling French, Spanish, Hebrew, and Latin, appeared from time to time to be fulfilled and still continue to create much controversy.

Therefore, it can be authoritatively stated from a Biblical perspective, that his was a Luciferian knowledge, **a clever mixture of truth and lies** e.g.

If you wish to administer poison to an enemy, do not hand him a glass of red liquid saying "Here, drink your cup of poison!" It is obviously far more appropriate to mix the poison with a pleasing drink and say "Here, have a drink of raspberry juice."

The result was that Nostradamus appeared to be correct in some cases but in others, wildly missed the mark.

Examples of <u>Possibly Correct</u> Prophecies

Century 2 no. 24:

> *Bestes farouches de faim fleuves tranner,*
> *Plus part du champ encontre Hister sera.*
> *En caige de fer le grand fera treisner,*
> *Quand rien enfant de Germain observera.*

Literal translation:

Beasts wild with hunger will cross the rivers, the greater part of the battlefield will be against Hitler. He will drag the leader in a cage of iron, when the child of Germany observes no law.

Possible meaning:

Adolph Hitler leading the Nazi party observed no laws of humanitarianism. From Germany, his ruthless army moved across many rivers into various parts of Europe causing destruction and havoc wherever they went.

Century 2 no. 6:

> *Aupres des portes & dedans deux cites*
> *Seront deux fleaux & oncques n'apperceu un tel:*
> *Faim, dedans peste, de fer hors gens boutes,*
> *Cirer secours au grand Dieu immortel.*

Literal translation:

Near the harbour and in two cities will be two scourges, the like of which have never been seen. Hunger, plague within, people thrown out by the sword will cry for help from the great immortal God.

Possible meaning:

Could this be a reference to the two atomic bombs, i.e. the Fat Man and the Little Boy, that were dropped respectively by the Americans on the two cities of Nagasaki and Hiroshima?

News reports from Japan, at that time, told us that the victims' bodies were burned black, very similar to the results of plagues which have hit Europe over the years, causing these miserable survivors in their death throes to call out to God for help in their misery.

Examples of <u>Apparently Failed</u> Prophecies

Century one no. 17:

> *Par quarante ans l'Iris n'apparoistra,*
> *Par quarante ans tous les jours sera veu:*
> *La terre aride en siccite croistra,*
> *Et grans deluges quand sera aperceu.*

Literal translation:

For forty years the rainbow will not be seen. For forty years it will be seen every day. The dry earth will grow more parched and there will be great floods when it is seen.

Possible meaning not clear.

A check on world weather statistics does not reveal a forty year drought nor a forty year flood, and it would appear to be highly unlikely that this would ever take place.

Century nine no. 14:

> *Mis en planure chaulderons d'infecteurs,*
> *Vin, miel & l'huile, & bastis sur forneaulx*
> *Seront plonge sans mal dit mal facteurs*
> *Sept. fum extaint au canon des borneaux.*

Literal translation:

The dyer's cauldrons put in a flat place, wine, honey and oil and built over furnaces. They will be drowned, without saying or doing an evil thing, seven of Borneaux, the snake extinguished from the cannon.

Possible meaning:

On a farm in Borneaux, seven fine men concoct a mixture of wine, honey, and oil, into which they quietly sink and are drowned. One of their wives wishing to draw attention to the plight of her husband fires off a cannon which unfortunately disturbs and kills a snake which is sleeping in the barrel.

Footnote: it is clear that none but the Sages, the Elect, and the Adepts, will be able to utilise the information given in this prophecy in a constructive manner.

Question: At this point, the question may well be asked "How did Nostradamus manage to correctly predict **any** major events at all, at least 400 years beforehand?

Answer: Lucifer (Satan), his illuminator has major plans for this world in the form of a complete takeover. He, who is called the god of this world, simply revealed some of his plans to the occultist Nostradamus with the purpose of leading as many as possible away from the true prophecies.

However, a challenge:

[1]***"We have also a more sure word of prophecy, whereunto ye do well that ye take heed, as unto a light that shineth in a dark place."***

It's a fact. The Bible, the Word of God, is far more accurate than Nostradamus.

Footnotes

1 II Peter 1:19; The Holy Bible.

Recommended Reading

Encyclopaedia Brittanica – Nostradamus

The Prophecies of Nostradamus by Erika Cheetham; ISBN 1 85152 480 0 Bath Press.

Nostradamus – The End of the Millenium by V.J. Hewitt and Peter Lorie; ISBN 0 7475 0945; Labyrinth Publishing, South Africa.

CHAPTER THREE

A MIRROR FROM THE PAST

From "The Handwriting on the Wall" by David Jeremiah (pg 62).

When the thirteen colonies were still part of England, Professor Alexander Tyler wrote about the fall of the Athenian republic, over 1,000 years ago.

*"**A democracy cannot exist as a permanent form of government**. It can only exist until the voters discover that they can vote themselves money from the public treasure. From that moment on, the majority always votes for the candidates promising the most money from the public treasury, with the result that democracy always collapses over loose fiscal policy, followed by a DICTATORSHIP.*

The average age of the world's great civilisations has been 200 years. Those nations have progressed through the following sequence –

> *from bondage to spiritual faith*
> *from spiritual faith to great courage*
> *from courage to liberty*
> *from liberty to abundance*
> *from abundance to selfishness*
> *from selfishness to complacency*
> *from complacency to apathy*
> *from apathy to dependency*
> *from dependency back to bondage."*

THE REVERSE SIDE OF AN AMERICAN $1.00 BILL

CHAPTER FOUR

THE HISTORY OF THE SEALS

Although these two odd looking seals appear on the back of every US$1 bill printed since the year 1933, I have asked many American friends the meaning of the seals, yet **not one** could give me an answer.

24 April 1995 – for example, as I put my pen to paper in my little office in New Zealand, my mind goes back to the evening of 19th April where we awaited our next flight in the transit lounge of L.A. International Airport. I was having a discussion with the airline ground staff behind the desk. I had a US$1 bill in my hand and asked "Can you please tell me the meaning of these two strange seals on your dollar bill?" The three American airline staff members in full uniform looked blankly from one to another as the youngest of the group murmured that he thought they had something to do with **'truth'**.

Can you believe what I am telling you here? Some years ago, we took 40 airplane rides, criss-crossing the U.S. on a lecture tour. Not one person we spoke to (and there were many of them) knew about the existence of these seals.

In the words of many – **"We spend 'em, we don't read 'em."**

Now, should you feel to criticise these citizens, for their lack of knowledge, let me enquire "What is written on your currency?" Most honest readers will agree that unless you are absolutely desperate for reading material, you do not usually read your bank notes.

Believe me, the young man at L.A. airport was miles off when he said that he thought it had to do with the truth. It is actually the very opposite.

A VERY DETAILED
EXPLANATION OF THE TWO SEALS

I have just been handed a letter by our office manager, Keith Jones, from an American citizen living in Texas. I quote:

"Greetings from North-West Texas....I was blessed to be in attendance at your meeting in Tauranga (New Zealand) about a month ago. You told more truth about the U.S. government, our economy, our currency, and the plan of the enemy, than I have ever heard in this country.

We have heard bits and pieces of the truth about .... the symbols on our dollar bill, but have never heard such a complete presentation. Thank you and keep up the good work.... Texas 4.13.95."

Now, what you are going to read here has never, and can never ever be taught in any U.S. school. The ramifications would be catastrophic.

WHAT YOUR TEACHER NEVER TOLD YOU!

Dates to Memorise: **1776, 1778, 1782, 1784, 1792, 1870, 1884, 1933, 1991**.

[1]**1776 – Illuminati of Bavaria**. (Encyclopaedia of Freemasonry by Albert G. Mackey M.D., page 405.)

"A secret society, founded on May 1st 1776 by Adam Weishaupt, who was professor of canon law at the University of Ingoldstadt.

*..... To give the Order a higher influence, **Weishaupt connected it with the Masonic institution**, after whose system of degrees of esoteric instruction, and of secret modes of recognition, it was organised.*

....Weishaupt....had originally been a Jesuit, and he employed therefore........the shrewdness and subtlety which distinguished the disciples of Loyola, and having been initiated in 1777 in a lodge at Munich, he also borrowed for its use the mystical organisation which was peculiar to Freemasonry.

In this latter task, he was greatly assisted by the Baron Von Knigge, a zealous and well-instructed Mason.

....on June 22nd 1784, the Elector of Bavaria issued an edict for its suppression. Many of its members were fined or imprisoned, and some, among whom was Weishaupt, were compelled to flee the country...." End quote.

This group, the Illuminati, were the designers of the two seals found on the reverse side of every U.S. one dollar bill, dated from 1933 onwards.

THE EYE OF LUCIFER

The eye in the triangle was called by Weishaupt ....**The Insinuating Brethren.** This simply meant that ultimately the Luciferian gnostic eye would represent the leaders of the One World Government who, under the control of their leader, Lucifer, would dominate every other group in society.

Can you believe this?

There is at present (1995) a card game available in both South Africa[2] and Australia called....wait for it – **"Illuminati New World Order"**, together with the pyramid and eye on the cover. What arrogance! (For more information, see Footnotes.)

The reader will discover that gleaning information on this secret society is extremely difficult, in spite of the fact that it is operating more intensely 200 years later that at its beginnings. I checked with a modern version of the Encyclopaedia Britannica but found that all the relevant information had been deleted. **Strange isn't it?**

However, all was not lost, because I had friends who still owned an older set of these volumes.

[3]Quotes from Encyclopaedia Britannica Vol 12 1963:

Illuminati

"....*Their founders' aim was* **to replace Christianity by a religion of reason**...

....*the order was organised along Jesuit lines and kept internal discipline and a system of* **mutual surveillance** *based on that model.*"
End quote.

(Author's note – The Communist regime in Russia, China, and other countries, has worked on similar principles over the years, which has resulted in the populations of those countries being full of fear and paranoia. **Spying on your neighbour is the name of the game.**

The illusion is now being presented to the world that Communism has collapsed yet what is not clearly understood is that Communism was a test case by the New World Order advocates before setting up a repressive global system which will restrict everybody's lifestyles and manner of living.

e.g. **Dob in your mates!** The British term used is 'Grass'.

George Orwell, you were so right!

Readers will understand that the above statement is an Australianism. From our very first days at school, generations of young people were taught that loyalty to one's friends was a basic principle understood by all. **Dobbers** may be variously described i.e. whistle-blowers, super-grasses, future potentates, power hungry or would-be Hitlers.

As we pen these lines in 1995, an alarming trend has developed in the two test countries of Australia and New Zealand and we make bold to say will soon appear also on your side of the world.

Read this section with great care, and marvel.

Example no.1

In the country of New Zealand, if you are out driving in your motor car and notice another driver exceeding the speed limit, or in your opinion, driving dangerously, you may pick up your cell phone and become an instant policeman by dialling *555. During the first week, the police were amazed at the number of drivers who used this facility.

The average Kiwi of course has no other avenue of exercising power over others. If you are a timid, nervous, driver, any person who overtakes you can easily be considered a dangerous driver, and thus should be reported.

Example no.2

During a recent lecture tour in Western Australia, we learned that should you observe a driver whose car has a smoking exhaust pipe, a quick call on the phone to the authorities concerned will see to it that this vehicle is removed from the roads. Again, the police were amazed at the response.

You understand now, don't you? Every driver is able to take on the role of instant detective. Oh, the feelings of power!!

Example no.3

We then moved down to New South Wales where bold headlines in the newspaper informed us that if we suspected that any person down the road was abusing their child, a special telephone number was made available so that that person could be reported, or as the Australians say – dobbed in.

So now, if you hate your neighbour, the facility is there to destroy him. Even if he manages to be found innocent, the mud still sticks.

Example no.4

A sign on a refrigerator in New South Wales read, "Dob in a dumper". This means that should you observe an individual throw refuse from their vehicle, all that is required of you is that you take their number and report them.

Example no.5

Arriving back in our own country New Zealand, to the amazement of people involved in the fitting of windscreens to motorcars, (and others of course), we discovered that a law change has been mooted which meant that extra dark tinting on vehicle windows would no longer be allowed unless a certain percentage of light was still able to penetrate. This would mean that thousands and thousands of dollars have been wasted and businesses could go to the wall through this seemingly petty law. Could the true reason for this new law be that certain individuals require clear vision into the interior of every vehicle e.g. speed cameras and law enforcement officers. At least 35% of light must be allowed through the windows.

Good news – As we go to press, the glass fitters report that there was so much opposition at this stage that the Government was forced to throw the bill out. Let us watch and see if they try again at a later stage.

Remember the New World Order rules. Introducing new policies is similar to the ancient method used for breaking in a horse. Move in quietly whilst continuously flicking around it with a sack or something similar. If the horse over-reacts and rears up, simply move back for a time, and later on, continue with the treatment until the horse accepts it.

Example no.6

In New Zealand, should you observe your neighbour cutting down native timber on his own private property, to be used in construction work of any type, you must dob him in. However, if he is using this timber for firewood, it becomes legal for him to do so.

At this time of writing, it is amazing how many trees are being chopped down for firewood.

Example no.7

The latest information to hand regarding **the Internet** is that the U.S. Government is saying "Yes, you can put bars on your windows, locks on your doors, put your jewellery and other valuables in a safe, but you have to give us the keys and the combination because you might be a crook." **The Government's wish to monitor communications** would supersede a citizen's right to be free from Government monitoring. **These people want to know who put what on the Internet**.

This is mutual surveillance '**par excellence**'.

To our further shock and chagrin, we read in the Christchurch 'Press', 15th December 1995, the headline – "*Law to protect whistle-blowers*.

Whistleblowers who disclose serious wrongdoing in the public or private sectors, will be protected by law, under law changes planned by the government.

*....the Government had decided to act on recommendations of an independent review team into **whistleblowing**. The group's report issued yesterday, believes such moves are justified, although it argues against creating a specific whistle-blowers' authority....*" End quote.

Now, if there ever was an opportunity to get even with someone you dislike, this is it. Spying is now becoming legitimate. Please add to this list your own observations, as spying and dobbing in become the norm.

Back to our quote:

"....From 1778 onwards they (the Illuminati) began to make contact with various masonic lodges, where under the impulse of A. Von Knigge (O.V.), one of their chief converts, they often managed to gain a commanding position...." End quote.

Author's notes – Now what have we learned?

The date in Roman numerals – 1776, on the base of the pyramid does not stand for July 4th (Declaration of Independence) but for the inauguration of the Illuminati, May 1st. The reason for this is that Weishaupt and his society designed both seals in Bavaria.

The word 'Illuminati' means the 'Enlightened Ones' or the **'Illumined Ones'**, pregnant with the **mystical gnosis** or secret knowledge of Lucifer (the bright and shining one himself).

1778 – Von Knigge infiltrates Freemasonry but only has influence in the upper degrees where preside the **Sages** – the **Elect** –the **Adepts**.

A man shouted at me and complained about my expose during one of my lectures in Australia." I asked "Which degree are you in?" He replied "The 18th", to which I answered "Would you please sit down sir, you do not know enough yet."

His wife encouraged him to sort me out at the conclusion of the meeting. He failed to do this and within a month, the woman was a widow. Her husband died in very mysterious circumstances in a car park.

1782 – In this year, the small group of Illumined Masons who designed the two seals, handed them in a red velvet bag to a messenger. **This messenger, now hooded**, handed the velvet bag to Thomas Jefferson on the 17th June, in his drawing room in Virginia.

1784 – Thomas Jefferson was **appointed U.S. Ambassador to France** where he was able to study European Illuminism in great detail. Both Weishaupt and Jefferson adopted a common policy and Jefferson returned to the U.S. and became Secretary of State.

1789 – On September 15th, the **Congress accepted the Great Seal** of the United States of America. This was in two parts of course, but until 1933, only the so-called 'eagle' was the emblem of the U.S.A. The pyramid with its 'eye in the triangle' capstone was not used officially until much later on.

1792 – During this period of time, the Congress debated the cancellation and deletion of the pyramid and eye seal. Embarrassing questions were being asked. **"What has an Egyptian pyramid to do with the U.S.A.?"** Strangely enough the objections were squashed and the seal remained.

THE TWO SEALS ON THE REVERSE SIDE OF
THE AMERICAN $1.00 BILL

22

1870 – The anniversary of the day on which Rome became the capital of Italy. This is also a great Masonic date for **it marks the organisation of a supreme rite, introduced into Freemasonry** to lend a satanic character to the vague divinity, more or less well-known, by the name of **The Great Architect of the Universe.**

[4]An Italian Freemason called Mazzini, in a letter to Albert Pike in America, on January 22nd 1870, wrote the following –

*"We must allow all the federations to continue just as they are, with their systems, their central authorities and their diverse modes of correspondence between high grades of the same rite, organised as they are at the present, **but we must create a supreme rite, which will remain unknown, to which we will call those Masons of high degree whom we shall select. With regard to their brothers in masonry, these men must be pledged to the strictest secrecy. Through this supreme rite, we will govern all Freemasonry which will become "one international centre", the more powerful because its direction will be unknown....***

*The two founders divided their powers according to the following plan. To Pike was given dogmatic authority and the title of **Sovereign Pontiff of Universal Freemasonry**, while Mazzini held the executive authority with the title of **Sovereign Chief of Political Action**....*

*This degree was called **The Palladium** or **The Cult of the Triangles**. It is essentially a **Luciferian rite**. Its religion is neo-gnosticism, teaching that **divinity is dual** and **that Lucifer is the equal of Adonay**, with Lucifer the god of light and goodness, struggling for humanity against Adonay, the god of darkness and evil."* End quote.

This latter statement was made by Albert Pike, a 33rd degree Mason and Grand Pontiff of Universal Freemasonry on the 14th July 1889, to the 23 Supreme Councils of the World.

It is for this reason that the dualistic nature of the Lodge reveals itself in the chequered floor of every Lodge building.

The Latter Day Saints Link

An interesting note on **Mormonism** tells us that Joseph Smith and his brother Hiram were promoted to the upper degrees of Freemasonry in one day and their doctrine teaches that **Lucifer is the brother of Jesus**.

In their Temple rituals, candidates also go through the Masonic witchcraft, cutting of the throat, tearing open of the chest, and the slitting of the stomach.

It is for this reason that we can now clearly understand **Freemasonry and its brother Mormonism are purely occultish, satanic, and Luciferian**.

Any man who is in either Masonry or Mormonism is in terrible spiritual danger of Hell fire. **Stay in the Lodge at your peril. You have been warned!**

Take careful note – shouting, swearing and outbursts of anger at this point, will in no way change the facts. The Palladium is there and every Mason is therefore under the direct influence of Lucifer (or Satan).

[5]In the late 1970's, William Schnoebelen was **initiated into the Palladium degree in Chicago**.

We quote – "I am ashamed to admit it, but I, myself, stood in the Lodge and joined in the traditional Palladium imprecation, which is (translated from the French): "*Glory and love for Lucifer. Hatred! Hatred! Hatred! to God accursed! accursed! accursed!*" End quote. He then went through four of the five steps. It makes frightening reading.

He was blessed in that a Christian woman prayed for him and he was delivered through our Lord Jesus Christ.

We understand that Masons reading this book will no doubt be extremely grateful to this author for doing what they should have done before joining this society – checked it out, however, letters of thanks are not necessary – it is my pleasure.

1884 – Again, debate raged in the Congress over this odd looking seal. Sure enough, its opponents were defeated and it is still there today.

1933 – A key date. **Franklin Delano Roosevelt**, a 32nd degree Mason **had both these seals printed on the reverse side of the US$1 bill** just as the U.S. was climbing out of the stock market crash of 1929. The general public were not particularly interested as to what was printed on the currency, provided it had some value.

1990 – **George Bush** in his pre-Gulf War speech spoke the words over and over – **New World Order, New World Order, New World Order**, thus publicly announcing to the world at large, that Weishaupt's 200 year old plan was now to be put into operation.

According to Mackey, Weishaupt said "My general plan is good, though in the detail there may be faults."

Remember the key dates –

1776 - Adam Weishaupt inaugurates the Plan

1990 - George Bush announces the Plan

We are not rushing on with this information as there is a great deal more material we need to share. This book is going **GLOBAL.**

Footnotes

1   Encyclopaedia of Freemasonry by Albert Mackey; 33rd Degree; McClure Publishing Co., Philadelphia, U.S.A.

2   Stamped and addressed envelope to Steve Jackson Games, P.O. Box 18957, Austin, Tx 78760, U.S.A.

3   Encyclopaedia Britannica, Vol 12, 1963.

4   Occult Theocracy by Lady Queenborough; page 208; Midnight Messenger, P.O. Box 472, Altadena, Ca 91001, U.S.A.

5   Masonry – Beyond the Light by William Schnoebelen; page 194; Chick Publications, P.O. Box 662, Chino, Ca 91708 – 0662, U.S.A.

Recommended Reading

Morals and Dogma by Albert Pike; Kessinger Publishing Co., Box 160, Kila, Mt 529920, U.S.A.

Prophecies of the Presidents by Timothy Green Beckley and Arthur Crockett; Inner Light Publications, Box 753, New Brunswick, N.J. 08903, U.S.A.

The Secret Teachings of the Masonic Lodge by John Ankerberg and John Weldon; Moody Press, Chicago, U.S.A.

(A prayer to release yourself from these oaths may be found elsewhere in this book.)

Predictions

The U.S.A., with an altered Constitution, will be admitted into the New World Order along with Europe and Japan.

GEORGE WASHINGTON – NOTE LUCIFERIAN EYE ON APRON

CHAPTER FIVE

A DETAILED DESCRIPTION AND MEANING OF THE SEALS

1. The pyramid has 13 layers of stone, representing the 13 initial states, yet 13 is also an important number in witchcraft.
2. The 'eye in the triangle' is not the eye of the Christian God. This is the 'Eye of Horus' in Egyptian mythology and in reality represents the eye of Lucifer or Satan.

Having visited, on two occasions, the ancient temple on the Nile River at Luxor, we have been able to verify our information on Horus. **Do not take this information lightly!**

Proof, proof, proof:

a. The God that we Christians serve does not have one eye.
b. Our God's eye is not in a triangle. This triangle on the dollar is connected with the Cult of the Triangles – the Palladium. You'll find plenty of detail on all this in chapter eight.
c. Our God's eye is not illumined.

Any person skilled in esoteric teaching or occult practice will tell you that if you open your eye partially, you have psychic knowledge. If you open your eye completely, you have the divine illumined gnosis or illuminated secret knowledge of Lucifer, the bright and shining one. **(Satan is another name for this devil.)**

By the way, the Rosicrucians also use a triangle which they refer to as the Law of the Triangle. One side equals Thesis, the other side, Antithesis, and the base is Synthesis.

WHERE DO WE FIND THIS EYE IN THE TRIANGLE?

It is sometimes referred to as the "Third Eyes of Illumination".

a.[1] On every US$1 bill since the year 1933.
b.[2] Worn as part of the Grand Master of the Freemason's Lodges' jewellery. They see it as an important symbol of the Supreme Being and it was borrowed by the Freemasons from the nations of antiquity. They call it the eye of the Great Architect of the Universe. The Egyptians knew it to be the Eye of Osiris or Horus. **Our title is much shorter – 'Lucifer'.**

LUCIFERIAN EYE ON WALLS OF CHURCH OF THE
ANNUNCIATION IN NAZARETH

28

c.[3] It is found on the walls of many churches today, thus showing that Luciferianism has infiltrated into this field also e.g. Come with us on our annual Middle East tour and we will escort you to the church that is built over the supposed site of Joseph and Mary's house, where Jesus was possibly raised as a boy. On the wall very clearly is this eye in the triangle looking down on the dove (Holy Spirit) and the Cross (Jesus and His death for all mankind.)

The guide told us that it represented the eye of God, so I replied, "You are an Arab, aren't you? You know that it is not the eye of God, but the Eye of Horus, or the Eye of Lucifer."

"Quite right, sir", he replied. "**Then why are you telling lies to the tourists?", I asked. He said "We don't want to upset the people, sir.**"

d.[4] It is clearly emblazoned on the front wall of Hitler's bunker at Eagle Nest.

It may interest the reader to also learn that Hitler was a Luciferian and believed in reincarnation. Adolf Hitler taught that by murdering 6 million Jews, he was doing them a favour as they would return to a far better existence.

Please do not write and tell me that Hitler was a Christian and a worshipper of the true and living God!

[5]By the way, it is written "*It is appointed unto man once to die, but after death, the judgement.*" Therefore, **don't get too excited about reincarnation.**

3. Now, let us translate the two lots of Latin words – '**Annuit Coeptus**' – announcing the birth of –

[6]'**Novus Ordo Seclorum**' – **a secular, heathenistic, ungodly, One World Government, One World Religion, One World Law System, One World Economic System, or N.I.E.O. (New International Economic Order).**

Hello, hello – the eye of the Christian God is it? Isn't that interesting? **According to these dear, deluded folk, God is now announcing the birth of a secular world system over which He will no longer have any control.** Come on please – you are too intelligent to believe that lie any longer.

However, let us not linger here any longer. Let us examine seal no. 2.

Here we see a bird with its head turned towards its right wing and

HITLER'S BUNKER – EAGLE NEST

there is a ribbon in its mouth with 3 Latin words written there for all to see – 'E Pluribus Unum' – **Out of many – One.**

The right wing denotes a strong dictatorship. The 13 arrows in the bird's talon, a time of war. The 13 olive leaves in the other talon – a time of peace from the year 2,000.

The original aim was to unite the 13 original colonies into the United States of America. A would be Presidential hopeful, Jack Kemp, and now running mate with Bob Dole (1996 Presidential race), made a very interesting comment, recorded in a British newspaper[7], that I picked up in Great Britain. ***America", he said, "was not created to be one great power among many. It was created to be the novus ordo seclorum – a new order for the age. Our nation has come to a defining moment. A time when our choices will be hardened into history."*** End quote.

Now, let us give credit where credit is due. This man knows something of the meaning behind those three Latin words. Unfortunately, the task falls to this author to assist with the explanation. Whilst engaged in the school-teaching profession, I worked with many university graduates and others who were brilliant in their knowledge of certain subjects but were hopeless in their efforts to pass on that knowledge to others. In other words, they were **poor communicators**.

What Mr Kemp is obviously trying to pass on to us is that the words 'novus ordo seclorum' did not only apply to the task of uniting the 13 original colonies in America. This was to be a trial run for E Pluribus Unum – Out of many – one.

At a certain time in history, he suggests, **the plan will expand,** and out of many nations, will come a **Global Village**, with a One World Government, a One World Religion, a One World Law System, and a One World Economy. We thank you Mr Kemp, for your thoughts.

At this point, no doubt, angry readers will say that we are adding to Mr Kemp's words.

Don't give up. We encourage you to read on. As far as this author is concerned, the fight is on and it is **gloves off.**

Information that I have kept confidential for years is now going to be revealed.

Now, let us proceed.

Thomas Jefferson, Benjamin Franklin and John Adams, all top degree Masons with links to the Illuminati authorised 'someone' to call upon illumined artists to design the two seals. (By the way, the U.S.A. is the only country in the world to have two official seals. You will shortly see why this had to be.)

Thomas Jefferson was the principal architect of the 'Declaration of Independence'.

At this point, I wish to clarify a most important point. In your mind you may be wondering **"Is this man suggesting that the founders of the United States of America were influenced by occultic devilish forces?"**

Until one year ago, I could not prove this to be the case – now I can!

Footnotes

1   The U.S. $1 bill – reverse side.

2   Note "eye" on George Washington's Masonic apron.

3   The eye in the triangle – Church of the Annunciation in Nazareth.

4   Hitler's bunker – Eagle Nest.

5   Hebrews 9:27; The Holy Bible.

6   'Night and Day', Great Britain, 14th August 1994.

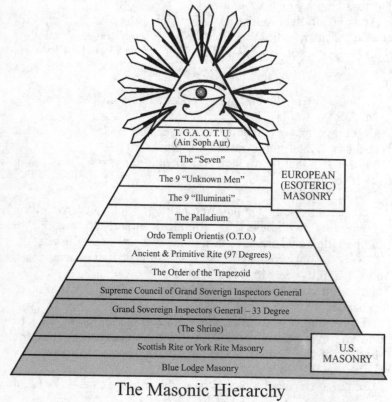

The Masonic Hierarchy

PYRAMID SHOWING VARYING DEGREES IN FREEMASONRY

CHAPTER SIX

THE PALLADIUM

Please refer once again to level nine on the Masonic pyramid. We have already learned of the Palladium under the date 1870.

[1]In the month of January on the 21st day in 1870, an Italian mason, named Mazzini, wrote the following note to the American mason, Albert Pike. We quote in part - "....*we must create a supreme rite WHICH WILL REMAIN UNKNOWN, to which we will call those masons of high degree.*" End quote.

Early in 1996, we were interviewed on the Gold Coast, Australia, and the videos subsequently went to air. The majority of viewers thought the programmes were great, but some folk called up and denied that there was any such degree as the Palladium. All this did was to further reveal their ignorance.

I'm so sorry to shatter your illusions in this way, but I must.

You will understand that at a date determined by Almighty God, in the not too distant future, **this author and all other human beings will be embarking on a journey through a dark valley, yet there is one who has promised to guide us through**. It is my duty therefore, to inform you as to the results of my investigations on YOUR BEHALF.

I just cannot bear to think of any man, whoever he may be, **writhing and screaming out for mercy on his death-bed**, when I had the information which could have set him free.

If you have risen even to the degree of Master Mason in the Blue Lodge, or possibly only to Fellowcraft or Entered Apprentice, you now understand that you are an object of laughter and derision to those above you, who have BRANCHED OUT into the Royal Arch or other avenues.

Esoteric Masonry, which is never discussed or even alluded to in the Blue Lodge, **is in complete control of all the degrees in every Lodge**.

Over the years, we have seen a number of 32nd degree men come out and be set free through the power of the true Light i.e. the Lord Jesus Christ, yet one such 32nd degree man in South Africa, in spite of my warnings, was so deluded and determined that within one month of our meeting together, proceeded on up to the 33rd degree. May God have mercy on his soul.

We outline herewith the esoteric groups in Europe which remain anonymous to the vast majority of Freemasons who remain in deep spiritual darkness.

To any men who are in the 33rd degree or lower, just look where you are placed on the pyramid.

Please, at this stage, pick up your US$1 bill and recount the layers of stone on the pyramid on its reverse side. Did I hear you say 13?

I mean to say, what **normal man** among us wouldn't begin to ask questions as he proceeds to:

a) have his shirt rolled up over his breast
b) have his trouser leg rolled up
c) have a slipper placed on his foot
d) have a black hoodwink placed over his eyes
e) have a rope with a running noose placed on him
f) feel the point of a sword pricking him above the heart
g) find himself repeating blood-curdling witch-craft oaths whilst at the same time drawing his right thumb across his throat, and mumbling out some words about having his throat cut, and his tongue torn out, etc etc.

Sickening isn't it? Why, even your small son would be struggling to exhibit such crass stupidity. Some say it is merely a game or a charade. Ask any witch!

However, it gets worse. **He then blasphemes against Almighty God** in Heaven by sealing this demonic witchcraft oath **in the kissing of the Bible.**

To add insult to injury, he then defends himself against any critics by repeating the senseless cliche which has been taught to him – "**It was not for real. I didn't really mean what I was saying**. It was merely symbolic."

My question is – "Symbolic of what?"

It is my unfortunate duty to now inform you that in any court of law, you would be charged with perjury, and according to the Word of God, **you have just put a demonic curse on a) yourself** b) your wife c) your children d) and your descendants to the third and fourth generations.

"Thou shalt have no other gods before Me."[2]

This statement applies to all men; actually more so to ministers of religion, priests, deacons, elders, and church members, who should have known better and investigated this devilish aspect before joining.

It will now become apparent to all readers, that it is for this reason that some so-called Christian churches are struggling.

In their ignorance, they have allowed witch-craft advocates into positions of leadership. Some churches' foundation stones were laid by the enemy's men. These dear, ignorant mis-guided men have damned themselves with their own lips.

How would you like to have a man guiding you in your spiritual life who has done and said such horrible things?

But wait, it gets steadily worse. Mazzini's and Pike's communications show us that every Freemason's Lodge is under the direct influence of LUCIFER. That's correct Sir! Even your Lodge and it matters little whether it is in Europe, the Americas, Africa or Asia.

In simple language, I suggest you ask your minister or priest if he is a Freemason. If so, give him this ultimatum.

"Either you resign from the Lodge, or I leave your church!"

Footnotes

1 Occult Theocracy by Lady Queenborough; page 208.
2 Exodus 20:3-5; The Holy Bible.

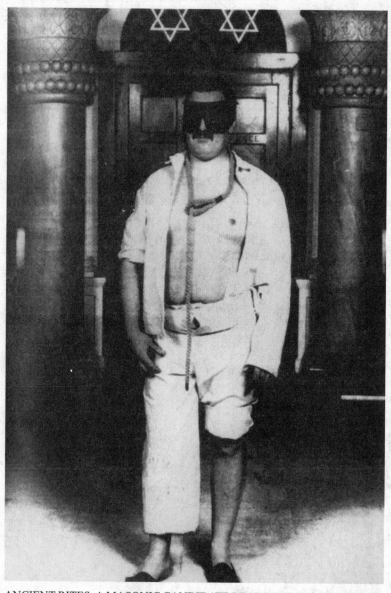

ANCIENT RITES: A MASONIC CANDIDATE READY FOR HIS INITIATION TO THE FIRST DEGREE, PREPARED EXACTLY AS A CONDEMNED MEDIEVAL HERETIC ON HIS WAY TO THE GALLOWS.

Yorkshire Post, 11.5.96

CHAPTER SEVEN

WHAT IS A FREEMASON?

A man who joins a society which he knows nothing about.
The two authors of the book "The Hiram Key", Chris Knight and Robert Lomas, bear this statement out in an article printed in the Yorkshire Post, 11 May 1996. Please bear in mind that what you are reading herewith is not a criticism, but pure fact. Both these men are Freemasons.

"*They write: "A compelling reason for silence amongst Masons is not so much a compulsion to adhere to their sacred vows, or a fear of macabre retribution from their fellows: it is more that they do not understand a word of the ceremonies they participate in, and their only fear is that people would laugh at the apparently pointless and silly rituals they perform...*

Our biggest criticism of Freemasonry is its sheer pointlessness. It does not know where it came from, no one seems to know what it is trying to achieve, and increasingly it seems improbable that it can have much of a future in a world that demands a clarity of purpose and benefit." End quote.

Had he made a thorough investigation of the beliefs and ultimate aims of this group, it is clear that, unless he was lacking in either morality or intelligence, he would never have thought of joining such an organisation.

Imagine for a moment, the man who has spent night after night of his valuable time, sitting up in bed, manual in hand, repeating the beliefs and obligations contained there-in, to his long-suffering and patient wife, who obviously feels her time could be more usefully employed.

(**A note to the wives of Freemasons** – please have a look at the picture on the opposite page and tell me whether it answers the question "Why does my husband never tell me what goes on in the Lodge?")

The shock must be absolutely devastating to such a man in any of the three initial degrees in the Blue Lodge when he finds out (and sometimes he never does) that all this learning was in vain as he reads the following statement from Albert Pike.[1]

"**The Blue Degrees are but the outer court or portico of the Temple. Part of the symbols are displayed there to the initiate, but** *he is intentionally misled by false interpretations. It is not intended that he shall understand them, but it is intended that he shall imagine he understands them. Their true explanation is reserved for the Adepts, the Princes of Masonry."* End quote.

I would suppose that any red-blooded Mason would immediately fly into an uncontrollable rage and storm out in a search and destroy mission, on those who allowed this deception to continue.

All readers, who have taken the vows, and repeated the obligations of any of the first three degrees in the Blue Lodge, please stand in front of a mirror and repeat out loud to yourself:

"I've been taken for a ride. Was I not lacking in wisdom to join a society that I knew nothing about. To make it worse, I believed the lies they fed me. How do I get myself out of this mess?"

But wait – that's not all!

During the course of his initiation, the demonic oaths, obligations, and actions, much akin to a witchcraft initiation, have such a mind-bending effect on him, that normally speaking, he will no longer be in any state to any think or reason clearly, and will in most cases, still endeavour to defend those who have so cruelly deceived him.

Mind you, the sin of **pride**, must come into it somewhere. Who in their right mind wishes to be branded a mentally challenged individual? Possibly the words of one Mencius could apply at this stage.

"To act without clear understanding; to follow a path all one's life, without knowing where it really leads, such is the behaviour of the multitudes."

So you see that although the Freemasons' libraries contain **thousands of books** in such places as the Grand Lodge in Washington D.C., filled with information that only a tiny percentage of men would ever see, let alone read and digest, it is little wonder that a large percentage of them are ignorant of all these details.

[2]Scottish Rite Masonry tells us: *"Grand Commander, Albert Pike, established the Library of the Supreme Council in 1888, when he donated his personal library of some 8,000 volumes which form the nucleus of the present collection.*

....Today, the Library contains more than 175,000 volumes, all **non-fiction***. The collection on Freemasonry in all its branches is the most complete in the world, and comprises about one-third of all the volumes in the entire Library..."* End quote.

175,000 divided by three equals 58,333. To any critics of this expose, we must ask the question – **how many of these books have you read**?

It therefore, has become the unfortunate task of others to inform and instruct, unenlightened men who still think Freemasonry is to do with the building of hospitals, orphanages, and homes for the elderly and widows, or is merely a society which makes good men better.

Do you sincerely believe, Sir, that all those books referred to above are filled with information on building codes and regulations and instructions on how to care for the underprivileged?

On your initial visit within the Lodge walls, as you dressed down for your initiation, didn't you smell the proverbial rat?

Remember the black hoodwink, the running noose, the dagger pricking you above the heart. Remember your right hand acting as a knife drawn across your throat. You do remember – don't you?

The N.S.W. Masons in Australia, of course, tell us that the following words have been added after the traditional oath. No doubt this was done to make the witchcraft oath more palatable.

"This was the penalty of this obligation in ancient times. We neither could, nor would, improve them, but rely instead on the moral obligation attached to this vow...." End quote.

'Gobble de gook' is the relevant comment in this case.

I feel at this stage to point out to any Freemason reading this section, to do as this author did. (Please refrain from flying into an uncontrollable rage, which by the way, is a significant feature of the movement, but thoughtfully exercise your God-given intellect.)

Find yourself a copy of an 861 page book called "Morals and Dogma", written by the Masonic authority, Albert Pike and check the information that you are now reading.

How do you feel as you read this further statement by Albert Pike on page 104 in this same book.

[3]*"Masonry, like all the Religions, all the Mysteries, Hermeticism, and Alchemy, <u>conceals</u> its secrets from all except the Adepts, and Sages, or the Elect, and uses false explanations and misinterpretation of its symbols to mislead those who deserve only to be misled, to conceal the Truth, which it calls Light, from them, and to draw them away from it.*

....So Masonry jealously conceals its secrets and intentionally leads conceited interpreters astray." End quote.

This being true, the candidate is led away from Jesus Christ who proclaimed Himself to be the 'Light of the World'. This is not only serious but also blasphemous!

William Schnoebelen in his very clear book "Masonry, Beyond the Light", has a heading which reads, **"Welcome to the World's Largest Coven"**.

To Sum Up

It has now been revealed to you that:

a) you were not wise to join a society that you knew nothing about;

b) the vast majority of the information you learned was full of lies and deceit;

c) if you remain a moment longer in the Lodge, you become more unwise than you were when you joined;

d) it becomes progressively worse as you ascend the various degrees culminating in the shocking revelation that the god of Freemasonry is Satan, known in the Bible as Lucifer!

[4]*"The theological dogma of Albert Pike is explained in the 'Instructions' issued by him, on July 14, 1889, to the 23 Supreme Councils of the world and have been recorded by A.C. De La Rive in La Femme et l'Enfant dans la Franc – Maconnerie Universelle (page 588) from which book we translate and quote as follows:*

"That which we must say to the crowd is – We worship a God, but it is the God that one adores without superstition.

"To you, Sovereign Grand Inspectors General, we say this, that you may repeat it to the Brethren of the 32nd, 31st and 30th degrees – The Masonic religion should be, by all of us initiates of the high degrees, maintained in the purity of the Luciferian doctrine.

"If Lucifer were not God, would Adonay (The God of the Christians) whose deeds prove his cruelty, perfidy, and hatred of man, barbarism and repulsion for science, would Adonay and his priest, calumniate him?

"Yes, Lucifer is God, and unfortunately Adonay is also God. For the eternal law is that there is no light without shade, no beauty without ugliness, no white without black, for the absolute can only exist as two Gods: darkness being necessary to light to serve as its foil as the pedestal is necessary to the statue, and the brake to the locomotive.

"In analogical and universal dynamics one can only lean on that which will resist. Thus the universe is balanced by two forces which

maintain its equilibrium: the force of attraction and that of repulsion. These two forces exist in physics, philosophy and religion.....

"*Thus, the doctrine of Satanism is a heresy; and the true and pure philosophic religion is the belief in Lucifer, the equal of Adonay; but Lucifer, God of Light and God of Good, is struggling for humanity against Adonay, the God of Darkness and Evil.*" End quote.

Take a tip from a friend, you had better leave this organisation immediately.

"Why?" you ask.

Whilst writing this chapter, I have sought to remain calm and unemotional. We are dealing with an incredible deception here.

It must also be recognised that my reader's final destiny could well be determined by what is written on these pages.

1. The problem commences with the Entered Apprentice Degree –
   1st Degree. The Tyler presents the candidate to the Master, who then asks, "Whom have you there?"

The Tyler replies, **"A poor candidate in a state of darkness"**. The implication is quite clear – this means 'spiritual darkness'. Freemasonry can therefore be described as a **journey towards, and constantly seeking for – Light**.

2. It now becomes clear to us that no born-again, committed, believer to our Lord Jesus Christ, could ever continue on beyond this point.

   Religious people – yes.
   Relationship people – no.
   You see, we know and understand clearly that:

a) God is light.
b) Jesus said "*I am the light of the world. He that followeth me shall not walk in darkness but shall have the light of life.*"[5]

Excuse me – do I correctly presume that you skipped over these vital statements found in God's Word?

Would you please stop right here. Go back and read them thoroughly – preferably out aloud. Thank you!

A Baffling Question

How can seemingly intelligent men, from all walks of life, including ministers and religious leaders responsible for the spiritual welfare of others, belong to a society, many of whose leaders state quite openly, "Lucifer is God".

I've found the answer!

1. Remember exactly what Albert Pike said. "*The doctrine of Satanism is a heresy and the true and pure philosophic religion is the belief in Lucifer, the equal of Adonay, but Lucifer, God of Light and God of Good, is struggling for humanity against Adonay, the God of Darkness and Evil.*"

2.[6] Texe Marrs tells us "*Indeed I frequently hear from hardened New Agers, witches, druids, and other occultists, who doggedly insist that their hellish master, Lucifer is a god of good and not evil.*

    It is a fascinating fact that higher-level Masons and Illuminists also profess that their great deity is the glorious and radiant "Father of Light", giver of good things. He's definitely not the devil." End quote.

3. We further learn that "*Today, the Illuminati continue to believe in two principles, Satan and Lucifer. Satan is the evil one, Lucifer is the good side of the Force.*

    *...Part of the benevolence done by Satanic organisations and Satanists is part of their belief system to maintain a **balance** within their lives of the **dual principles**.*

    These good works are not entirely done to deceive (such as Freemasonry with their Schriner's hospitals.)

    In contrast to this, Jesus Christ told the gnostic religious leaders of His day that evil would be judged by God, and that all the good deeds of men are but filthy rags." End quote.

    Albert Pike makes it very clear. He says "***Lucifer is 'god of light'*** and warns Masons, '*doubt it not*'.

4. Here is the main part of the reason for this massive diabolical deception.

The authoritative King James Bible inserts **the key word "Lucifer"** into this passage.

"*How art thou fallen from heaven O Lucifer son of the morning.*"

The vast majority of modern translations however omit the word 'Lucifer' and herein lies the problem.

Let me show you by way of proof.

The Emphasised Bible – "*Oh Shining One, Son of the Dawn.*"

American Standard Version – "*Oh daystar*".

Jerusalem Bible – "*Daystar, son of the dawn*".

Amplified Bible – "*O light bringer and day-star, son of the morning.*"

New English Bible – "*Bright, morning star*".

An Important Question

How can we prove that this being Lucifer is Satan and not the God of Light?

Easy – open up your King James Bible at Isaiah 14:12-15.

Verse 12 – *"How art thou fallen from heaven, O Lucifer, son of the morning. How art thou cut down to the ground, which did weaken the nations."*[8]

Explanation – the true and living God never fell from heaven. The true and living God was not cut down to the ground nor did He ever weaken the nations.

Verse 13 – *"For thou hast said in thine heart, I will ascend into heaven."*

Explanation – What for? If he is already God, he lives in heaven!

"I will exalt my throne above the stars of God. I will sit upon the mount of the congregation in the sides of the north.

Explanation – Hey, this is God's throne-room he's talking about here. This guy is obviously not God. **He's a filthy usurper!**

Wait – the arrogant wretch hasn't finished yet.

Verse 14 – *"I will ascend above the heights of the clouds. I will be like the most High."*

Explanation – If he was truly God, he would be looking down not up. He wouldn't need to ascend above the clouds as he would already be there. A further sign of this pervert's intention are revealed in that he, a created being, has plans to take over from his Creator.

He has to be joking!

Verse 15 – *"Yet, thou shalt be brought down to hell, to the sides of the pit."*

Explanation – All Freemasons, occultists, New Agers, and witches, please take note of where your god is going to end up.

Read on at your leisure. Verses 16 & 17 tell us that Lucifer, the Freemasons' god, the devil behind the New World Order, will be mocked and scorned as a 'loser'.

Do you wish to follow a loser and to finish a loser? Then ignore this information.

Who is this Albert Pike? Are his statements reliable? The 'Scottish Rite Journal', November 1992 includes an article by the **Grand Commander....**

Albert Pike – Debit or Credit?

Quote...."*I recently heard an outspoken Scottish Rite Brother refer to Albert Pike as a **debit** to our order. Pike, he asserted, in no way benefits the contemporary Scottish Rite. In contrast, Pike's **epic work**, Morals and Dogma, he thinks, weakens our every Masonic action and causes members to leave our ranks....*" End quote. (Emphasis added).

The Grand Commander later on says: "*It must be understood that Morals and Dogma is an expression of Pike's personal opinions. The book does not represent official Scottish Rite philosophy. ....The Ancient and Accepted Scottish Rite uses the word "Dogma" in its true sense, of doctrine, or teaching, and is not dogmatic in the odious sense of that term.*" End quote.

**But wait, later on in the article he says: "*Pike's great work is not the book of an hour, a decade or a century. It is a book for all time...*

Abandon Morals and Dogma? Never! The book disclaimed is often the most useful after all..." End quote. (Emphasis added.)

What do you make of this type of reasoning? He appears to be telling us that in Freemasonry you can believe what you choose. If this be the case, why bother joining? I believe what I choose to believe and I'm not a Mason.

Could the uncertainty and ignorance of their beliefs be one of the reasons why Masons get so angry when they are challenged?

They apparently enjoy going to the Lodge, but very few of them wish to understand what they are involved in.

If you wish to be a winner in this race of life, MAKE A CLEAN CUT and from now on, serve the God who deserves to be served. The true and living God, and His son, the Lord Jesus Christ.

It is written, "*Know ye not, that to whom ye yield yourselves servants to obey, his servants ye are, to whom ye obey, whether of sin unto death, or of obedience unto righteousness.*"[9]

"*For what shall it profit a man if he gain the whole world and **lose his own soul**?*"[10]

Footnotes

1   Morals and Dogma; Albert Pike; page 819.

2   A Presentation 1990 – Presenting the Ancient and Accepted Scottish Rite of Freemasonry; page 42; House of the Temple, 1733 Sixteenth St, N.W. Washington D.C. 20009-3199, U.S.A.

ONLY CHRIST CAN REMOVE THE CURSES

3   Morals and Dogma; Albert Pike; page 104.

4   Occult Theocracy; Lady Queenborough; pages 220-221.

5   John 8:12; The Holy Bible.

6   Flashpoint; January 1996; Living Truth Ministries, 1708 Patterson Rd, Austin, Texas 78733, U.S.A.

7   The Duality of Good and Evil by Fritz Springmeier; Endure to the End; volume 2, Issue 6; 1327 9th Ave S.E. Olympia, Wa 98501, U.S.A.

8   Isaiah 14:12; The Holy Bible.

9   Romans 6:16; The Holy Bible.

10 Mark 8:36; The Holy Bible.

Special Note to all Masons

This book is in no way to be considered as a personal attack on individuals. This author has access to vast amounts of information which is non-accessible to the majority of people. However, consider this – **if the hierarchy of your society makes outrageous statements in writing**, it is only right and proper that you should be made aware of these statements and act accordingly.

By now, the reader will have gathered that this whole book has been written from the perspective of a twice-born, Bible-believing Christian. Therefore, it immediately becomes clear that any reader who has doubts regarding the final authority of God's Word, the Bible, will struggle with some of the material found herewith. – So be it!! Facts remain as they always have – facts.

1. The Freemasons started well – a male club, or fraternity of, in the main, stonemasons.

2. Their social work is commendable however, so also is the work of other groups such as the Salvation Army (who thankfully do not utter blood-curdling oaths and obligations.)

3. The Freemason's Lodges were infiltrated by persons involved in the curious arts, occult practises and Luciferianism, as their own writings make clear.

4. These esoteric aspects are not openly discussed in the Blue Lodges so these men remain in ignorance.

CHAPTER EIGHT

THE COUP DE GRACE - A MASON REVEALS ALL

On page 96 of our book "Second Warning" I tell the story of a Mason who attended one of my meetings in New South Wales, Australia.

I was part way into my explanation of these matters when he interjected that it was hardly fair of me to hit the 'craft' as he called it. I replied "Which craft?", which sounded like a pun, yet was not meant in cruel way. He answered, "You know what I mean" as he felt that he should have the right of reply.

I said to him, "Come on up and bring us a word of explanation." I allowed him to publicly state his case in our meeting. The man couldn't believe it and neither could my audience. We parted that night on good terms, as I had done the honourable thing.

The next night we arrived at the building where the 2nd lecture was to take place. There he (the Mason) was again in the front seat. I said "Back again?" and he replied "Yes". (Fairly remarkable observation but the English language and custom lend themselves to these little oddities.)

I said "I was good to you last night. You be good to me tonight. Are you a Christian?" He replied that he was a Methodist lay preacher, which in no way answered the question, as John Wesley, the founder of the Methodism said in his pre-conversion days, "*I went to convert the heathen but who will convert me*?"

I then asked, "What degree are you in?" to which he replied "the 32nd". I answered excitedly "You are the man I'm looking for. Have you heard of Albert Pike?"

Mason: "Yes".

Self: "You are aware of his statement, Lucifer is God and Adonay is also God?"

Mason: "Yes, of course I am."

I'll be quite frank at this stage. **I was convinced that, as many others have done, this man would try to dodge the issue by one of the following means**.

a. Albert Pike never made such a statement. Enemies of Masonry attributed the statement to him.

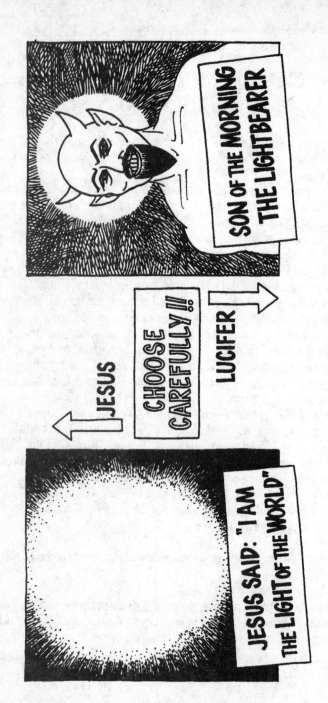

b. That statement applies to some U.S. Lodges but we here in Australia, Great Britain and the other colonies are not linked etc etc.

My dear reader, did you note what this Australian man said? – **He knew this statement of Pike's yet it didn't bother him**.

Self: "Can you please equate your belief in God, with a belief also in Lucifer?

Mason: "I will". He then turned me to the two following Scriptures in the Bible.

"*I Jesus....I am the root and the offspring of David and the bright and morning star.*"[1]

Then he said, "*We will now read from the prophet Isaiah. "How art thou fallen from heaven oh Lucifer, son of the morning...."*[2]

Mason: "There you are Mr Smith. They are the same person."

Self: "**What?** Jesus said "*I am the bright and morning star.*" Lucifer is called "son of the morning".

[3]I continued on, "God, through Jesus (the Word) created Lucifer who was the anointed cherub involved in music and the praise and worship of **heaven**. Because of his pride, he was thrown out of **heaven** and fell to the earth along with one third of the angels.

Jesus never fell from **heaven**.

Lucifer will burn in **hell** forever with his followers.

The Lord Jesus Christ will reign forever with His followers."

I was angry, yet happy at the same time as I now understood where these guys were coming from.

The New South Wales Freemasons, as you possibly now already know, got to hear of this public revelation but botched their explanation badly, making things much worse. They engaged the services of a Committee of Chaplains, who in my humble opinion would all have been better off employed in another line of business. The article is quoted in our book 'P.S.' on pages 25-26. It was entitled "A Response to Specific Criticisms of Freemasonry", part two (The New South Wales Freemason Vol 20), no.5, February 1988.

[4]They wrote, "*In Revelation we read "I Jesus am the bright and morning star." This means Jesus has identified Himself with the qualities of the morning star, or Lucifer, a fitting title for Him whom Christians regard as the 'Light of the world'.*

Some Masonic degrees are restricted to Christians whose members refer to God as Jesus, or as Pike stated "Lucifer".

Are you still concentrating? This statement was not devised by enemies of Freemasonry but by their own appointed committee of Chaplains. Can you believe it?

These men blew it! **Our Lord Jesus Christ is the true light and is the Creator**. Lucifer is the false light and was created!

Although Lodges in the old Commonwealth countries such as New Zealand, Australia, Canada, South Africa, India, parts of Africa etc, are linked to the Grand Lodge in England, never again let me hear the lie that Albert Pike's statement was not really from him, nor that U.S. masonry is not linked to world masonry in general.

Never again forget the highly secret global Freemasonry headquarters named the Palladium.

Freemasonry and the Law

An article in the 'Weekly Telegraph', 21-27 August 1996 has the headline "*Freemason chosen for justice body.*

The Government has defended its appointment of a Freemason to head the new commission to investigate miscarriages of justice.

....Sir ...., the chairman of the Criminal Cases Review Commission, was confirmed by Freemasons Hall in London as both a Freemason and a member of the Royal Arch, a group interested in studying the 'philosophy' of Freemasonry....

....The nub of concern is a 'ritual' involved in the Royal Arch which states that a Freemason should "relieve and befriend" any brother Freemason in need of help and should "suggest the most kindly and the most palliating and the most favourite circumstances in extenuation of his conduct, even when justly liable to reprehension and blame". End quote. (Emphasis added).

It is little wonder that such involved language was used in this statement. If simple English had been used, people would immediately be very upset with this clear manipulation and **misuse** of our law system.

Explanation of the above ritualistic statement:

Should for example, a Freemason, be guilty of a crime, it would be the task of the police Freemason, the judge Freemason, and the lawyer Freemason, (and any other Freemasons who belong to this Royal Arch degree), to get the charges against their fellow Freemason dropped.

Therefore, this could well be a clear case of the '**goat guarding the cabbage patch**'.

But that's not all!

North American Freemasons in the third degree swear "*I will keep a worthy brother Master Mason's secrets inviolable, when communicated to or received by me as such, murder and treason excepted.*"

In the Royal Arch degree of the York Rite, even that small qualification is summarily removed. The candidate swears that "*I will keep all the secrets of a Companion Royal Arch Mason (when communicated to me as such, or I knowing them to be such), without exceptions.*"

At this degree, the candidate also swears that "*I will not speak evil of a Companion Royal Arch Mason, behind his back nor before his face, but will appraise him of all approaching danger, if in my power.*"

Therefore, an officer of the court who knew of an arrest warrant sworn out against a brother Mason would have to warn him immediately so he could flee the jurisdiction.

A Mason who was told of a brother Mason's crimes, even including rape, robbery, or child abuse, would have to keep his knowledge of those crimes a secret, even in a court of law!

A Royal Arch Mason who knew of a Companion Mason's being a murderer or a traitor would have to keep his knowledge a secret.

If a Mason appears in court against a non-Mason, all he has to do is give any number of obscure gestures or words to a Masonic judge, and this man will be obligated to rule in his favour.

No one in the court room will be the wiser (except another Mason who would be forbidden from bringing the incident to light.)

In the light of this information, it is clear that any person connected with the law system of any country, should be forbidden to join any Lodge or secret society which could in any way interfere with his duties.

'London Times', 27 September 1996 – "*Police to declare Masonic link.*

All police officers will be asked to declare whether they are Freemasons under plans being prepared by chief constables to curb the organisation's links with forces.

Any officer who reveals he is a Freemason or a member of any other semi-secret organisation would have the details entered on a force register of interests. The declarations will be voluntary but if

FOLLOW YOUR LEADER

52

an officer stays silent and later faces allegations involving Freemasonry, his silence would count against him...

The guidance will make it clear that officers must avoid membership of any group which might lead to questions over their impartiality...

Many senior officers believe that the influence of the Freemasons is declining..." End quote.

It is little wonder then that from time to time unusual court rulings baffle the general public.

A Confused Minister Writes From Canada:

"Both Mackey and Pike's publications were largely disagreed with on a universal basis as soon as they were available a century and a half ago".

Author's comments –

1. Please notice that this man did not come up with the names of any of those who disagreed.

2. In the light of his statement, why is it then that the New South Wales Committee of Chaplains in Australia, write in their official magazine "*some Masonic degrees are restricted to Christians, whose members refer to God as "Jesus" or as Pike stated "Lucifer".*

3. As Mackey and Pike's publications are '*largely disagreed with on a universal basis*', does this mean that an official public announcement has been made throughout all the Lodges that these mens' works, including Mackey's Encyclopaedia of Freemasonry, should be taken from their bookshelves and destroyed?

4. If this minister is correct regarding Pike's and Mackey's works, we can therefore assume that basically, a Lodge member can believe anything he wishes to, and disregard anything that the Lodge hierarchy tells him.

This being true, imagine what would happen if a would-be member refused to go along with the initial obligations involving the ceremonial cutting of the throat, and the tearing out of the tongue, and instead decided to preach the gospel, referring to Jesus Christ as the only way to God.

This would be akin to anarchy and the whole system would rapidly fall apart.

Thus, to any reader who feels strong emotion getting the better of him at this point, please answer all these questions and then ask yourself this one.

5. Do I, any longer, wish to associate with any society which includes members who truly believe that Lucifer is God?

Who is Lucifer? He is the arch-enemy of Almighty God.

His other names are 'Satan' or the 'Devil'.

A final note.

None of this is to prove that one is right and one is wrong, but an opportunity to use our God-given intellect in an exercise of clear thinking.

Does this minister know something that the Australian Committee of Chaplains did not know?

Of course, no Christian minister has any right to belong to any organisation where **even some of its members** declare openly that Lucifer is God!

This is outrageous, as Jesus made it clear, that light and darkness never mix.

One observation I have made over the years is that Freemasons struggle with woolly thinking and find it difficult to face facts, and strive to the very end to protect what they '**think**' is the truth – after all, what intelligent man wants to confess that he was mistaken?

This no doubt is a spiritual problem and comes from the oaths that they took upon themselves at their initiation.

I well remember visiting a Freemason who asked for help after reading one of my books, but upon entering his office, he began to talk and talk and talk, never leaving me space to comment apart from 'yes' and 'no'.

He later stood to his feet and said "I'm sorry but I must go now as I have another appointment."

His secretary, a born-again Christian believer, came to me with a look of amazement on her face and said "I have never ever seen him behave like that before. What came over him?"

I was able to explain.

Who is to blame for all this deception?

During the year 1996, a concerned lady sent me a tape recording of a Masonic Service held in a Uniting Church in Australia, to persuade me that I had got it all wrong.

I was dumbfounded as I listened to the minister go along with all this woolly thinking, using the word **tolerance**, over and over again.

Since listening to this tape, I have concluded that the Masons are no more spiritually lost than the poor church adherents who attend such gatherings, **but the chief culprit would appear to be none other than the Minister who obviously is posing as a Christian**. It would appear that he has not discovered the basic premise of Christianity, that **Jesus Christ Himself is God's only Lamb, and that only His precious blood cleanses from all sin**.

[5]When Jesus said, "*I am the way, the truth, and the life. No man cometh unto the Father but by Me*", He wasn't joking.

Here are the possibilities:

a) He was deluded.
b) He was a madman.
c) He was evil.
d) He was telling the truth and was who He said He was.

Any minister in a so-called Christian Church who doesn't subscribe to section d), should resign immediately. Better to go to the Lake of Fire by yourself than drag a whole congregation and some Freemasons along with you.

Jesus made this clear in His day – "*But woe to you, scribes and Pharisees, hypocrites! For you shut up the kingdom of heaven against me; for you neither go in yourselves, nor do you allow those who are entering to go in.*"

If I can discover all this information, any minister can do the same and should do so.

I say this kindly – but for the grace of God and circumstances, I could have been caught up in this Luciferian plot myself.

The author of this book is not God, and we can rest assured that those whose hearts are genuinely towards the true God, both Masons and non-Masons, will (at some time throughout their lives) be given an opportunity to repent and turn to God's Lamb, the Lord Jesus Christ.

Who really knows what takes place in those last few seconds before death?

Advice – Advice

Men, face it. The moment they hoodwinked you, it was not only a physical event. **It was a spiritual hoodwinking also**. As you drew your thumb across your throat and uttered those dreadful words, you put a curse on the following:

a. yourself
b. your wife
c. your descendants to the third and fourth generations

"*I the Lord thy God am a jealous God, visiting the iniquity of the fathers upon the children unto the third and fourth generation of them that hate me.*"[7]

Only Jesus Christ the Lord can break the curses. The prayer of renunciation needs to be prayed with witnesses (see prayer at the end of this chapter.)

Fruit of Masonic Curses

1. The man's wife becoming increasingly lonely and angry as the husband is apparently continually 'out with the boys'.
2. The wife and children open to spiritual attack, and nightmares.
3. The wife can have feelings of insecurity and creepiness while her husband is at the Lodge meeting.
4. Alienation within the family.
5. Children disobedient and hard to control.
6. Restlessness, mental confusion.
7. Financial problems.
8. Covert sexual deviancy and frigidity.
9. Mistrust and lack of compassion.
10. Physical ailments especially in the three main areas connected to the Masonic oaths, which open a man and his family up to demonic influence i.e. Throat cutting – pulmonary area; chest ripping –cardio-vascular area; stomach slitting – bowels and related organs.

For further help, please contact:

Mr Phil Bennett
85 Leinster Ave
Raumati South
Kapiti Coast
NEW ZEALAND
Ph/Fax (04) 297-3040

Our grateful thanks to him for this added information.

We do not need any more religion. What we now need to do is to enter into a relationship with God Himself, through His Son Jesus Christ. He died for you and His precious blood alone will be accepted by God as payment for every evil thing you have ever thought or done.

Please turn immediately to the back of this book and pray the other prayer which will help you to receive the **Lord Jesus Christ who is the true Light of the World** – not the illumined gnostic light of Lucifer (Satan) you opened yourself up to when you joined Freemasonry.

[8]**Born again – this is the experience you are really seeking. Jesus said you must be 'born again'.**

Then, **write a letter to the registrar of the Lodge** saying "Please strike my name from the register. I am now a 'born-again' believer in Jesus Christ as my Lord and Saviour. I no longer require a Masonic funeral. Thank you. Yours faithfully...."

A Formula to Follow

1. Have the candidate (either a man having taken the masonic oaths, or a female relative who has been oppressed by these oaths) stand next to you and repeat after you:
2. "I renounce the spirit of Freemasonry with all its oaths, secrets and curses.
3. I renounce every ancestral spirit of Freemasonry in my family line.
4. I confess Jesus Christ is my Lord and Saviour."

   (At this point, stop and ask candidate if they are truly born-again. If not, lead them in the sinner's prayer found at the back of this book, or one of your own involving:
   a) Repentance from sin
   b) Believing that the Lord Jesus Christ died for me
   c) Receiving Him into my life now and confessing this with my lips. Romans 10:9-10.

5. For those in, or who have taken the oath for, the **first degree** – "I renounce the spirit of the Entered Apprentice Degree as taken by me (my father, my grandfather, etc). I renounce all these curses with the oaths in the Name of the Lord Jesus Christ. I reject the cutting of the throat, and the tearing out of the tongue. This no longer belongs to me."

   For those in, or who have taken the oath for, the **second degree** –" In the Name of the Lord Jesus Christ, I renounce the oath and the curses of the second degree as taken by ....(insert name). I reject the tearing open of the chest, and the ripping out of the heart. This curse no longer belongs to me."

For those in, or who have taken the oath for, the **third degree** – " In the Name of the Lord Jesus Christ, I renounce all the curses connected with the oath of the third degree. I reject the slitting open of the stomach, the tearing out of the bowels and the burning of them to ashes.

I reject the demonic name Ma Ha Bone.

I reject the spirit of death from the death blows to the head.

I reject falling into the stretcher and observing the death symbols.

I reject the blasphemous kissing of the Bible, on a witchcraft oath.

I reject the spirit behind a false resurrection. Only Christ rose from the dead of His own free will."

For those in, or who have taken the oath for, the **Royal Arch** degree – "In the Name of the Lord Jesus Christ, I renounce the false, secret name of God.

I reject Jah Bul On as the demonic monster that he is.

He is not the living and true God.

The God that I worship is the Lord.

The God of Abraham, Isaac and Jacob.

The Father of our Lord Jesus Christ.

He is my God and my Father through the new birth.

I renounce with my lips, any other subsequent oath or curse taken by .... and I confess that Lucifer will go to the lake of fire where he will burn forever.

My Lord Jesus Christ is in heaven from whence He will reign forever over all – King of Kings and Lord of Lords."

Leader, then invite candidate to breathe out gently, long breaths. As he continues like this, leader should speak to the spirits –

a) "In the Name of the Lord Jesus Christ whom I serve, I speak to the spirit of the **Entered Apprentice degree**. Come out on the breath and set ......(insert name) free in the Name of the Lord Jesus Christ. In the Name of Jesus, I break this oath and this curse over ....'s (insert name) life and pronounce him/her free.

b) I come against the spirit of the **second degree** in the Name of the Lord Jesus Christ. I break the oath and the curses of the second degree in Jesus' Name. You are no longer welcome here – come out on the breath.

c) I speak to the demonic spirit of the **third degree** with the oath and the curses. I release .... (insert name) from these cursed things, in the Name of our Lord Jesus Christ. Set him/her free now. His/her body is the temple of the Holy Ghost. You have no right to be in him/her. Leave on the breath, now in Jesus' Name. Spirit of death, leave him/her.

d) In the Name of the Lord Jesus Christ, I come against the false name of God. Jah Bul On is false. You devil, come out in Jesus' Name. I set this man/woman free in the Name of the Lord Jesus Christ. What God hath cleansed, let no man call unclean. Praise the Lord!"

You may also need to pray over his/her family.

Footnotes

1   Revelation 22:16; The Holy Bible.

2   Isaiah 14:12; The Holy Bible.

3   Ezekiel 28:11-18; The Holy Bible.

4   Revelation 22:16; The Holy Bible.

5   John 14:6; The Holy Bible.

6   Matthew 23:13; The Holy Bible.

7   Exodus 20:5b; The Holy Bible.

8   John 3:3; The Holy Bible.

Recommended Reading

Masonry – Beyond the Light by William Schnoebelen; page 194; Chick Publications, P.O. Box 662, Chino, Ca 91708 – 0662, U.S.A.

They Took the Oaths by Roger and Sydney Mytton-Watson; Lot 16, Saunders Way, Karragullen, Western Australia 6111.

Freemasonry on Trial by many authors; Internet address – http://www.monger.com/mason.

We highly recommend these publications.

Prediction

As more and more people become aware of the Luciferian aspects in Freemasonry, they are pulling out, and the Lodge is seeking new members.

If you belong to Rotary, Lions, the local yacht club, etc, do not be surprised if you receive an invitation to attend an open night.

Although not encouraged years ago, a subtle form of recruiting is now taking place.

CHAPTER NINE

THE MYSTERY REVEALED

THE TWO SEALS ON THE REVERSE SIDE OF
THE AMERICAN $1.00 BILL

In the year 1993, during a lecture tour of Western Samoa, we were contacted by the Prime Minister of that country to visit his home the next morning for prayer and discussion regarding some problems which had emerged.

Later on the next morning, after all the business was dealt with, I pulled out a US$1 bill from my pocket and explained the mystical occult symbolism including the eye of Lucifer above the pyramid.

His first question was one which is being asked by many around the world. **"If that is indeed the eye of Lucifer, how is it that right alongside, we have the words clearly written, "In God We Trust"?"**

Ask any American who knows a little of their history and they will explain the reasons John Robinson and the **Pilgrim Fathers** left their native England. The basic reason was for 'religious freedom'. Hence, '**In God We Trust**'.

Now, the next question also requires an answer. "What has an Egyptian pyramid to do with the U.S.A. and what is the eye of Lucifer doing in that position, obviously waiting to come down on the pyramid (representing the world structure as it is today) and thus to become the capstone of history? What arrogance is this?"

Author's special note – From my reading of the ancient prophecies, **there is another far greater than Lucifer who will be the capstone of history. His Name is Jesus Christ, who is also Lord.**

So far, it appears that a **devilish coup** has been planned by a created being, who in his pride and foolishness wishes to usurp his Creator's plan and ultimate position of leadership.

We continue.

During the year 1991, we were lecturing in Seattle, in the north west state of Washington. Entering our host's house one evening, a young lady also arrived at the same time, carrying a very large book under her arm. This book was entitled "**The Secret Teachings Of All Ages**" by Manly P. Hall, a well known Masonic writer.

Some may say that the meeting with this girl was an accident; however, I prefer to think otherwise. I was so excited about the information contained in this book that I immediately offered her $20.00 U.S. and she went off to purchase another copy.

We make bold to say that without a copy of this book, or one like it, the reader would continue to remain in ignorance about the true meaning behind the seals.

THE JIGSAW COMES TOGETHER

Just as I have drawn on the knowledge of others, I am pleased to be a link in the chain that others may draw on what I have written here, and make **choices** as a result, that will extend far beyond this life into eternity.

Sufficient information is necessary first of all, so that a reasoned and intelligent **choice** may be made.

Do not underestimate the value of the information you will discover in the following chapter.

Recommended Reading

The Secret Teachings of All Ages by Manly Hall; ISBN No. 0-89314-830-X; The Philosophical Research Society Inc; 3910 Los Feliz Boulevard, Los Angeles, Ca 90027, U.S.A.

THE TWO SEALS ON THE REVERSE SIDE OF
THE AMERICAN $1.00 BILL

62

CHAPTER TEN

THE OCCULT NATURE OF THE SEALS EXPLAINED

[1]Quote from "The Secret Teachings of All Ages", pgs XC and XCI –

*"European mysticism was not dead at the time the United States of America was founded. The hand of the **mysteries** controlled in the establishment of the new government, for the signature of the **mysteries** may still be seen on the Great Seal of the United States of America. Careful analysis of the seal discloses a mass of **occult** and **masonic symbols** chief among them, the so-called American eagle. ......the American eagle upon the Great Seal is but a conventionalised **phoenix**...."* End quote. Emphasis added.

Now, what is a **phoenix**? It is a mystical bird that rises from man's first attempt to set up a similar system of One World Order, namely '**the Tower of Babel**'.

[2]Referring to the New World Order, the 'Weekend Australian' newspaper, 1st September 1990, printed the large headline – '***How to make our tower of Babel work properly***'.

Sometime later, Margaret Thatcher passed the comment when referring to the European Union aspect of the New World Order, that *"....it was an even more utopian task than the building of the tower of Babel. At least, when they built the tower of Babel, **they all started speaking the same language**...."* End quote.

These planners are obviously very aware as to what they are doing. However, Manly Hall isn't finished with his explanation yet. Let us read on.

"Not only were many of the founders of the United States government Masons, but they received aid from a secret and august body existing in Europe...." (Break quote.) Please read slowly and thoughtfully.

*"....which helped them to establish this country for **A PECULIAR AND PARTICULAR PURPOSE** known only to the initiated few."* (Emphasis added.) Break quote – Who are the initiated few? **The Elect, the Sages, the Adepts** i.e. men who have gone well beyond the publicly known upper degrees of Freemasonry.

Now you can understand why Blue Lodge Masons get excited and violently angry when they first hear this information. They were very unwise not to seek out this occult aspect before joining.

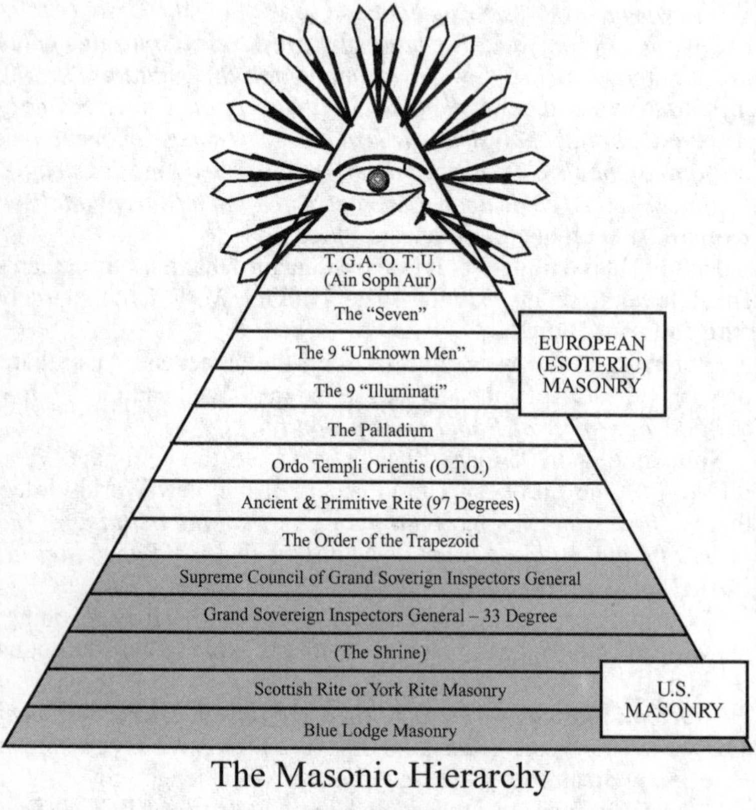
T. G.A. O. T. U.
(Ain Soph Aur)
The "Seven"
The 9 "Unknown Men"
The 9 "Illuminati"
The Palladium
Ordo Templi Orientis (O.T.O.)
Ancient & Primitive Rite (97 Degrees)
The Order of the Trapezoid
Supreme Council of Grand Soverign Inspectors General
Grand Sovereign Inspectors General – 33 Degree
(The Shrine)
Scottish Rite or York Rite Masonry
Blue Lodge Masonry
EUROPEAN
(ESOTERIC)
MASONRY
U.S.
MASONRY

The Masonic Hierarchy

PYRAMID SHOWING VARYING DEGREES IN FREEMASONRY

Look once more at the pyramid structure of Masonry.

Therefore, any Mason reading this information, must realise that if you have been admitted to any degree in the blue or red Lodges, this knowledge is not for you to know.

If you think this chapter contains strong material, just wait until you finish the following section.

Question: What is the 'peculiar and particular purpose' for which America was established by **occultists and Masons**?

Answer: **To put Lucifer (Satan/the devil) on the throne of the world** and thus set up a secular, ungodly, heathenistic, New World Order, over which the true and living God will have no say. (Remember the key word 'seclorum'.)

It is very important to realise that **the U.S.A. was created to lead us into the New World Order, whilst Russia would apply the pressure that would make all that possible**. This is the Hegelian dialectic in operation i.e.

a) The U.S.   = Thesis
b) Russia   = Antithesis
c) Link the two = Synthesis

Humanity is to be **convinced through fear** of the need for a One World Government. Then they will sacrifice national sovereignty of states. Hence, wars, terrorism, military aggression, are made to occur, and ever proliferate just prior to the new millenium.

However, just to prove that we are not speaking out of order here, let us take only two examples to prove our point.

At the base of the pyramid is the date 1776 written in Roman numerals. Remember, this does not stand for the U.S. Declaration of Independence on July 4th, but rather for the inauguration of the Illuminati on May 1st.

Just as a matter of interest, **who else appreciates this date? Witches and top men in secret societies** are initiated into upper

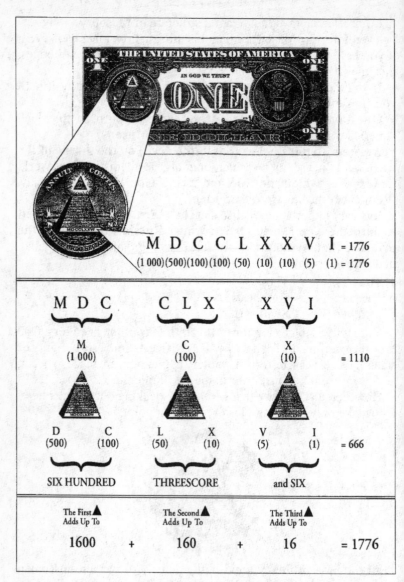

MDCCLXXVI = 1776
(1 000)(500)(100)(100)(50)(10)(10)(5)(1) = 1776

MDC   CLX   XVI

M
(1 000)

C
(100)

X
(10)

= 1110

D   C
(500)   (100)

L   X
(50)   (10)

V   I
(5)   (1)

= 666

SIX HUNDRED   THREESCORE   and SIX

The First ▲ Adds Up To   The Second ▲ Adds Up To   The Third ▲ Adds Up To

1600   +   160   +   16   = 1776

OCCULT NUMEROLOGY

66

degrees on this day, and communists always have their May day parade.

Now to find a secret esoteric message, first draw 3 pyramids.

M - 1000   D - 500   C - 100   C - 100   L - 50   X - 10
X - 10   V - 5   I - 1   = 1776 *(May 1st)*

a. Place M at the apex of the first pyramid. Now place D & C on the base line.
b. Place C at the apex of the second pyramid. Place L & X at the base line.
c. Now, place X at the apex of the third pyramid and place V & I at the base line.
    Add all the numbers along the base line. They equal 666.

Where else do we find this number?

Are you aware that there is an ancient prophecy written by a man called John, who was banished by the Roman authorities to a Greek Island called Patmos? He speaks of a **one world political leader** who arises at a certain time in history. This man is called by a number of names, one of them being '**The Beast**'.

There is also another religious man who is predicted to arise and he is called 'The Second Beast' or '**The False Prophet**'.

In the light of the esoteric mystical numerics shown above, it is now imperative that we link this information with the prophecy dated 96 AD.

Remember this prophecy was predicted in the book of Revelation 13:16-18 in the year 96 A.D. and is being fulfilled between the years 1990 and 2000.

[3]Verse 16 – "*And he causes all, both small and great, rich and poor, free and bond, to receive a mark in their right hand or in their foreheads.*"

Verse 17 – "*And that no man might buy or sell, save he that had the mark, or the name of the beast or the number of his name.*"

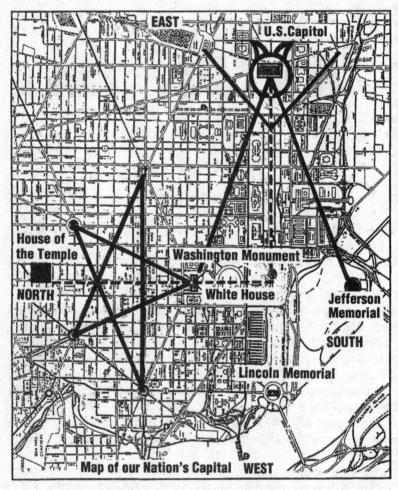

EAST

U.S. Capitol

House of
the Temple

Washington Monument

White House

NORTH

Jefferson
Memorial

SOUTH

Lincoln Memorial

Map of our Nation's Capital   WEST

A MAP OF WASHINGTON D.C. SHOWING MASONIC
SYMBOLS BUILT INTO STREETS

Question – "Do we know the number?" Get ready – yes, you guessed it.

666

Verse 18 – "*Here is wisdom. Let him that hath understanding count the number of the beast, for it is the number of a man and his number is six hundred, threescore and six.*" (End quote.)

Meanwhile – Back to the Occult

Here is Manly Hall again. "....*The Great Seal is the signature of this exalted body – **unseen** and for the most part **unknown,** and the unfinished pyramid upon its reverse side is a trestleboard, setting forth symbolically the **task to the accomplishment of which, the United States government was dedicated from the day of its inception.***" (Emphasis added). End quote.

How are your emotions at this point? Frightened – stunned – baffled – confused – angry?

Let me be very frank. This author becomes very upset at revealing this information as he has many special friends living in that great country – **the United States of America**. However, the truth must be told.

Whilst visiting another country, I spoke at a Presidential breakfast on these subjects and in the middle of my address, one of the diplomats present arose and along with his wife, stalked out of the conference room, obviously muttering unspeakable phrases.

The other diplomats wisely kept their seats as they represented 8 other sovereign nations who desperately need this vital information.

The newspapers in Australia and New Zealand made a big deal of this drama of course. Let's face it – the plan is so clever, and the information so vast and devilish, that unless it is presented in a logical manner, you are written off as having psychological problems.

The offended diplomat was duly sent a copy of my book 'P.S.' but it probably got no further than his secretary. Poor man – the old 'ostrich with its head in the sand' trick.

Let us continue.

Prove This Information Yourself – A Challenge

You may establish the veracity of this information by photostating the seals and placing them on a transparency. Then cut the transparency in half and place one circle on top of the other and you

GOATS HEAD INSIDE SATANIC PENTAGRAM

will be amazed to find that by carrying out these instructions various esoteric messages appear.

[4]A friend of ours here in New Zealand, also an author and a researcher, Bruce Cathie, has written a number of exciting books on subjects hidden from the majority of the populace. His area of expertise is harmonics, and his books are worth reading for his highly detailed mathematical formulae.

Bruce Cathie tells us that Washington D.C. was built on a reclaimed swamp. He also reveals that with regard to harmonics in communications networks, this city is exactly where it has to be. The harmonic communications link ups are absolutely amazing between, for example, the White House, the Pentagon, the Russian Embassy, the Naval Bases, etc, etc.

Not only that, when the Freemasons and occultists designed Washington D.C., they incorporated their masonic symbols into the streets of the city. On p 68, please observe the map of the city. The masonic compass and square are actual streets, as are also the streets making up the satanic inverted pentagram, inside which, the goat's head is placed.

I showed this map to **a leading Mason**, who replied "**It must have happened by accident**."

Of interest is the fact that the goat's horns fit into the two top areas of the pentagram, his face in the middle, his ears to the sides but please note where **the beard stops - right at the White House**.

Now, look at the compass. One end stops at the Jefferson Memorial (remember - this was the man who received the hooded messenger, and received from him the two Illuminati seals in the red velvet bag.)

Where does the other end stop? You guessed - **right at the White House**, so ultimately, let's face it, the President of the U.S.A. is spiritually affected from at least two areas of the occult world.

Therefore, is it not reasonable to assume that **the city of Washington D.C. is under a terrible Luciferian curse**?

The chickens are coming home to roost.

[5]As I write these lines on the 25th April 1995, there is in front of me on my desk, a cutting taken from the 'Australian' newspaper dated 19th April 1995 (6 days old). The bold headline reads "*Clinton steps in to rescue Washington.*

President Clinton yesterday authorised a partial federal takeover of the nation's capital hoping to stop the embarrassingly crisis-ridden city from sliding into financial collapse.

....Mr Clinton yesterday signed 'legislation' to create a five member oversight board with broad powers to sack thousands of city workers and control spending by the mayor of Washington, Mr M....n B....y and his city council.

....the federal intervention will allow the district to borrow hundreds of millions of dollars from the Federal Treasury to help pay its bill but will also force it to balance its budget within three years." (Author's note - these are called '**conditionalities policies**'.)

"*....the mayor and council have been forced to concede that they can no longer finance all of the schools, prisons, hospitals, and other services over which they won control.*

The new control board has been described in Congress as the strictest financial oversight, ever imposed on a U.S. city...." End quote.

Don't worry Washington D.C., I predict herewith that very soon, your whole country will privatise and sell out your ailing businesses to others who can do the job better. You will follow the New Zealand plan shortly after your 1996 elections with Mr Bill Clinton still at the helm. (Predicted 25th April 1995.)

As I revised this section of the manuscript during the month of August 1995, the previous paragraph, spoken prophetically in the month of April, began to turn into history in the month of July as **the U.S. Congress visited New Zealand to learn how to restructure and to follow the New Zealand model** (see elsewhere in this book for further proof).

NOW, BACK TO THE SEALS

Through books like this one, the general populace are beginning to ask questions right across the world.

1. Why is there a pyramid on the U.S. dollar bill?
2. What does the eye represent?
3. What is the meaning of all those Latin words?

In the light of all these questions it would appear that the enemy, Lucifer, **has had his cover blown**. How can these secret world-manipulators stop people asking these embarrassing questions? **Remove the dollar note of course**. The plan is too far on now, to be spoilt by a lot of inquisitive people demanding answers.

A Mind Boggler

[6]A short time ago, we were in London where I picked up a copy of the London 'Times', 19th April 1995. Please note the headline -I almost flipped out. "*America weighs up demise of $1 bill*.

*In their drive to restore America's greatness, Washington's Republican revolutionaries are **seeking to abolish** the ultimate symbol of their country's global supremacy, the "greenback". ....N....t G.....h and his fellow Republicans want to do away with the world famous dollar bill and replace it with a coin.*

....Fighting to abolish the dollar bill is the "Coin Coalition" comprising vending machine companies.

...They argue that dollar coins would be cheaper and more convenient....

*Currency experts also point out that **America is one of the last developed countries to retain a banknote now worth so little** – barely 60 pence (Great Britain). In fact, America has had a dollar coin for much of its existence.*

The silver dollars lasted until 1965, although the "greenback" introduced in the 1860s was the more common currency." End quote. (Emphasis added).

As I have mentioned before, the US$1 did not bear the two Illuminati seals until 1933 when the top degree Mason, Franklin Delano Roosevelt, authorised their printing.

How do I know?

I have a note in my possession dated 1928 – no seals! I have in my possession a note dated 1935 – 2 seals!

Whilst travelling on a river boat up the Mississippi River with some friends of ours who happened to be linked with the Freemason's Lodge, I brought out these two US$1 bills and very swiftly silenced their protestations.

Heavy information you will agree. Yet even now, we are not finished. Let us entitle this next section –

Footnotes

1   See footnote chapter 4.
2   Weekend Australian; 1st September 1990.
3   Revelation 13:16-18; The Holy Bible.
4   The Bridge to Infinity – The Energy Grid and Harmonic 371244 by Bruce Cathie; America West Publishers, P.O. Box 986, Tehachapi, Ca 93581, U.S.A. Ph: (805) 822 9655.
5   Australian Newspaper; 19th April, 1995.
6   London Times; 19th April, 1995.

CHAPTER ELEVEN

A STRANGE PHENOMENA

In the early 1940's, the firm of E.W., Cole situated in the Book Arcade, Melbourne, issued redeemable coupons with the following inscriptions:

"*D40*   *United States of the World*
(C31)   *Tis Coming, Tis Coming*
           One Government, One Religion
           One Language, Before the Year 2000."

And on the reverse side:

        "*The Government of Right*
        The Religion of Goodness
        The English Language
        Improved by the Best Words
        of all other languages."

The second voucher said:

"*D42*   *The Whole World is the Fatherland*
 C33   *of the Noble-minded*
         (And within the rainbow)
         Federation of the World Medals
         Issues by E.W. Cole, Book Arcade, Melbourne."

And on the reverse side:

> "*Country and Religion*
> *Let the World be your Country*
> *And to Do Good Be your Religion*"

WELCOME TO THE NEW WORLD ORDER

CHAPTER TWELVE

THE ANNOUNCEMENT

At the end of 1990, George Bush in his Gulf War speech, spoke of a **mystical 1000 Points of Light'**. He did not explain this any further.

The Aim

To cleverly, unobtrusively, surreptitiously, using Fabian Socialism practices, relieve each country of

a) **first of all its national assets**
b) **its governmental ability to govern**
c) **its sovereignty and independence**
d) **and link each country into an INTERDEPENDENT GLOBAL VILLAGE whilst the citizens are still asking the question "What's happening?"**

The Plan

a) Do not on any account advise the citizens of the electorate what you are about to do or are doing.
b) Select **key government departments** and announce that these are about to be **corporatised, privatised**, then later on of course, these can be **sold up to new overseas owners**.

During the month of May, 1995, I heard a lady being interviewed on the radio who said: – "I've often longed to know the future so that I can live in the light of that knowledge."

Never fear Madam, we are here to help you.

THE STOOGES – There are at least 1000 groups with the gnostic, illuminated, secret, knowledge.

These are Mr Bush's "1,000 Points of Light".

Many of these persons involved must be connected with societies such as the Freemasons, who **in many cases, yet not all**, give more allegiance to their own obligations than to the laws of the country. Sad, yet true. (Read 'The Brotherhood' by Stephen Knight.) It has been suggested that almost all men given a knighthood thus enabling them to be called "Sir", are Freemasons. Should any reader of this book be able to prove that this is incorrect, please contact the author.

It is of significance that one of the first to speak of a "global concept" was Dr Henry Kissinger. He is now involved in world restructuring. **Could this be the reason why he recently received a knighthood from the Queen**?

Wairarapa 'Times Age', 14th June 1995 – "*Honorary Knight.*

Henry Kissinger, the veteran statesman, and former United States Secretary of State, is to be awarded an honorary knighthood....The award is to be presented to Mr Kissinger by the Queen in London on June 20th.

As an American, he will not be allowed to call himself "Sir", an honour reserved for British citizens.

The detailed reasons for the award were not given." End quote. (Emphasis added).

It is also of note that on occasions, various writers have referred to this man as a **public relations advocate for the New World Order**.

The ancient prophecies make it exceptionally clear that **this New World Order will continue on for only three and a half years once it comes to full power, under the complete control of a powerful leader**.

Are these proponents of the New World Order evil?

Not all. Mostly very **sincere but ignorant** of the end results of their enterprise.

[1]In the guinea pig country of New Zealand, 40 politicians belong to a group called P.G.A. – 'Parliamentarians for Global Action'. Without reading books like this, the majority of these people would not have a clue as to the aims of the little-known group.

(All who belong to this society should now seek out their own literature, outlining aims and objects of P.G.A. Then, upon becoming suitably shocked at what they read, resign immediately.)

Footnotes

1 The list of names was broadcast on a Sunday evening, over a New Zealand radio station on February 19th, 1995.

I have waited patiently for this information for a period, not less than 26 years.

Herald Sun Australia, **November 26 1996**

Nixon aides top job chance.

HENRY KISSINGER, international affairs dove and former aide to Richard Nixon has emerged as a serious contender for Secretary of State in President Bill Clinton's second term.

. . . the 73-year-old . . . refused to deny he'd been approached by the White House, which is keen to employ prominent Republicans in the Democratic President's team.

"I'd like to serve with a president who also speaks with an accent" Mr Kissinger said to the paper, referring to Mr Clinton's southern drawl.

. . . Mr Clinton added fuel to the Kissinger rumour last week by saying he favoured a name not yet printed. That name, the *New York Times* reported, was Mr Kissinger's. - End quote

Authors note:
Insert, The point is that Kissinger is now back in the public eye.

Footnote
See also Chapter 23, "Who is He?" on p 158.

THE ORDER

Antony C. Sutton

322

Wednesday Evening, June 28th, 1882.

CHAPTER THIRTEEN

SETTING UP THE NEW WORLD ORDER SUBTLY PUBLICISE IT

The scene was San Diego International Airport on February 18th, 1991.

I boarded a flight which would take me through to Dallas, Fort Worth, then on to Midland and finally to a small town called 'Big Spring', Texas. An invitation had been issued to conduct a series of lectures.

Whilst dashing through the airport, I just had time to pick up a copy of the Los Angeles 'Times'.

Prior to this date, we had watched the television screen with great interest as George Bush had introduced the words **'New World Order'** to us on a number of occasions whilst also discussing Saddam Hussein's attack on Kuwait.

Over and over, the same words 'New World Order', 'New World Order'...what did it mean?

By this time I was also aware of President Bush's involvement with a secret fraternity called the **'Skull and Bones'**, during his days at Yale University. Entrance to this society was highly selective and only two authors seemed to know anything about it.

a. Ron Rosenbaum
b. Antony C. Sutton

The initiations to this German-based society were reported to be:

a. wrestling, while completely unclothed, in a bath of mud;
b. lying in a coffin revealing the personal secrets of your life to the other members of the club;
c. being locked in a tomb for a season, wailing like a banshee;

By the way, it should be noted at this point that the motto of Yale University is the same as that which is written on the base of the pyramid found on the reverse side of the US$1 bill – '**Novus Ordo Seclorum**' i.e. a secular, heathenistic, ungodly, New World Order.

When the members graduate from Yale, they then move on to another highly secret group called **'The Order'**.

[1]Antony Sutton, in his brilliant expose, tells how **The Order manipulates politics, education, religion, and economy, towards one end i.e. a complete takeover of every person's individual freedoms**.

Being of German origins, the philosophies of two great thinkers were strictly adhered to:

a. Kant

b. Hegel

Quoting from Antony Sutton's book, we read – "*From this system of Hegelian philosophy comes the historical dialectic i.e. that **all historical events emerge from a 'conflict' between opposing forces**....*" End quote.

In other words, there is no chance of setting up such a monumental change in society without a "**very significant war**".

Operation Desert Storm

Now, enter one Saddam Hussein. A man who no doubt, morning by morning, views himself in his bedroom mirror, smiles at himself and says "Here I come, you lucky people."

The world planners saw to it that **this man received wrong advice from the two super-powers**, prior to his invasion of Kuwait.

Russia – General Makashov – "Yes, go on Saddam. You will become the hero of the OPEC nations. They all despise Kuwait as being the fat cat of the Middle East. The Kuwaitis continue to set their own oil prices in defiance of all the others in the area. Yes, go for it, my boy" (or words to that effect).

Saddam smiles. His only worry now is "What will the U.S. reaction be? Will they intervene and spoil my plans?"

A meeting is arranged between Saddam and the representative from **the United States of America** – one **April Glaspie**, who also appeared to give him the 'okay'; whether intentionally or not, we cannot say.

Whilst in the States a little after this event, we watched television coverage of April Glaspie being interviewed by the Congress.

Congress: "*What advice did you offer to Saddam Hussein, Ms Glaspie?*"

Ms Glaspie: "*Arab problem – Arab solution*".

Obviously Saddam took this as an 'okay', thumbs up style message. He invaded Kuwait and was immediately attacked by the combined armies of the **Novus Ordo Seclorum** (New World Order).

In fact, George Bush made this fact abundantly clear, that for the first time in history, a common aggressor had been dealt with by the armies of the major nations of the world.

This was to serve as a lesson to any other nation that may feel inclined to get 'stroppy' and out of hand. "What we gave Saddam, we are also capable of giving to you."

This is a perfect example of the Hegelian Dialectic in operation!

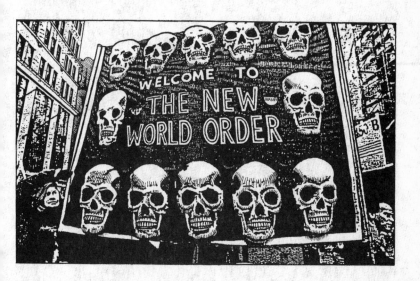

Military Bases Closing Down World-Wide

It is for this reason, the U.S.A. began the trend in closing down military bases left, right, and centre. Under the New World Order, or the 'Global Village', we will no longer need to fight one another, as our hearts are all going to change and be full of love, one for the other. Any miscreants will be dealt with swiftly and harshly by the international armies of the New World Order.

Notice for example how 'decisively' and 'swiftly' the United Nations' forces dealt with the problems in **Somalia** and then in **Bosnia**. (Tongue in cheek, of course.)

If this is how the United Nations' Army operates, heaven help us!

Oh yes. We will ultimately all join hands with Gaddafi, Saddam Hussein, Idi Amin, and each other, moving our bodies rhythmically and singing "We are the world".

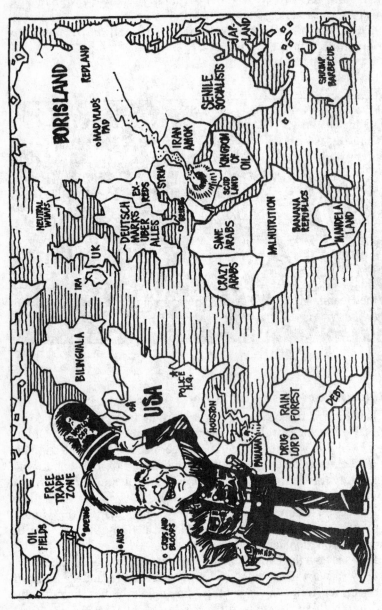

CARTOON FROM SEATTLE NEWSPAPER

84

Meanwhile, back to the L.A. Times article – 18th Feb 1991

Flying over Texas at about 30,000 ft, I lazily turned to the inside pages of the newspaper and figuratively speaking, almost fell out of my seat. The first thing that struck my eye was a demonstrator's picture with the words, *"Welcome to the New World Order"*, with a border of human skulls all the way around the outside. The amazing article which was written below the picture read in part.

"Policy – The President found a slogan for his Administration. But neither he nor anyone else can seem to define it." End quote. (Emphasis added.)

In other words, the message is so heavily coded, people do not understand it.

("Excuse me – that is the main reason for this book".)

Continue quote – *"....Go and ask them upstairs", urged a senior State Department official, whose job, at least on paper, includes building large parts of the New World Order.*

"I can tell you what I think it is", another senior official confessed, "but I'm not sure that it is the same as what the President thinks it is...." End quote.

On the 31st March 1991, we were in Seattle and picked up a copy of the Hearst paper, 'P.I. Focus'. There was a very revealing cartoon showing George Bush as the policeman of the world. A map of the world done as a comic strip showed up the New World Order as a type of comedy.

A psychologist in New Mexico once told me that if you wish to put over a very terrifying message in an acceptable manner, they would recommend the use of:

a) **music and song**
b) **humour**

For example, in this comic strip we see each country portrayed in a light-hearted manner.

Los Angeles = Crips and Bloods (gangs)
N.W. South America = Drug Lords
N.E. South America = Rain Forest – to be paved
Central and South America = Debt
Central Africa = Malnutrition
South Africa = Mandela Land (later proven to be correct)
Russia = Gorbyland (later proven to be incorrect)
Australia = Shrimp barbeque

Then surprise, surprise, in the month of June I was handed a copy of the Robert Maxwell newspaper – 'The European', 14-16 June 1991, with the heading "*Old New World Order*". Reader please listen to me. **The things which I have been saying for years are, in part, now in the public domain.**

Quote in part – "*Yale's founding slogan is Novus Ordo Seclorum (New World Order). Could it really be that simple? The President is known to be a keen Yalie, full of school-spirit. He endures a good deal of teasing about his membership of 'Skull and Bones', the most arcane and exclusive of the college's many 'men-only' dining clubs.... Of course one notices the obvious, one finds it assailing the sense at every turn.* Novus Ordo Seclorum *is also inscribed on the Great Seal of the United States. In that exalted capacity, it appears on the reverse side of every dollar bill....*

....Mikhail Gorbachev made a speech at the United Nations December 7 1988, weeks after the election of George Bush to leadership of the free world.

"Today, the further world progress is only possible through a search for a universal human concensus as we move forward to a New World Order."

....Did Thomas Jefferson, as a U.S. founding father, beat Bush and Gorbachev to the phrase?...." End quote. (Emphasis added.)

Please take note that the author of this article, one Christopher Hutchins, asks this final question at the conclusion of the article. I suspect he knows the answer.

Footnotes

1   An introduction to the Order by Antony Sutton; State Publishing Co., Montana, U.S.A.

Prediction

Your country will also experience ethnic unrest as tensions are stirred up by factions who themselves are secretly primed by New World Order agents, following the plans of the Hegelian dialectic.

Remember – Thesis versus Antithesis.

At a suitable time in history, repressive laws are introduced, thus controlling both groups.

Hegel called this – Synthesis.

CHAPTER FOURTEEN

THE TASK TO HAND
TRY OUT THE PLAN

If you were a planner, looking for a country to test out your diabolical plan, which one would you choose?

a) A little known place, as far away as possible so as to be inconspicuous.

b) A country whose activities are considered so unimportant that the world's media barely gives it a thought.

c) A country situated as close to the international dateline as possible so that the day's trading for the world could start there each morning.

d) A country with possibly a fair sized land mass (shall we say about the size of Great Britain) but with a tiny population.

e) A population of people who are not in the main vocal, demonstrative, or vociferous in their condemnation or opposition of anything they find offensive. Their national motto could be summed up in the words, "She'll be right".

f) A population who, in the main, know very little of activity in the outside world, only that which is carefully fed to them by the media.

g) Preferably an island nation where border controls do not pose a great problem.

h) A country looked upon as a poorer brother to a larger nation nearby. The plan could therefore be tested on both nations in tandem. The larger nation situated alongside this test case country, could have as their motto, "She'll be right, mate."

Can you visualise such a nation?

I can because I was born there. I am saddened to tell you, it is my birth place - New Zealand.

Using the American programme, "That's Incredible" as an example of the average N.Z.ers laid back and slack attitude to life, our programmers designed their own show entitled, "That's Fairly Interesting".

Proof 1 – see page 135 of our book 'Final Notice'. Quote – "*In the late 1980's, the President of the World Bank visited New Zealand. He said on that occasion, "New Zealand's economic restructuring was a role model for other countries which also had to adjust their policies to achieve growth", the World Bank president, Mr Barber Conable said....*" End quote. (Emphasis added.)

Proof 2 – The "Australian" newspaper, 25th August 1995, makes this point very clear with the giant heading -

"*The Kiwi Experiment – New Zealand's robust approach to micro-economic reform has been held up as a model for the country. But research has cast doubt on whether the gain has been worth the pain. Detailed analysis undertaken by a New Zealand economist has concluded the country's growth performance has been the worst of any industrialised country.....since the country's economic reforms were begun in 1984.*" End quote. (Emphasis added.)

Proof 3 - "*The New Zealand Experiment. Harsh ABC's of Frugality.* 'Edmonton Journal', 14th November 1995:

"*The public seems largely resigned to the irreversible nature of the reforms. But there is still bitterness and distrust of Government...*" End quote.

Alberta, of course, is following the New Zealand Rogernomics plan.

Now, it is quite simple for you, the reader, to understand all this information written in extremely simple English. However, it took over 24 years to put it all together. I can assure you that this is **not conjecture**. It is all **fact**.

Come with me on this fascinating journey as we search to find out why our country has been so drastically torn apart. **Readers from other countries**, take out your pen and make notes, as many of you by now have followed this same path, or at this very time are following it to the letter.

Predictions

Other countries' citizens will sometimes claim that their country in particular was also a test case. This could well be true on occasions, as the new World Order folk do not put all their eggs into one basket. This would make the 'plan' too obvious too quickly, and angry citizens may attempt to put a stop to it.

For example, although the initial plan commenced in New Zealand in 1984, we need to point out the following facts.

Australia – 1984: Henry Kissinger flew into this country and gave talks to financial institutions and politicians. Just after he left, EFT POS (Electronic Funds Transfers at the Point of Sale) commenced.

Singapore – harsh penalties for littering, smoking, chewing gum, etc, are now in place. This could soon go world-wide.

With the **Australian** elections over, Mr John Howard and his government are now free to follow the New Zealand plan - closing down hospitals and post offices, getting rid of Unions and the ACTU, and replacing them with Individual Personal Contracts. Not only that, the Welfare System must go and folk will be encouraged to take out Private Insurance cover.

In **Great Britain**, Mr Tony Blair is being groomed to follow the same path. Goodbye Mr Major.

CHAPTER FIFTEEN

THE PLAN

1. Lend each country a great deal of money to assist them with development.

We have travelled and lectured world-wide for over 30 years. In each country I pose the question **"Are you in debt?"** and the answer comes back strong and clear from many voices, **"Yes"**. This is called audience participation. Please notice, they don't have to think before they answer as this condition has become part of each individual's knowledge.

However there are exceptions where the audience has shouted "No" e.g. Singapore, the Isle of Man, the Channel Islands (i.e. Jersey and Guernsey).

Until the year 1961 when New Zealand borrowed from the I.M.F., we had not only full employment, but were seeking workers from outside this country to assist us.

2. Who are the best known money lenders?
    a) The Bank for International Settlements. Within this group we have the G10 and the **G7**. For information on these groups, please read our book 'Final Notice', pages 242-244. N.B. G7 is the main power group. They meet in the main in Basle, Switzerland.
    b) The World Bank.
    c) The International Monetary Fund.

Forget about the G10, they are relatively unimportant. The Group of Seven (G7) are the key players.

Should the IMF (International Monetary Fund) or the World Bank wish to lend money, they must come to the G7, '**cap in hand**' for the authorisation to do so.

3. This is the most important point of all. Do you remember ever borrowing money from a bank or a finance company? Did they require security? Yes, of course. It is called **collateral.**

When national governments borrow from the money lenders, do they require security? Yes, of course.

Take note now. Their security lies in '**Conditionalities Policies'**, all signed and sealed at the time the money was borrowed by previous, sometimes forgotten, or even deceased, politicians. In the case of New Zealand, **17th April 1961**.

The plan was deadly; slow, but sure. Time was on the side of the planners. Although George Bush referred to the plan as the '**New World Order**', Jimmy Carter referred to it as '**Global 2000**'. By the year 2000 therefore, the planners' aim is to have everything set up.

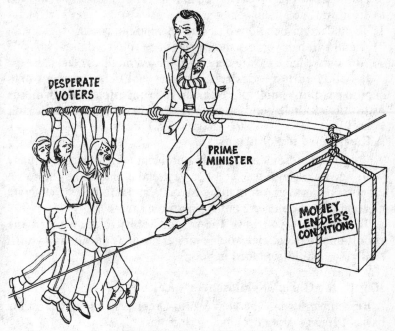

WALKING THE TIGHTROPE

a) A One World Government
b) A One World Religion
c) A One World Law System
d) A One World Currency
e) A One World Computerised Tracking System to deal the death blow to objectors to the system.

"Far out", you say. Keep reading!

We are herewith presenting a basic premise, then we will establish this as a fact, beyond a shadow of a doubt.

Politicians – trustworthy or not?

Have you ever wondered why it is that when you elect a politician to power, he never seems to keep his pre-election promises? Why is this?

Many of them are highly honourable people yet, when they arrive at the halls of power, they are quietly taken to one side and given a list of the **conditionalities policies** to read.

Politicians today are trapped and therefore are merely allowed to decide on such menial subjects as:

1) Should shops be allowed to stay open on Sundays?
2) Should all baby prams and carriages be fitted with seat belts?
3) Should we increase the benefit to unwed mothers? etc. etc.

It is this author's desire that every politician in the world should read this book and clear up the confusion in their minds as to why all their good intentions seem to come to nought.

A Clear Word to Politicians

They have presented you with a problem which faced me many years ago as a school-teacher of 15 years experience. They removed corporal punishment from the classroom, and left the teachers with no final line of defence against classroom saboteurs.

To sum up – you have the responsibility, but owing to the conditionalities policies, you no longer have the authority to fulfil that responsibility placed in you.

Hegel – the German philosopher speaks

Remember again. The New World Order is being set up on the basis of Hegelian philosophy or principles.

By printing the following paragraph, I am not in any way taking a swipe at politicians or leaders of any country on earth. My sympathies lie with you in your frustration to beat off continuous criticism of those who **simply do not understand**.

Sadly, when politicians get trapped during a television or radio interview, they angrily reply, **"The reality is...."** but none of them really understands the reality, unless they read books like this.

[1]Antony Sutton in his book 'The Order', goes on to say: *"What then is the function of a parliament or a congress for Hegelians? **These institutions are merely to allow individuals to "feel" that their opinions have some value** and to allow a government to take advantage of whatever wisdom the "peasant" may accidentally demonstrate.*

*As Hegel puts it, by virtue of this participation, subjective liberty and conceit, with their general opinion, **individuals can show themselves palpably efficacious and enjoy the satisfaction of feeling themselves to count for something**...."* End quote. (Emphasis added.)

LUCIFER'S EYE

RUDE, RUDE, RUDE, EXTREMELY RUDE!

So you see then, the political, financial, and social agenda for our country is now in the hands of those who initially lent us the money.

Wherever we lecture, we tell the people – "Stop criticising your government and leaders. **Pray for them** as this problem which confronts them is spiritual but most of them are not aware of it.

Remember this eye – Lucifer.

[2]*"I exhort therefore that, first of all, supplications, prayers and intercessions, and giving of thanks be made for all men.*
For kings and for all that are in authority....that we may lead a quiet and peaceable life in all Godliness and honesty...."

Pray for a politician – never; why should I? What positive benefits can we expect by praying for them?

Answer – 1. **A quiet and peaceable life**
2. **A Godly, honest life style.**

There is therefore a spin-off from this exercise.

Footnotes

1   The Order; Anthony Sutton – pg 119

2   The Holy Bible; 1 Timothy 2:1-2

GOVERNMENT
POLITICAL
LEADER

MONEY LENDERS'
CONDITIONS

NEW WORLD ORDER
MONEY LENDERS

YOU BORROW – YOU PAY!

CHAPTER SIXTEEN

THE CONDITIONS

These are geared so that gradually each country on earth who gets caught in the money-lenders web then is forced to follow a certain line.

The New Zealand guinea pig experience

In the early 1980's, New Zealand had been selected by the 'planners' and the G7 were somehow involved in the plan.

5 men in the New Zealand Labour Party at the time agreed to the plan, and instead of informing the rest of the party, went ahead, and secretly implemented the policies which would later lead to the selling out of the country and enslavement of its people.

We herewith quote proofs of this action with no animosity, anger, malice, or emotion. These are the facts as recorded by the New Zealand media. You have heard of Reaganomics in the U.S.A.? Read this and marvel. (See also page 46 in our book 'Final Notice'.)

[1]*"The Plan.*

By piecing together statements and documents it can be shown that "Rogernomics" was a plan imposed by a small group of ministers on a party which had confused ideas as to what it was letting itself in for....Ultimately, the L.....e, P....r, C......l, P......e, D......s view of the economic policy had been endorsed before the snap election. Even the Prime Minister D.....d L.....e acknowledged that the **agenda of Rogernomics** *had been* **withheld from the party** *which had campaigned for his election...."* End quote.

Why did I not write down their full names? There is no reason to bore overseas readers with any names, as these men were obviously not the architects, merely the perpetrators.

Some may feel very angry having read the above article and begin to think in terms of wild west scenes where bodies jerk on the end of ropes, **but surely we can show some grace to these deluded individuals and forgive them for what they did**. Anyway, hanging for treason was struck from our law books just prior to these restructuring events taking place.

Wait a moment, we aren't finished yet.

In our book 'Final Notice', on page 46, we draw attention to another media article which helped our understanding.

[2]"*Rogernomics kept secret from the party.*

*The Labour Party hierarchy kept "Rogernomics" **secret from party members** for the 1984 General Election, the Prime Minister, Mr L.....e has told Australian television.*

*Mr L...e said Labour's economic policy had to be sold to the party and the country in **various disguises** the newspaper said....*" End quote. (Emphasis added.)

That gives you confidence in the democratic system doesn't it? And to think that disillusioned voters, at the time, laid the blame on the Labour Party as a whole. New Zealand people will remember that ultimately we kicked them out, then brought in the National party who by this time understood that it would be political suicide not to continue '**the Plan**'.

My concern is this. New Zealand being the test case, was conned by **secrets and various disguises** and now, all you others in many different countries will go like sheep to the slaughter unless folk read and understand what we are writing here.

What did they do to New Zealand?

Precis of the plan:

1. Government departments targeted **for restructuring**
2. Corporatisation
3. Privatisation
4. Shares 49% overseas initially (i.e. locals and foreigners joint control)
5. Overseas raiders come in and buy up local shares until over 51% goes foreign
6. State-owned Enterprises and assets called '**the family silver**', has gone forever
7. Investors must be found to stop the country collapsing
8. National sovereignty is an illusion and a thing of the past
9. As the future governments have little or no assets to work with, the final stage is a change to M.M.P. which involves many little groups forming coalitions as they can no longer govern the country anyway. The coalition group voted to power gives the illusion of

governing and thus keeps the ignorant masses happy. True control now comes from our New World Order masters, overseas.

In the year 1996, both Israel and Italy have coalition governments, and are proving to be ungovernable. You obviously can't satisfy everybody!

As we do our final check on this manuscript, the New Zealand elections are over and 'The Economist' newspaper from Great Britain, makes the following comment – *"Politics crashes on head. The ambiguous result of the New Zealand election should provide Britons with enough evidence to reject proportional representation...*

...the state of New Zealand politics was a disaster all democratic societies should fear...

Mr Tony Blair, the leader of the British Labour Party, intends to hold a referendum on election reform if he wins the British election next year.

The Economist said **the New Zealand experience, which could well see the country reverting "to the rule of fudge and mudge", is likely to vindicate Mr Blair's personal reservations about proportional representation***...*" End quote. (Emphasis added.)

Do you have government departments? Yes, we used to have them too, and if you looked them up, they could be found in the front of our telephone directories. Not now though. They've disappeared.

Citizens of other countries, take careful note.

Stage 1 – We awoke one morning in the early 1980's to find that 6 government departments had been targeted for "**restructuring**".

Stage 2 – The catch word was '**corporatisation**'. The clever folk explained to the not so clever folk that this would **increase efficiency**. Any old fool knows of course that government departments world-wide are notoriously inefficient. All the Kiwis (New Zealanders) said "**Oh good!**"

Illustration: A gardener, an architect and a public servant had a debate as to who was the most important.

Gardener: "The first man that was created became a gardener therefore, I am the most important."

Architect: "The great architect of the Universe designed this world of order out of chaos, therefore, I am the most important."

Public Servant: "**And who do you think created the chaos**?"

Stage 3 – We woke a few mornings later to see a new word in the paper. It was '**privatisation**'. The learned ones told the non-learned

98

ones that this would **increase efficiency**, and all the Kiwis said "**Oh good!**"

<u>Stage 4</u> – We awake and upon reading the morning paper, see a new word appear – '**shares**'. At this point, we smell a rat, and quickly write letters to our leaders asking whether they are selling these shares to overseas people.

"Oh no", is the hasty reply. "We are only selling 49% overseas and thus the remaining major shareholding stays in New Zealand", and all the unsuspecting Kiwis said, "**Oh good**."

<u>Stage 5</u> – By a further act of Parliament, or by hostile share takeovers, the overseas investors buy up 51% of the ex-government departments with their assets and those valuable commodities, often called the 'family silver', bought with the tax money paid for through my grandfather's sweat, my father's sweat, and my sweat, go overseas, never to return again. And all the Kiwis said, "**Oh dear**".

In future therefore, when you read the word '**privatisation**', please add the word '**goodbye**' and another word '**forever**'.

Overseas readers may be interested to read that the Christchurch 'Mail', 20th December 1993, reported "*New Zealand 40% foreign owned.*" Also note a 'Press' headline 10 December 1994, "*Most of major firms' shares, foreign owned.*"

> New Zealand Railways – U.S. owned
> New Zealand Ferry Service – U.S. owned
> Wellington Buses – Scottish owned
> New Zealand Herald – Irish owned
> Wellington Electricity – Canadian owned

Now should there be a neighbouring Australian laughing up his sleeve and saying "New Zealand, you only have 11% to go and you've lost your sovereignty and independence, let us turn to the Austrade figures reported from a magazine called "Fight", dated July 1994. These were the levels of foreign ownership in various areas at that time.

Processed food	*95%*
Motor vehicles	*100%*
Pharmaceuticals	*100%*
Confectionary and Beverages	*84%*
Manufacturing	*57%*

Building Materials	88%
Mining	97%
Electrical	98%
Banking	86%
Chemicals	98%
Insurance	82%
Hotels	75%
Oil and Gas	92%

And that is not all – read on.

Let us divide these percentage totals by the number of industries listed and it would appear that Australia is approximately 88.62% in overseas hands, at least as far as these industries are concerned.

Recap the Stages

1. Restructure Government Departments
2. Corporatisation
3. Privatisation
4. Shares – initially only 49% overseas
5. Shares – Increase to over 51% overseas
6. Investors from overseas

Notice now, that without these investors, your country will collapse economically as you have been already cleverly conned into the selling up of your major assets.

Will you believe this, that in the guinea pig country of New Zealand, certain politicians introduced a bill, (and I rejoice to say that it was thrown out) to make it a criminal offence to speak against foreign ownership of land.

These world government characters never give up. Do not be surprised at a later date to see another attempt made to silence those who speak up in defence of their country and its assets.

An Australian commentator wrote a fascinating article during the year 1994, to the 'Sydney Morning Herald'.

"While both sides of Australian politics carry on about the Queen, **plans are emerging for a de facto form of global government** *that will make the republic debate a quaint irrelevancy.*

Last week, the leaders of the world's richest countries, the Group of 7 (G7), agreed to proposals which are likely to increase greatly the power of the International Monetary Fund **(IMF) to discipline governments "who don't do what it says".**

The G7 also accepted proposals to boost the power of the World Bank **to make third-world countries adopt "free market policies."**

....The plan to give the IMF and the World Bank more power, *has been devised by a group of bankers calling themselves the Bretton Woods Commission.*

....You mightn't get to be crowned at Westminster Abbey, but if you want to exercise **real sovereignty**, *you could do worse than join* **the de facto world government**, *now being constructed by the international bankers...."* End quote.

Question – Did the social experiment called Rogernomics that was secretly sold to us in various disguises help us at all? A wealthy colleague of mine said that this was the best thing that ever happened to the country. Not being in the wealthy group, I personally dispute his findings.

A Wellington economist writing to the newspaper in 1995 agrees with both of us.

Quote – "*Recent government policies have certainly favoured the rich.*

....The majority of the population are still worse off than they were in the 1980's.

....The rich of course, are much better off. *The tax cuts ensured that. No wonder they are triumphant about their recovery.*" End quote. (Emphasis added).

Overseas readers also take note that when government departments become privatised, in many cases you will find them being sold off at **'mates' rates'** to insiders (those in the know) – sometimes at a price less than half their value.

Protestation will avail little.

The Global Scene

Let us offer up some proof about all this from other countries around the world. Remember first of all, those **conditionalities policies**.

Please take note of the key rules of the New World Order planners.

Rule 1 –

**BY CONTROLLING ENERGY
WE CAN CONTROL NATIONS.**

**BY CONTROLLING FOOD,
WE CAN CONTROL INDIVIDUALS.**

Rule 2 – By excessive rates and taxes, destroy all small business. **Merge all big business until about 6 companies control the commerce of each country**.

This is called 'centralisation of control'. Thus **merge, merge, merge**, is the name of the game.

Rule 3 – The first area to be privatised in each country and sold overseas to agents of the New World Order planners must be **telecommunications** (Telecom in New Zealand, Telstra in Australia, Telekom in Malaysia etc). Sell it for a song if necessary but get rid of it. This is so that a global dossier on every individual can be set up.

Footnotes

1   The Listener N.Z.; 19th December 1987
2   The Christchurch 'Press'; 26 June 1987

CHAPTER SEVENTEEN

CONDITIONALITIES – WORLD-WIDE ILLUSTRATIONS

<u>Proof 1</u> – 'Sunday Tribune', South Africa, 29th July 1991 – "*IMF funding likely **but with strings**.*

Conditions may be too severe for South Africa.

*.....For many debt-ridden African countries, receiving IMF assistance has meant subjecting their economies to a brutal form of shock therapy prescribed by the IMF as a **condition** for receiving financial assistance.*" End quote. (Emphasis added.)

<u>Proof 2</u> – 'Auckland Star', 2nd February 1990 – "*Telecom sale only weeks away.*

*.....This year, we intend to **complete** our privatisation programme",* Mr C....l said, but his office later circulated another version of the speech in which the word **complete** had been changed to **continue**...." End quote. (Emphasis added.)

<u>Proof 3</u> – We then flew across to Great Britain and picked up a copy of the 'Daily Telegraph', 12 March 1990 – "*Telecom seeks sell-off for expansion overseas.*

British Telecom is pressing the government to sell its remaining 49% state holding before the next general election.

*...The Labour Party has listed British Telecom as its **main privatisation target**...*" End quote. (Emphasis added)

Link that information with this information – 'Australian', 25 May 1992 – "*Selling off government businesses to the private sector once would have raised fury in large sections of the community. These days it is regarded as inevitable.*

Even selling off government services such as prisons and roads seem to have gained wide-spread acceptance although there are still some pockets of resistance.

*Most people acknowledge that governments simply do not have the **discipline** nor the **expertise** to run business operations **efficiently**.*

....the British Government's privatisation programme started in the early 1980's.

***In the U.K. more than 200 government businesses have been sold off...*" End quote. (Emphasis added.)

<u>Proof 4</u> – 'Daily Nation', Nairobi, Kenya, 14th July 1993 - "No new U.K. aid to Kenya. Minister: IMF conditions must be met." End quote.

<u>Proof 5</u> – 'The Age', Melbourne, 28th April 1993 - "*Africa faces ruin says report.*

...Oxfam suggests that unless IMF's **terms and conditions** *are fundamentally altered, it would be better to extricate the IMF from Africa altogether...*" End quote. (Emphasis added.)

Would you like something a little more up to date?

During a recent trip to Ghana, the local people were very upset by the introduction of VAT. The same problem arose in early 1995 in Western Samoa, where there was an attempt to unseat the government of the day.

In Ghana, West Africa, I was able to assure both government and people that conflict was useless as the **conditions** have been in place for many years i.e. Value Added Tax (VAT) or a Goods and Services Tax (GST).

A politician in Australia, in the year 1994, whilst battling to become Prime Minister, **foolishly told the electorate, "When I get into power I am going to introduce GST."** This is very similar to saying – **"Vote for me and I'll shoot you in the head."**

<u>Rule</u> – You must never announce a new tax until you first secure the job. The poor man was doing so well too, and even to this day probably wonders what went wrong.

Now, let us return to the Ghanaian illustration.

<u>Proof 6</u> – Stage 1 – 'The Independent', Ghana, 12-18 April 1995" We can't avoid VAT - Dr B....y.

The Minister for Finance and Economic Planning, Dr B...y has called on Ghanaians to endure the effects of the Value Added Tax (VAT) and that "No matter how difficult it is a current (sic) and *we must join.*

He said the industrialised nations including African countries such as South Africa, Nigeria, and Malawi, are all practising VAT.

...."If we stop collecting VAT, and then go to the IMF to collect money, they will not take us serious (sic) because we were unable to implement the policy", *Dr B...y added*." End quote. (Emphasis added.)

Thank you Dr. In all my years, I have not ever heard of a politician who laid it straight on the line as this man did.

Understanding an issue brings a measure of trust and credibility. But no, the others bumble on, deceiving and being deceived.

Stage 2 In the 'Daily Nation' newspaper, 15th July 1995, we read, "*Ghanaian President.....**urged his finance minister** who has steered the country through years of economic reform, **not to resign** while the country was trying to entice in foreign investment...Minister B...y had tendered his resignation a week ago....*" End quote.

Stage 3 – 'Zambia Times', 23rd July 1995, "*Ghana's President ...... accepted the resignation of Finance Minister B....y......*

*The 50 year old lawyer has **received praise for championing the economic reforms** which halted the slide in the economy and built the foundation for a take-off. But he has **also been bitterly criticised by others who blame the reforms** sponsored by the International Monetary Fund and World Bank, for difficulties, especially the high cost of living and unemployment.*

***B...y has not stated publicly why he is leaving** but he did say that he had thought about it long and hard.*" End quote.

No person with understanding should ever criticise any politician wishing to leave their job. The pressures are, in many cases, insufferable.

So then, who is the big bad wolf? Is it the IMF, the World Bank, the Bank for International Settlements or G7?

No – let's go back to the beginning.

Do you sincerely believe that a little known New Zealand politician who had his own business collapse, could possibly dream up such a clever scheme? It was alive before this man was born. Credit only where credit is due.

An interesting excerpt from a U.S. paper called EIR, 23rd September 1988. "*....The overall approach was laid out by IMF Director General..... in a recent interview to a German newspaper. **"If a country thinks the IMF is a big satan or a criminal organisation, we can't do anything for such a country. Naturally, we only work with those countries that want to work with us.***

*....That kind of approach doesn't leave anybody any choice. Work with the IMF and **get wiped out by its conditionalities policies**, don't work with the IMF and get **destroyed**.*" End quote. (Emphasis added.)

That's an interesting choice isn't it? Your country will be **wiped out**, or **destroyed**.

This is not in any way a criticism of the IMF as they are also locked inextricably into the plan. They do what they are told.

LUCIFER'S EYE

Heavy stuff eh?

Do you somehow feel at this point that the information is becoming irrefutable?

No? Then read on!

Some of you may feel that yours is the only country in the world that is privatising and thus has these problems. We have established quite clearly, I feel, **that privatisation is simply one of the conditions.**

Enter the Rothschilds family – the House of the Red Shield. At this time of writing (27th April 1995), they are going through some fairly deep waters regarding their involvement in the privatisation and subsequent selling out of British Coal to a group who were not the highest bidders – This type of behaviour is not limited to Great Britain.

Did you know that the Rothschilds have a **privatisation unit**?

<u>Proof 7</u> – 'Weekend Australian', 2-3 January 1988 – "*Rothschild and Sons drops its guard.*

....Mr O.....r L........n and Mr J.....n W.....e, members of the Rothschilds International Privatisation unit.

....Mr L....n had been a member of the Prime Minister's policy unit.

....Since arriving at Rothschilds, they have worked on a slew of privatising projects.

*Mr L....n has written a book..... called '**Privatising the World**'."* End quote. (Emphasis added.)

<u>Proof 8</u> – 'Daily Mail', 13th April 1990 – *"The great sell-off. **Russia** paved the way yesterday for massive privatisation that will send shockwaves through the Soviet economy.*

President Gorbachev's economic advisers announced that 70 per cent of the state sector would be privatised." End quote.

And who do you think travelled to Russia to teach them to privatise? None other than the ex-New Zealand Minister of Finance.

<u>Proof 9</u> – 'Herald', 20 February 1992 – *"The former Minister of Finance, Sir R....r D.......s, is off soon to talk to the Russians about **privatisation**......Sir R.....r said he would be part of a three man privatisation advisory committee organised by the WORLD BANK...."* End quote. (Emphasis added.)

What further information do we learn from this article? There were two others involved, suggesting clearly that **this is not one man's plan**. Others are in on the deal as front men in different areas of the world. Try and deny this part if you will, but we know who the rotten apple in the barrel is!

<u>Proof 10</u> – 'Citizen', Johannesburg, South Africa, 7 August 1993 – *"**Zambia** to step up privatisation.*

Deputy Director of the Zambia Privatisation Agency.......Zambia, whose economies....ravaged by 27 years of misdirection and mismanagement under State control, plans to privatise more than 150 companies over five to ten years.

*.......He said ....**redundancies** would be minimal...."*

(Author's note – "Ha, ha, ho, ho...")

"....He said.....its privatisation legislation placed no restriction on who could invest in Zambia, or the number of companies which could be bought...." End quote. (Emphasis added.)

<u>Proof 11</u> – During the early 1990's, we stopped off at the Island of **Mauritius** on our way to South Africa. We came across a demonstration being held, where workers, fearful of losing their jobs, violently waved placards and screamed out unmentionable things in the French language. One banner was very clear with only four words

on it. Although French is not my natural language, I did indeed take some pride in translating this to my wife – "*Non a la privatisation*!"

Proof 12 – 'Citizen, Johannesburg, South Africa, – "*Madagascar privatises.*

....Madagascar is to sell of its state controlled companies as part of reforms agreed with the World Bank and the International Monetary Fund...." End quote. (Emphasis added.)

Proof 13 – 'Financial Times', London, 10 April 1991 – "*IMF Egypt in $350m accord.*" End quote. (Emphasis added.)

Proof 14 – 'Financial Times', London, 11 January 1991 – "*Israel may turn to IMF...*

...the country is likely to have to borrow $20 billion over the next several years." End quote. (Emphasis added.)

Proof 15 – 'Financial Times', London, 15 January 1991 – "*Strong demand for shares in Polish privatisation.*" End quote. (Emphasis added.)

Proof 16 – 'Financial Times', London, 4 January 1991 – "*Brazil privatisation countdown begins.*" End quote. (Emphasis added.)

Proof 17 – 'Financial Times', London, 25 January 1991 – "*Prague begins property privatisation.*" End quote. (Emphasis added.)

Proof 18 – 'Financial Times', London, 1991 – "*Czechs hang "for sale" sign on 50 of republic's key companies.*" End quote. (Emphasis added.)

Proof 19 – 'Financial Times', London, 13th June 1991 – "*Argentina's talks with IMF reach a critical stage...*" End quote. (Emphasis added.)

"What else is there to be privatised?" I hear you cry. Oh, not very much really – just the **hospitals, jails, town water, railways, trams, airlines, freeways, bridges, electricity, airports, government banks, government shipping lines, gas companies, serum laboratories, scientific laboratories, inland fishing rights, ocean fishing rights, defence facilities, etc etc etc....**

Proof 20 – 'Edmonton Journal', 15 May 1994 – "*Jails on the road to privatisation.*" End quote.

Proof 21 – In an advertisement in a magazine called 'Airline Business', a conference was to be held in London 28-29 March 1988. The title of the conference was "*Toward the Global Airline*".

LUCIFER'S EYE

Whilst speaking in Johannesburg, South Africa, in the year 1992, on August 13th, a staff member from South African Airways heard what I had said, went back to work later that evening, and punched the keys on the computer under 'General Information'.

He was astounded at what he had read and came back the next night to tell me. **"Only 6 major airlines will remain."**

This will explain why we regularly read the word '**merge, merge, merge**'.

This book is not written with the express aim of frightening anybody, but it is important to bring this section to a close with a damning piece of evidence to show that we are indeed on the right track.

When I revealed this information to about 2,500 people in Ghana, West Africa, during the month of April, an audible gasp went through the audience.

South Africa and Nelson Mandela are so well-known worldwide, that this information will now clarify the issue to hand.

<u>Rule</u> – **Obey the conditions or you don't get the money**.

Before being elected President, Nelson Mandela allayed the fears of his voters in the ANC party and said that he would in no way yield to the money lenders and privatise, thus ultimately selling out the country's **independence and sovereignty**. Now, please take note.

Proof 22 – 'Business Day', 11 July 1994 – "*G7 leaders pledge financial aid for South Africa.*

.....European officials said South Africa was likely to obtain aid from a number of countries, but cited no numbers. They stressed that "the G7 countries" (author's comment – please note this phrase), had actively backed the resumption of financial support for South Africa by the IMF and the World Bank...." End quote. (Emphasis added.)

Note here the clear **link** between G7, the IMF and the World Bank. Put on your safety belt.

Proof 23 – 'Weekend Australian', 5-6 November 1994 – "*ANC to privatise in shock reversal.*

The African National Congress has been forced into several policy reversals since becoming the leading partner in South Africa's government on national unity, but few of its conversions have been more dramatic than its recent decision to embrace privatisation to generate funds for social development.

Only a month after the country's April election, President Mandela was vowing he would never support a programme that would merely channel more wealth into the hands of the country's white minority. As recently as August, Mr J....y N.....o, minister in charge of implementing the Government's centrepiece reconstruction and development programme, condemned privatisation as a method of "sacrificing long term assets, for a short term benefit...." End quote. (Emphasis added.)

Good man – clear thinking!

Illustration – I have a very close friend who owns a saw-milling business. Wishing to visit his home country, he enquired as to whether or not, in my opinion, he should sell his saw mill to raise enough money for the airfare. I said "**Don't do it**. You collect your air fare money, of that there is no doubt, but when you return back again, you no longer have your asset to use for generating further finance."

To those of you persistent enough to continue on this far in the reading of this book, I herewith state the obvious –

Old (**you know who**) here is so smart that he can see what very few politicians and others cannot see. By selling up the family silver, **it is goodbye to sovereignty and goodbye to independence** as the governments of these countries will have nothing left with which to work with or generate finance.

Hey – **We are in dire trouble!**

Believe it or not, in the little country of New Zealand in the year 1995, **some of the leaders in this diabolical plot, along with their cohorts, are trying to set up a political party to finish the job; some may even say "To finish us off!"**

We suspect that they will still do well in the polls as apparently only elephants have good memories.

A good analogy in this case could be 'the battered wife syndrome' – 'Hit me again, I needed that'.

A further note from the role model country of New Zealand. We originally had two major political parties who took turns at the helm of our country's politics.

M.M.P.

Today, on 27th April 1995, the leadership of the country is further weakened by setting up a mass of little parties, none of them with any 'clout' (power). Remember the old phrase – "United we stand, divided we fall."

The new system is called M.M.P. (Mixed Member Proportional). I asked a friend the meaning of these three letters to which he replied **"Many Mixed-up Politicians"**.

We need help, and we need it urgently.

Prediction

Your country will follow the New Zealand plan. As they have also borrowed money, they must also fulfil the conditions.

Gradually, circumstances will be developed, so that political power moves from each nation to the international New World Order ruling elite.

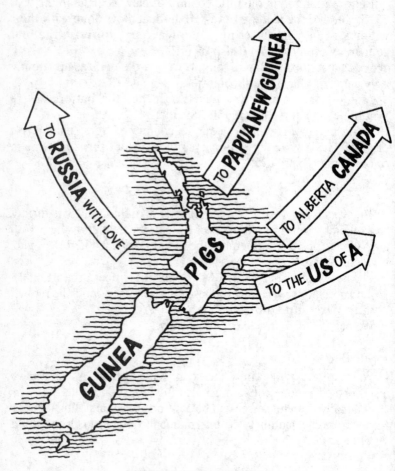

EXPORTING THE PROBLEM

112

CHAPTER EIGHTEEN

THE GLOBAL VILLAGE – EXPORTING THE PLAN

It was Henry Kissinger who first coined the phrase – **A GLOBAL CONCEPT**. He made it quite clear, many years ago, that as far as he was concerned, small nations no longer should be seen as important.

The idea was simple.

1. **Choose a little insignificant, laid back nation**, whose national motto is "She'll be right". Whatever you do, don't choose a volatile group such as the French, the Spanish, the Italians or the Greeks. The whole thing would quickly become far too complicated as they would all, with a great waving of arms and legs, protest every single step of your **restructuring** of their lives.

By the way, on our return from Israel, we passed through Sydney on our way to New Zealand. Guess who was giving a lecture in that city on 14th November 1995? You guessed it – Henry Kissinger. But, please spare me a moment and read his words.

"Australian Financial Review", 14th November 1995 – "*He said it had never previously been the case that **the entire global system was up for restructuring**.*

National leaders now had to deal simultaneously with universal issues...." End quote. (Emphasis added.)

Very important – read this carefully and thoughtfully.

2. Then of course, once the role model has been suitably subdued to the degree that there is no fight left in them, **either the plan is then exported to the rest of the world or the rest of the world could visit the role model to find out how to do 'it'.**

Is this pure conjecture or can it be proved?

Here we go again.

To save boredom creeping into our midst, we will take only **5 examples as proof**, yet there are far more of course.

Proof 1 – Russia

Sir R.....r giving talks in Russia.

New Zealand 'Herald', 20 February 1992 – *"The former Minister of Finance Sir R...r D....s is off soon to talk to the Russians about privatisation.*

*He expects to leave on March 1 for six days of discussions. Sir R....r said he would be part of a three-man privatisation advisory committee **organised by the World Bank**.*

He was appointed a consultant to the bank in March 1990." End quote. (Emphasis added.)

As a result of this restructuring and privatisation of Russia, the country has fallen apart, and is now run, in many cases by Mafia like criminals. Many Russians hate the changes so much, they wish to return to a repressive communistic form of government or even to a dictatorship.

A friend of mine visited Russia in 1995, and said that when he entered a bank to change some money, the teller pointed him to a suspicious looking character seated behind a desk in the bank. She said she was afraid that this other money changer would harm her if she proceeded with the transaction.

True to type, the Russian banks are also in trouble. The 'European' newspaper, 31st August-6th September 1995 –

"Russian bank crisis may return to dictators.

Economists in Russia say the country's banking crisis is so critical that it could lead to a political upheaval and an eventual return to a dictatorship.

....A run on the banks by depositors demanding their money back would effectively paralyse the monetary system...." End quote.

A possible future contender for the position of dictator is Russia's ex-security chief, Alexander Lebed, the man with the deep voice.

Former Soviet president, Mikhail Gorbachev, has said that this man could lead a new democratic Russian government. Possibly a co-alition style government, which in its weakness would fit in with New World Order concepts.

Whoever comes to power at this crucial time in world history, will, according to the prophecies, invade the land of Israel, and thereby seal his own country's doom.

Thus the two superpowers of Russia and America, must decline and make way for the European Union and its leader - Antichrist.

Could ultra-nationalist Vladimr Zhirinovsky win a future election???

Maybe later on as a coalition partner. Time will tell.

The New Zealand 'Herald' reported an outrageous t.v. interview with 'Mad Vlad' on 22nd June 1995. Entitled "*Turbulence on the airwaves.*

Russian far-right leader Mr Vladimir Zhirinovsky clawed his way back into the headlines yesterday, scuffling with a top talk show host and throwing orange juice in the face of a fellow guest during a live broadcast.

....Mr Boris Nemtsov, whom Mr Zhirinovsky had called a 'scumbag' and a ..?%!!.., replied in kind." End quote.

At least his antics lend a little light refreshment in the political arena. His ambitions may well come to nought. Who cares?

Yeltzin has won again but only for a season and we now await a new leader to take over. **Please see the predictions at the end of chapter eighteen**.

Proof 2 – Canada

During the year 1994, we did a lecture tour across from Vancouver to Central Canada. Arriving in Alberta with our information, we were somewhat startled to find out the following:

a. Canada was absolutely broke. 'Globe and Mail', Canada, 12th May 1994 – "***Canada a third world debtor, think tank says***.

The growing debts of the federal government and all 10 provinces has now pushed Canada past Argentina into the company of poor-house nations like Ethiopia and Bolivia.

....puts Canada in 46th spot with a "worsening" debt trend narrowly ahead of Morocco and a couple of notches behind Burundi in eastern Africa.

Mexico, Ghana, Burma, Brazil, Poland and even war-ravaged Rwanda all fared better in the ranking....

*....Of the seven leading industrial countries, **only Italy scored worse**...*

*...The (Frazer-think-tank) institute presented a 72 page report along with a list of **suggestions** to put the country back on the road to frugality...*" End quote. (Emphasis added.)

I read the list of so-called '**suggestions**' which to my highly-trained eye, **looked very similar to the conditions** which apply to every other country. Take this 'suggestion' for example.

Continue quote. "***Sell all self-supporting Crown corporations***." End quote.

We lectured in a number of towns and cities, one of them being Fort McMurray which is situated well to the North in the province of Alberta. During the winter, the temperature drops to minus 40 degrees and I was told that when you speak, your words freeze as soon as they leave your lips and your friend needs to de-frost them in the micro-wave to find out what you said – a slight exaggeration some may feel.

Now, guess who had been there before us?

You've got it. The man from New Zealand. Our ex-Minister of Finance.

'Today', Fort McMurray, Canada, 31 October 1993 – "*Change or face the music. New Zealander speaks from experience.*

Canada must go back to fundamentals and remove barriers against international competition or face the same crisis that devastated New Zealand's economy in the mid-1980's.

This was the message delivered by Sir R...r D.....s, the former New Zealand finance minister, credited with turning that country's near bankrupt economy around."

(Author's note – Observe carefully the next statement.)

"Running a business distracts politicians from the policies of the country to what is best for industry", he told members of Fort McMurray's Canadian Club...

While his policies took their toll on some, D.....s said job losses weren't as bad as first feared...." End quote.

I guess it is okay to tell a bunch of Canadians that, but try telling it to the guys who committed suicide and the families that were left behind in New Zealand absolutely devastated.

Now, there are two sides to the argument:

a. Those who are promoting this system, in many cases (not all), would be called **reprobates**. They have the bit between their teeth and books like this absolutely packed with information to show them the folly of their ways, are tossed aside with scorn and disdain. Their lives may be full of excitement at the moment, but what will all this yield in the end? I'll spell it out clearly. The date of writing, 27th April 1995.

Their own grand-children could well grow up and curse them as the next generation will experience.

1. **No personal freedoms**
2. **No religious freedom**

THE UNGODLY SEAL

3. **No right to own your own home**
4. **No right to own your own children**
5. **No right to run your own business**
6. **No right to hold your own beliefs at all**
7. **God becomes the earth and the cosmos**
8. **The true God as a separate Creator has no place – remember the word 'seclorum'.**

The question may now be asked – What do these people think of people like us?

We are labelled '**conspiracy nutters**' by these individuals who consider themselves the world's gift to mankind. **These are the elite, the illumined ones. They know what is best for the peasants of the world**. We need them to rule over us and tell us what is best for us and our families. How privileged we are to have such giant intellects helping us. Of course, they control all the media, except a few independent newspapers, but these do not amount to any threat.

Of course, their 'advisers' do not fly into the normal airports. Oh no, they arrive at airforce bases, travel in black limousines to the city, converse secretly in offices which have been carefully checked for bugs, as the 'peasants' must not learn of their fate.

Too late! The peasants will find out now because long after this author is dead and gone, these words will still be about. Friends have agreed to print innumerable copies of this book should the need arise. Remember the rhyme about spilt milk.

If this plan is, as we have learnt from Oxford University, a seclorum (ungodly, heathenistic, secular with a pronounced absence of the true and living God), what does God think about all this? Is He upset or agitated? Does all this cause Him to bite His fingernails in despair? Not really.

[1]*"Why do the heathen rage and the people imagine a VAIN THING?*

The kings of the earth set themselves and the rulers take counsel together, against the Lord, and against His Anointed saying, Let us break their bands asunder, and cast away their cords from us."

Paraphrase of the above – The only threat to a completely secular, godless, carefree society where everyone does that which is right in their own eyes are a certain group of people and their annoying Victorian style morality. They quote regularly from the Bible and remind us the Almighty God is still in His heaven and still has laws.

Let us set up a new system – a secular, New World Order, with no Bible-based moral laws, then we can do what we like and be answerable to no one. We will continually cause governments worldwide to sign and ratify our United Nations charters which gradually erode the individuals' freedoms.

By the way, it has happened before at the Tower of Babel. The Phoenix is rising. It's happening again. Is God impressed?

[2]*"He that sitteth in the heavens shall laugh. The Lord shall have them in derision."*

God's committed, born-again, true believers in Jesus Christ as their Lord and Saviour will also laugh. In fact as I sit at my desk pouring all this on to paper, I continually chuckle to myself and wonder why it is not clear to all.

Surely you were there when powers of deduction were given out.

One does not need to be an Einstein to understand all this yet, no human being will ever stop the plan continuing on to its appointed conclusion. **These New World Order people may be likened to a runaway horse** looking desperately for water.

I know where there is some spiritual water, which, if you drink of it, you will never thirst again.

But we digress. Let us return to the U.S.A.'s poor brother Canada, as we see how Australia's poor brother New Zealand, is influencing its future.

An Alberta news magazine in 1993, invited New Zealanders to pass their opinions on in the form of letters. Entitled – *"The New Zealand Model creating poverty*.

The Alberta Government is pursuing the same economic agenda New Zealand has been following since 1984. The architect of the New Zealand program, S.r R.....r D......s, (knighted by Margaret Thatcher), has been a frequent guest of the Klein government." End quote.

Let us quote from of these letters. We will not quote the rude ones which attack personalities as they are here today and gone tomorrow.

"The national debt has risen from $12 billion in 1984 to $65 billion in 1993. Unemployment was 60,000 in 1984. Now it is over 200,000." End quote.

You have heard of **Reaganomics** – U.S.A.

You may have heard of **Rogernomics** – New Zealand

The Premier of Alberta at this time was Mr R.....h K.....n. Hence the play on his first name. 'Alberta Report', 31 January 1994. There is a picture of the Premier, chin in hand, in a thoughtful pose and above in bold letters the word – **"Ralphonomics** – (Alberta of course)".

We had meetings in two venues in Edmonton, also Kelowna B.C. and Fort McMurray, then on to Winnipeg, Manitoba, and Winkler, Manitoba. We told the audiences that there were some **key CATCH WORDS** to bear in mind.

1. **Restructuring** – which means getting the sack in three stages.
   a) Leak it
   b) Deny it
   c) Do it
2. **Redundant or retrenched** – getting laid off, sacked.
3. **Pain** to be endured – only by the victims, not by the organisers.
4. **Light at the end of the tunnel** – a mystical illusion. As far as we can see now, the only light at the end of the tunnel is the second coming of our Lord Jesus Christ.

Sure enough, we had only just spoken these warning when the papers began to report these happenings.

'Edmonton Journal', 21st May 1994 – *"University of Alberta Hospital to lay off 200.*

...We have talked with the employer about trying to look at some innovative ways of providing services in a cheaper way..." End quote.

You know the end result of this ploy, don't you? Kill two birds with one stone.

a. Lay off unionised workers
b. **Employ contract labour** who will never again strike. They can't afford to. Result – **goodbye Trade Unions – forever**.

Mid 1996 in the guinea-pig country of New Zealand, the mopping-up process continued as workers suddenly discovered that the collective bargaining days were over for ever. From now on, it was to be, "**personal contracts**" or nothing.

One of the biggest oil fields in North America is situated at Fort McMurray. It was great fun riding in their giant earth-moving machines, built about 3 stories high. The main employer out there is called 'Syncrude'.

'Edmonton Journal', 21st May, 1994 – "*Syncrude jobs to shrink by 500.*

....International investors from Japan and Korea have said they wanted to see such changes before pouring money into the oil sands development." End quote.

You see – **sacking masses of workers is one of the conditions. This is the true meaning of restructuring.**

'Edmonton Journal', 19th May 1994 – "*Fear of job cuts causing terrible stress.*

During the French Revolution, many aristocrats never knew when they would face Madame Guillotine.

Today in budget cutting Edmonton, many workers don't know when they'll face the axe. And experts say, uncertainty is more stressful than the actual chop.

...people must be able to control what will happen to them. That's why they always plan and hope for a good outcome.

*....but take away that stability, and **the result is stress.***.

Everyone's tense at work. It just spoils the work situation. It's just like a cloud hanging over you.

...workers face a grieving process.

...You see people getting laid off and there's a sense of mourning for loss of friends. In Edmonton, we're really feeling that at the moment.

LUCIFER'S EYE

....If there's too much, something gives. Either you get sick or exhausted and have to give up something. There is a clear connection between stress and illness." End quote.

New Zealand readers – does all this remind you of anything?

The planners fly in their first class seats over the top of all this, but believe me, **their day will come!**

Remember the Bible verses you learned at Sunday School?

[3]"*I will repay. Vengeance is mine sayeth the Lord.*" End quote.

[4]"*Be not deceived, for whatsoever a man soweth that shall he also reap.*" End quote.

[5]a) "*One dieth in his full strength, being wholly at ease and quiet.*

 b) *Another dieth in the bitterness of his soul and never eateth with pleasure.*" End quote.

Unless these wreckers of peoples' lives cut out their arrogance, I suspect dying will not be a peaceful, enjoyable experience for them.

Actually, we all can choose, even at the this moment, to follow the living God and His Son, the Lord Jesus Christ. (See the salvation prayer at the back of the book.) Or, you can continue on following you know who, and go to be with him forever.

Choices – choices.

Meanwhile, back to **Alberta, Canada.**

Things got so bad as a result of the Ralphonomics restructuring that was in turn exported from New Zealand, that we now read the following: 'Edmonton Journal', 21 May 1994 – "***Province asks churches to help victims of K....n's cuts.***

*Edmonton churches are being asked to return full force to one of their historical roots – **helping the poor**.*

And it's the provincial government that's doing the asking.

....Many local clergy believe there is no way churches can fill the void being left by government cutbacks.

...government needs to rethink its approach to cutting social service budgets.

*...**It's not governing. It's ruling by ideology. There is no room for the poor and dispossessed**.*" End quote.

Now, you see, we sometimes export this diabolical ideology, or nations come to us, to learn how to do it.

Proof 3 – Papua New Guinea

We travel to this country from time to time, and tell them what is to take place. For example, over ten years ago, on 23rd September 1983, during the course of a lecture given at Port Moresby, I spoke very clearly of that country being set up with computers etc. (See our book 'Second Warning', pages 12-13, for more details.) In those days, there was no hint of this happening. No wonder, when we turned up in 1994 for a lecture, the John Guise Stadium was packed to capacity, including the car park, for the biggest public gathering ever held there. The television people estimated well in excess of 50,000 people. The media however, showed very little interest until we were later ambushed and stoned at Wewak.

'Dominion', 22nd April 1995 – "*C....n to study NZ reforms for PNG.*

New Zealand's private sector reforms including the privatisation programme, will be studied by Sir J.....s C.....n and his officials during a four day visit.

*....Sir J.....s said, "I would like to focus on learning from and adapting for **Papua New Guinea**, where appropriate, **New Zealand's reputable and successful public sector reform programme**....*" End quote.

But wait – I have in my possession some information that is absolutely without precedent.

Where is the home of the Illuminati?

Europe indeed, but also the United States of America. Washington D.C. and New York City are the twin areas of interest.

<u>Proof 4</u> – The United States of America.

'NZ Herald', 30th March 1995 – "*Congress plans to visit to study N.Z. reform*.

*A delegation from the United States Congress is expected to visit New Zealand this year **to study the economic reform process first hand**. The idea was raised with the Prime Minister, Mr B....r during his tour of Capitol Hill yesterday.*

He said, "Plans were "quite advanced"...." End quote.

(Author's note – Since they have been planning since 1776, they should be "quite advanced".)

Continue quote – "*...the initiative is indicative of what Mr B.....r, described as the "**quite remarkable level of interest in New Zealand's reforms among United States policy makers**."*

....Mr B.....r spent the afternoon with Mr B...b D....e ..... and the speaker of the House Mr N.....t G.....h.

*....the American media continued virtually to ignore him. This was despite the EXTRAVAGANT PRAISE lavished on him by the highly newsworthy Mr G....h **(new speaker of the house) who referred to him as "THE GRAND MASTER" and said the Republicans wanted him to teach us "the NEXT PHASE"**.* End quote. (Emphasis added).

Can you believe what you are reading? Anybody familiar with **Freemasonry** knows the term '**Grand Master**', which according to Mackey's Encyclopaedia means 'the presiding officer who has the right not only to be present, but preside over every Lodge. He can inspect their books and must be received with the greatest respect.'

Now to continue. Any New Zealand citizen knows that much as we respect our leaders, our present Prime Minister (1995) was not the man in power when the plan was formulated and probably knows very little about it as the finance ministers and their advisers handle this side of things. We were glad therefore to see Mr B.....r allude to this fact.

Continue quote – "*While all this was gratifying to Mr B....r's ego, he said **he had been careful in his private discussions in Washington to SHARE THE CREDIT WITH THE LABOUR PARTY**.*" End quote.

Now, this is good honest thinking on his part and his is to be congratulated. Let's face it. Mr B....r would be the first to confess that the whole plan initially baffled him as it also baffled three and a half million people other Kiwis. **Even now, at this time of writing, it would appear that none of these politicians can see the end result. I hope this book gets to them in time and jolts them out of their starry-eyed euphoria**.

Continue quote – *"Mr G....h applauded the New Zealand experience of "rethinking its approach, re-establishing its competitiveness, looking at down-sizing and privatising and changing, saying "THAT WAS EXACTLY WHAT THE REPUBLICANS WERE GOING TO DO. We hope to TRAIL ALONG BEHIND AND LEARN HOW TO IMITATE NEW ZEALAND",* he said.

The contract with America – dubbed by its critics "The Contract on America" is a document from the hard right." End quote. (Emphasis added.)

Postscript

Do you want a laugh?

Read this latest gem from the British 'Sunday Times', 14 April 1996 – *"Russians teach Scots to Privatise"*.

Footnotes

1   The Holy Bible; Psalm 2:1-3

2   The Holy Bible; Psalm 2:4

3   The Holy Bible; Romans 12:19

4   The Holy Bible; Galatians 6:7

5   The Holy Bible; Job 21:23 & 25

Prediction

The Russian scene is unclear at this stage of writing in 1996. The successor to Yeltzin could be Alexander Lebed, Vladimir Zhirinovsky, Prime Minister Viktor Chernomyrdin, Ivan Rybkin, or a coalition led by some other demonic character.

The Christchurch 'Press', 29 October 1996 had as its headline – *"Lebed seen as leader.*

Former Soviet president, Mikhail Gorbachev, said yesterday the controversial army general recently sacked as a minister by Boris Yeltsin, could lead a new democratic Russian government.

"...I would myself help to form such a team", Mr Gorbachev said. ...Mr Gorbachev suggested Prime Minister Victor Chernomyrdin should take over presidential responsibilities from Mr Yeltsin for three months. There should then be an election..." End quote.

Never forget, the prophecies make it clear, Russia will invade Israel.

It's all getting ready to happen. Prepare yourself spiritually. See Ezekiel the prophet – chapters 38 and 39.

CHAPTER NINETEEN

FULL SPEED AHEAD FOR CONTINUAL CHANGE

To further illumine the situation on the necessity for speed, note this article from the 'Daily Nation' newspaper, Kenya, 18th July 1995 - "*The World Bank's Vice President for Africa....has decried the slow pace of structural adjustment efforts now underway across all Africa and said the reforms could move **faster**....adding that **reforming countries were partners with the bank.***

*...the bank was in the development business, and cannot be pre-occupied with countries like Zaire and Sudan which, he said were **not interested in reforms**.*" End quote. (Emphasis added).

This means Zaire and Sudan are not wishing to fulfil the conditions. Zaire already has the Ebola virus. What are the plans for Sudan?

WHICH PHILOSOPHY IS BEING USED?

Fabian Socialism, which has 3 main planks.

a) **Gradualism** – sneak up on the people, then hit hard. Never slow down your reforms or deviate or all your waiting has been in vain.

b) **Dispossession** – every book I have ever read on the New World Order make land and real-estate the valuable commodity to be taken over at all costs.

c) **Pauperisation** – destroy every sector of society using the best methods possible to achieve this.

Apparent Political Suicide

Residents of New Zealand, (the guinea pig country), will remember the Finance Minister of the day refused to slow down the reforms although they caused almost unbearable pain to many families. **Result, he lost his job**.

The next Minister of Finance, a woman, followed the same plan to a tee, as it was suggested that should she not stick to the rules, she wouldn't get the job. **Result – she lost her job**.

Keep raising taxes and rates until people can't keep up the

payments. Your friendly government man then knocks on your door saying "Sign your property over to us. We will pay the taxes and rates, whilst you become a tenant on the land that was originally yours."

Reader, please take note of the ruined sectors and watch your country follow the plan and go the same way.

Amalgamate county councils and quangos and control them from afar, so there is no longer any emotional involvement.

Sack thousands of workers and replace them with contract labour who sign a **contract** and thus cannot ever afford to strike again.

Thus **trade unions are undermined** and ultimately destroyed.

Remember Rule no.1. **By controlling energy we can control nations. By controlling food we can control individuals.**

On 13th October 1992, we read in Great Britain that **30 coal mines** were to be shut down with the loss of 30,000 coal-miners' jobs. We travelled to the **Rhonda Valley** in Wales and found that there was enough coal to supply that country for centuries. They then imported coal from Germany until the mines were privatised and began operations again with new overseas owners.

I received a call this morning from a man who had attended my lectures some time ago. He was told by his employer that their firm is to undercut all other trucking firms and carry food and vegetables nationwide on their fleet of older and many new trucks. (30th April 1995). I wonder where all the funds come from? New Zealand or overseas?

Destroy the primary producer – the farmer.

In the U.S.A., during the month of June 1991, a farmer was driven from his land every 25 minutes. Farming friends of ours in Great Britain and Iowa, U.S.A., refrained from growing crops on designated land as the government restricted them from doing so.

Small businesses, e.g. tractor and plough sales collapsed as a result.

Education came under attack. Government funds dried up. No discipline resulted in thousands of teachers leaving the profession whilst children left school with little knowledge of the basics of reading, writing, and mathematics. **Rebellion was taught as children learned their rights**.

Although all this appears to be a natural decline in standards, this is not the case. Education has been carefully designed to retard childrens' intellectual abilities, thus preventing them from reading and understanding events. Instead they are fed a diet of t.v. and videos.

In New Zealand, **parents no longer have the right to view their child's report card without the child's permission**. Men are leaving the teaching profession in droves, leaving women as the major role model. This is fine for the girls, but what about the boys?

[1]*"As for my people, children are their oppressors, and women rule over them. O my people, they which lead thee cause thee to err, and destroy the way of thy paths."* End quote.

Fishing – Commercial fishermen had to accept ITQ's i.e. Individual Transferable Quotas and were only allowed to catch the species that they were allocated. Result? Thousands of other species tipped overboard by angry fishermen and the price of fish rockets so that consumers can barely afford to buy it.

They call this **preserving the fish stocks**. Impoverished fishermen sell their ITQ's to those with the most money.

'Press', 21st November 1992 – *"Japanese could own all "fisheries".*
New Zealand's transferable fishing quotas are a recipe for disaster, according to a visiting expert on marine reserves.

....the system could result in the complete ownership of New Zealand's fisheries by Japanese companies.

*"**I don't think anyone should own what's in the sea**, therefore, a property right **is bizarre**", he said.*

*Any system that could result in the takeover of **fishing quotas** by overseas companies was **"lunatic"**, he said."* End quote. (Emphasis added.)

Obviously, this was a highly intelligent man who was not in on the plan.

Seeds manipulated – New bills are continuously being churned out by the New World Order people. This diabolical decree is entitled PBR or PVR – Plant Breeder's Rights or Plant Variety Rights. It requires that all seeds be **emasculated**, made into **hybrids** and fully controlled by the plant breeders.

In New Zealand today, the role model country has very few natural seeds left. This will bring the hippies out of the bush.

Note – For a catalogue of natural non-hybrid species, please write to Phoenix Seeds, Smithton, Tasmania, Australia.

Health – hospitals – thousands of staff were sacked and replaced with people on a **personal contract**. Result, poor service, pay for everything (user pays), and no more unions.

Psychiatric – patients were driven out on to the streets (under the guise of being 'rehabilitated and released into society to lead a normal life', as nobody wanted to be responsible for their care and upkeep.

It is of special note that just prior to the next general election in New Zealand in 1996, new funding is being provided to assist these poor folk. What a pity we don't have elections every six months. This is the old 'carrot on the stick' trick.

300 post offices were shut down virtually overnight. The post and telegraph department was **split three ways** and made into profitable businesses by contracting out much of its work. Charges consequently rose in an alarming manner. Postal rates are continually being increased.

Phone booths were changed overnight. Not only in colour but in mode of operation. 20 cent coins gave way to phone cards. Telecom, under privatisation, has the majority of shares with a large U.S. firm. A massive increase in charges was subtly dealt with by introducing colourful, plastic phone cards.

The tremendous profits that resulted could have helped our country but went to the new American owners.

In the year 1996, a television documentary told us that $620 million was sent overseas. The new owners defended themselves by saying that the **asset** can never be shipped overseas.

The elderly were mercilessly put under attack. Assets tests suddenly introduced caught many with too much saved up over the years and their government benefits, suffered accordingly. **GRI** – Guaranteed Retirement Income - New Zealand. **RIP** – Retirement Income Pension - Australia.

As a result, some elderly persons have returned to an old method of saving – **CIS** – **Cash In Sock**.

Savings for children and grand-children was taxed.

Collectors of moss or abalone (paua) shells off beaches were required to pay tax.

Welcome to the New World Order!

Electricity cards came next. User pays. You pay first then use the power.

Military bases closing down. These will be no longer necessary as we all become good friends and neighbours in our 'global villages'. U.N. forces can do the fighting for us.

New taxes came in i.e. G.S.T. - Goods and Services Tax. It started at 10% with promises that it would not rise. It did rise of course, to

12.5%. Other countries called it V.A.T. - Value added tax. This tax is inevitable as it comes under the heading conditionalities policies etc, etc... People in other countries are incensed at this tax and are in some cases organising protest marches against it. It is recognised as a political 'hot potato'.

Can you see it now? **Pick off each sector of society little by little. Sit back and watch your country go the same way.**

A note to those with no spiritual base to their lives. I recognise that this is quite heavy information.

As is often the case with those who are informed they have an incurable sickness, you, the reader of this book, may experience the following emotions:

a) Hot flushes and a 'trapped feeling'. "Stop the earth, I want to get off."

b) Self-pity. "Why wasn't I born in the days of the Waltons or the Little House on the Prairie?" (Author's comment - too late!)

c) Denial – "It isn't true. It isn't really happening. This
   author is a deluded, way out, doomsday cultist."

   (Author's comment - when you get to know me, you may find me to be a very nice, sensible family man with a very happy disposition.)

d) Anger – "It's not fair. Why does this have to happen to my generation?" (Author's note – **well, as it happens, you are living at a very important time in the history of this world**.)

Footnotes

1   The Holy Bible; Isaiah 3:12

Prediction

Watch as each sector of society in your country is restructured.

The **ex-government departments will all be given new names, which take many months to get used to**.

CHAPTER TWENTY

A MATTER OF SOVEREIGNTY

For some years now, some New Zealanders (or Kiwis, as we call ourselves), have known of quite a large group of Parliamentarians, originally calling themselves 'Parliamentarians for World Order' (PWO).

They soon discovered that this title contravened the Electoral Act as they had all sworn allegiance to uphold the sovereignty of this country. The name was then changed from Parliamentarians for World Order, to a new name i.e. 'Parliamentarians for Global Action' (PGA).

A list of 40 names was read over the air 19th February 1995. This author has in his possession a full list of these names, posted out by a current politician in the year 1996. The majority of these politicians would not have the slightest clue as to the true aims of the organisation. Some would see membership as an opportunity to take off to another all-expenses paid conference.

Most would see this group as presenting a united front against common "global problems".

The point is my friends; do not condemn these dear men and women out of hand. I will confess that **without a full knowledge of the ancient prophecies** and the end result of all this, **I also, no doubt, would cry "Oh, what a grand scheme**! It was worth all the pain for the glory of beholding the light at the end of the tunnel. A virtual Utopia where we attack global problems in a united fashion, and we will beat our swords into ploughshares," (as the Scriptural passage taken completely out of context, and written on the United Nation's building says).

The only thing that these planners have not taken into account is the heart of man from God's point of view.

[1] "*The heart is deceitful above all things and desperately wicked. Who can know it? I the Lord search the heart - I try the reins.*" End quote.

Please give the Lord credit for knowing a little more than we do. He had some difficulty with the Tower of Babel folk about 'four days' ago (1 day = 1,000 years in His sight), and now that the Phoenix is rising again, He says "Ho hum. Here they go again." We make bold to say that **the same mighty God who smashed the tower of Babel will also, at the right time smash the Luciferian new World Order, and set up His own system**.

Our son-in-law wrote to a current New Zealand politician in the year 1995 and this was his response.

"*Dear Mr K......*

Thank you for your letter of 26 January 1995 relating to my stance as a globalist.

I am sure that many intelligent New Zealander's share my views that a global government is inevitable and that it is to be welcomed. Unlike the conspiracy 'nutters' I see this as an opportunity to ensure global policies on health, technology, trade – and the chance to eradicate pestilence, famine and disease. I am unsure how many Members of Parliament feel the same way.

Yours sincerely

...............MP" End quote.

Proof 1

Please note the words "*a global government is inevitable*". They crash on blindly calling people like us '**conspiracy nutters**'.

I remember having lunch with a politician friend of mine in the New Zealand Parliament Restaurant called 'Bellamy's'. We looked around at the other politicians and my friend murmured "**The ignorance in here is appalling.**"

SOVEREIGNTY AND INDEPENDENCE ON THE LINE

Proof 2

New Zealand 'Herald', 27th July 1989 – "*....easier investing rules bring warning on sovereignty.*" End quote.

In our book 'Final Notice', pages 43 and 44, we list a number of New Zealand politicians who gladly and freely admitted membership to the group called PGA.

A politician called R.....d P.....e has his remarks written in Hansard (the New Zealand government records book).

Proof 3

Quote – "*We will not be able to tackle these problems unless we are prepared to co-operate and give up some of our national sovereignty.*" End quote. Date of statement – **16th July 1981.**

Now can you see why all was conducted initially in secrecy, then under various disguises. The people would go crazy if they found out.

Talk Back Radio

It is absolutely mind-boggling to listen, whenever I have a spare moment, to these talk-back radio shows where both host and callers do their best to put a handle on what is going on. **Each talk-back station in New Zealand will receive a free copy of this book, so they may discuss things intelligently in the future**. God bless them all.

Some years ago, New Zealand had a very authoritarian Prime Minister called S..r R.......t M.......n. He was deposed from his position through a situation which developed, yet never seemed to actively try to get back into power. I found that the reason was that **he was one of the 6 governors of the World Bank**, and regularly took overseas trips in this capacity.

Many people longed to have an authoritarian figure back in power and started a group called the "Sunday Club". Believe it or not, **the Sunday Club listed our books as recommended reading**.

Well did this cause an uproar in Parliament? A friend of mine named Bill, (now deceased), called me excitedly on the phone and said "Tune in to Parliament on the radio. They are arguing about your books."

It was great as they all started to fight and accuse each other of making certain statements. I couldn't help laughing when the speaker of the House rapped his gavel and shouted "Order, order. **None of you made those statements. It was this man Smith**."

Some days later, we received an invitation to visit the 'Beehive' (New Zealand's Parliament building) to have discussions with the Prime Minister.

Ethics prevent me from every making public what was discussed in his office that day but when we emerged, his secretary whispered "How did you last in there for one and a half hours? He always ushers people out after 20 minutes." I replied "If you knew what information I had to share, you would know why the visit was for one and a half hours."

Of course, R......t M......n was a New World Order man, very sincere, but like the rest, did not perceive the **end result**.

You will remember reading earlier on about the G7. Remember, they are the key players in this game. In fact, reading between the lines in the following excerpt, it would appear that the G7 could be the modern day authors of the whole restructuring plan, guided at all times of course by Satan.

THE EX-PENALTY FOR TREASON

134

New Zealand 'Sunday Star', 27th January 1987. (See 'Final Notice', page 245. Mr M.....n in this article spoke of 45 different representatives meeting in Rome.

"*...to see what we could do to mobilise public opinion in our various spheres of influence to give political support to the difficult decisions that have to be taken by the governments of the G7 to implement the policies that are seen to be necessary.....*

The G7 proposal involves some loss of sovereignty by the participants and that is where the political difficulty arises."

(Author's note – In other words, once the people of the country find out what you are up to, they won't let you continue with your plan. In fact, if the facility was still in the law books, they might even insist that you be hung outside Parliament building for treason, as when entering this noble institution, you took a vow strongly implying that you would protect and look after the **sovereignty** of this nation. Now you are secretly and nefariously selling it out.

What used to be called "Treason" is now called "Privatisation".

I wonder what would happen in New Zealand if all its citizens read this book, and discovered to their horror, that in the year 1993, 40% of this country was already in overseas hands. Of course, in 1996, the situation is far worse.)

Gradual Colonialisation by Multi-Nationals

A recent television documentary revealed that at the time of printing this book, more than 51% of our Stock Market is overseas owned.

Many foreign owners don't live in the community. Apparently New Zealand is to become an exclusive playground for the world's wealthy. Foreign owners will ultimately try to change New Zealand law.

Continue quote – "*If the public, or more correctly, the electorate of those countries can be persuaded that the result of that loss of sovereignty is higher standards of living for all the people of the world, the political difficulty will be overcome....*" End quote.

As I jot down these lines on 29th April 1995, I know that my country has lost over 40% of its sovereignty and we are far worse off than before. A great many very sincere folk are promoting the plan. It is sweet to the taste, but extremely bitter in the stomach.

Further proof – Have you heard of the Secretary-General of the U.N., B....s B....s G.....i? Quote from the "Agenda for Peace", paragraph 17, General Secretary's Report 1992 – "*The time of absolute and exclusive sovereignty, however, has passed...*" End quote. (Emphasis added).

SO, WHAT IS THE AIM?

"Interdependence" within the confines of the global village.

Explanation – No matter how well-known your particular country was at producing a product, the New World Order planners have now decided for us, what our particular **strong point** will be in the future e.g. New Zealand was well-known for dairy products, meat, and wool.

Under the New World Order plan, we have become well-known for **pine logs and tourism**.

Our wharves are packed with piles of logs awaiting export, mainly to Japan, as the price moves up from $150 cubic metre to $450 cubic metre. **Pine trees grow more quickly here than anywhere else in the world, with the exception of Chile**.

Proof 5

'Fiji Times', 11th June 1993 – "*Cattle make way for timber.*

A century after European settlers used fire and axe to wipe out most forests here, sheep and cattle paddocks are being turned into timber plantations.

Factors, including a ban on log exports from Sarawak to the fate of the American spotted owl, are producing record timber prices and a radical change in New Zealand's landscape.

Pruned radiata pine logs which were worth $NZ150 a cubic metre in May, are now fetching $NZ450.

....existing farmers are turning up to 25 per cent of their farms over to trees.

....It is not all rosy, and there are fears that the new prices for timber cannot be sustained...." End quote. (Emphasis added.)

Proof 6

'Dominion', 28th April 1995 – "**Trees displacing sheep and beef on hill country farms**.

The New Zealand Forestry Exchange has indicated that sheep and beef farmers are continuing to move from sheep and beef production to forestry." End quote.

The t.v. programme "Assignment", in August 1996, told us "Sheep and Cattle are being driven off the land. Over the past 25 years, pine trees have increased in New Zealand by 155%. the mayor of Wairoa says 5,000 hectares are planted in pines each year.

Question – Who now owns the Forestry?

<u>Proof 6</u>

'Dominion', 28th april 1995 – "*Foreign ownership pushes past 40 per cent.*

*The purchase of just over 50 per cent of Carter-Holt-Harvey by American based International Paper means **40.6 per cent of New Zealand's forest ownership** is **under foreign control**...*" End quote.

'Dominion', 10 June 1993 – "*Foreign investors move in on farms. ...most buyers being from Australia, Japan, Malaysia, the United States and Britain.....*" End quote.

As this book goes to press in the year 1996, it has just been revealed that the Americans now own most of the timber in this country. The American greenies love for the "spotted owl" made logging difficult in the north west of the U.S.A. so now these entrepreneurs have come to our fair shores.

SHUTTING THE DOOR AFTER THE HORSE HAS BOLTED

This very month, as I put pen to paper and write this book, it has just occurred to one of our quickly rising politicians that this is indeed happening. He is correct, but **too late!**

The problem is that he is now standing in the way of the New World Order plans. I regret to say that unless he changes tack, he could end up having an unfortunate accident. The New World Order planners are very determined people.

<u>Proof 7</u>

'Press', 22nd April 1995 – "*P.....s urges stand against **foreign ownership of resources**.*

*Foreign ownership of New Zealand resources is a "line-in-the-sand" issue that needs a strong Opposition stand against **quislings** and **traitors**, says New Zealand First Leader, W.....n P.....s.*" End quote.

Author's note – I have been longing to use those two words but I am not protected by **parliamentary privilege**. Which two words did he use again? **Quislings** and **traitors**. Could it be that this gentlemen feels that no politician has the mandate, right, or authority, to go against his **vows** and **sell up the sovereignty of his country, piece by piece?**

Now, some opponents didn't like this suggestion at all. Continue quote – "*Mr B.....n angrily rejected Mr P......s claims, classing the New Zealand First and Alliance stand on foreign investment as* **"grossly irresponsible distortions of reality**." End quote. (Emphasis added.)

The use of pseudo-intellectual language such as this, still leaves the number **40% firmly printed in our minds**. The ranting and ravings of apparent participants in this **sellout** leave reality where it always was – reality.

Aha! A clue at last.

The final paragraph in the article lets the proverbial cat out of the bag.

Proof 8

"*Foreign investment was still needed to help develop New Zealand's infrastructure if it was to capitalise fully on the* **potential growth areas such as tourism and forestry**....." End quote. (Emphasis added.)

What have we been saying for years in the course of our public lectures? **"If you want to make a buck in New Zealand, bring a chainsaw or cater for tourism**." Listen to the tapes. It is all recorded, over and over.

Other countries' roles in the New World Order

I have discovered my country's role. You can quite simply determine your country's role.

a) No matter how well-known a certain product may have been in the past, that will be allowed to lapse and die a normal death e.g. **Australia – steel, wool, meat, – dying**.

b) Then watch and see which industries have a lot of money being poured into them e.g. **Australia – wheat and minerals**.

Let us take a few examples and see what these countries have been set aside for:

Great Britain	finance, fashion and culture (architecture, music, cuisine, design, pop music, night life)
Argentina	beef

Uganda	coffee
Zambia	copper
Tanzania	diamonds
Germany	luxury cars
Japan	electronics
*Switzerland	clocks and watches, chocolate, storing stolen Jewish gold. Geneva is a New World Order headquarters and banking centre.
Spain	leather
Canada	wheat
Italy	designer clothes
Israel	fruit
U.S.A.	entertainment, Coca Cola, and pop culture
South Africa	minerals and diamonds
American Samoa	tuna fish
Papua New Guinea	gold mining
Canada	developing oil sands
Ghana, West Africa	timber, gold, bauxite, cocoa
Kenya, East Africa	tourism
etc etc etc	

*For many years, it has been our desire to visit the land of Switzerland. As a boy, I was friends with the son of the Swiss consul in Wellington. This family used to kindly invite me home over the weekends and I used to thrill to the sound of Swiss mountain music, yodelling, and visualise the fantastic mountain scenery in that lovely land.

Then later, some very dear friends of ours in Australia, Urs and Kathy Leimgruber, became our agents and from time to time would share with us information on that wonderful land.

The question may now be asked, "**What is Switzerland's role in the New World Order**?"

I did not know the answer to this until this month, when we made our first tour of the area, and we would like to share this information with you herewith.

The two areas which seemed to escape most of the problems from the World War, which concluded in 1945, were **the Vatican City** in **Rome, and Switzerland**. These two areas of course, have been famous for many years for banking, politics, and religion, and there is certainly some link-up between the two.

During the month of October 1996, our tour group visited Rome, then moved in to St. Peters and the Sistine Chapel, where we saw the **Swiss guards** looking after and guarding the entranceway. Previous to that, we had been crossing Switzerland from side to side and end to end, and learned the following.

In Geneva we found the headquarters of almost every group involved in setting up the global situation. There we saw the United Nations building, the World Council Church building, the Red Cross building, the UNESCO building, and many others that are situated in that great city.

We then moved on to other places, including Lucerne, which is called, in their language, 'Lucerna'. It is famous for supernatural lights, and possibly has a link-up with the word 'Lucifer'.

Not far away was the great city of Basle, where the G7 meet regularly. The G7, as many people know, is the headquarters for the money-leading institutions, and the World Bank and the international monetary fund cannot lend money without going first to their leaders, the G7, to gain permission.

In spite of all this, however, things are not going well for Switzerland. A headline in the 'Financial Times', 7th October 1996, reads thus: "*Swiss face 20 billion suit on Nazi gold.*"

And then in the 'Jerusalem Post', 6th October 1996, we read, "*Holocaust survivor files 20 billion dollar lawsuit against Swiss bank.*

A holocaust survivor living in Brooklyn has filed a twenty billion lawsuit in a U.S. Federal Court in New York against Swiss Banks for allegedly refusing to return victims' money and property....

She is seeking damages on behalf of herself and has invited other survivors, both Jews and non-Jews, to join the class action suit....

Weizhauss (from Romania) said her father got his money to Swiss banks before he was deported to Auschwitz in 1944....

She doesn't have account numbers. The suit is to force the disclosure of the numbers of the Swiss bank accounts from 1933 to 1945....Although such a case has been anticipated, it appeared to catch the banks, the Swiss government, and some Jewish advocates off-guard. It was unclear how the case would be co-ordinated or affected by the current efforts of the Volcker Committee, which is preparing to arrange an audit of dormant Swiss bank accounts from the holocaust era....

Named in the suit are: Union Bank of Switzerland, and the Swiss Bank Corporation, also known as Swiss National Bank, as well as more than a hundred unnamed banking institutions and individuals."
End quote.

To our surprise, we then read another headline in the 'Financial Times', 7 October 1996, which reads: *"Swiss Economy on the ropes. The chairman of the Swiss National Bank has inherited not one, but two problems...*

*"Internationally, he has been asked to explain the seemingly indefensible war time actions of his predecessors in buying looted Nazi gold. At home he is under pressure to solve Switzerland's worst period of economic stagnation since the 1930's.... For the last six years, Switzerland has been the **worst performing European economy**, apart from Finland, and the strains show."* End quote.

You had better believe it. From the time we arrived until the time we left, our hands were continually dipping into our pockets, and many of us left the country financially embarrassed.

Something fishy is going on! At this stage we should be very grateful to the man who invented "venetian blinds" because with Switzerland collapsing financially, it could be "curtains for us all".

Headline – *"Hitler hid profits from Mein Kampf in a Swiss bank."*

The 'Daily Telegraph' on 6 September 1996 reads *"Secret bank accounts were held in Switzerland for Adolf Hitler, into which the royalties from his book, Mein Kampf, were paid, it is alleged today....The accounts were handled by Max Ammann, head of the Nazi Party's Publishing Company...."*

A telegram dated October 1944 was passed to the 'Jewish Chronicle' and claims Ammann's account was held in the Union Bank of Switzerland in Berne.

It adds, "It is quite possible that Hitler's foreign exchange revenues from his book, and foreign exchange revenues of the Nazi Party abroad, are held at this Swiss bank in Ammann's name.

The disclosure comes amidst intense pressure on Switzerland to open up its notoriously secretive banking system, as part of a move to locate the assets of victims of the holocaust.

Earlier this year, Swiss bankers signed an agreement with the World Jewish Congress to let an independent commission investigate the war-time role of Swiss banks...."

In 1933, the year Hitler became Chancellor, the book sold a million copies and his income from 15% of the royalties was more than a million marks, making him the most prosperous author in Germany." End quote.

There's something very strange going on, and we do not pretend to know exactly what it is, but **world powers are certainly looking after these two areas, namely, Switzerland and the Vatican.**

Notice the World Bank is pouring millions into tourism in the land of Kenya, so when AIDS has done its job, the wealthy can enjoy the pleasures of Kenya's great safari parks.

At this stage, take a pen and write down the name of your country. Next, write down collapsing industries. Now, write down reviving industries, and those which are being built up through massive overseas investment.

It is quite simple really.

LUCIFER'S EYE

WE WILL ALL BE BROTHERS

Isn't it exciting. All joining hands, smiling and singing "**We are the world**..." We don't need the living God any more, they suppose. We have a substitute god in the form of ......

We cannot fight any more wars as we are now interdependent. If I make you my enemy, you may possess a product I need, so continued co-operation and harmonisation is essential.

Footnotes

1   The Holy Bible; Jeremiah 17:9

142

CHAPTER TWENTY-ONE

THE U.S. ROLE IN THE NEW WORLD ORDER

As we have pointed out in our other publications, U.S. Presidents are not elected, they are chosen by the New World Order planners.

Proof 9

See the quote in our book 'Final Notice', page 220. New Zealand 'Herald', 5th November 1980. *"Websters in Early for Last Word. The Republican challenger, Mr Ronald Reagan, has caused a major upset in the United States Presidential elections by beating Mr Jimmy Carter.*

*So in effect says the latest edition of Webster's Dictionary, even though **Americans do not go to the polls until later today to decide their President for the next four years.***

*....**Mr Reagan has been listed in the dictionary as the 40th President of the United States**, along with his 39 predecessors...*

The presumption or genuine mistake by the Chicago Publishers Consolidated Book Publishers, has dumb-founded the American Consul-General in Auckland. "Unbelievable", was his first word.

....Auckland representatives of the publishers were just as surprised and had no explanations." End quote. (Emphasis added).

Proof 10

Our first book 'Warning' had a 'Stop Press' on page 169. Quote-" *Obviously it is all planned that Reagan was chosen to be nought but a stepping stone for George Bush, the next One World Government man to ascend the throne of power."* End quote.

We were interviewed before the election via satellite. The programme was entitled 'Andrew Carroll at 7'.

Q. Who will win the election in the U.S. tonight?
A. George Bush.
Q. You sound very confident. How can you be so sure?
A. **It's in my book**. George Bush belonged to so many world government groups that there remains no doubt at all – Council on Foreign Relations, Bilderbergers (Europe), Director of the C.I.A., The Order (Yale University)" End quote.

Sure enough, he got the job.

You may wonder why he was replaced by Bill Clinton, after his doing so well in obeying his planner bosses and announcing the New World Order?

The answer is that he became stressed and ill with Graves Disease, and also unfortunately vomited on a high Japanese official. This did not go down well in diplomatic circles.

Is Bill Clinton a New World Order man?

Yes. His initial speech at his inauguration told us this. "Eye has not seen, ear has not heard, what we can do for you." This is called '**esoteric language**'. You take a Biblical text, mutilate it, and cause it to say something that it was not meant to say. The correct verse reads as follows and applies only to born again, committed believers in our Lord Jesus Christ.

[1]*"Eye hath not seen, nor ear heard, neither have entered into the heart of man the things which God hath prepared for them that love him."*

Bill Clinton attended the New World Order Bilderbergers Conference in Europe where all was explained. His role was to fill in, keep people occupied discussing his unorthodox and flamboyant lifestyle, then be prepared to step aside if necessary.

In spite of the number of scandals against him, he has already been chosen to move on into a second term. Should he be a good boy and does what he's told, he will be allowed to stay on. His running mate, Vice-President A...l G.....e, is a New World Order man also, geared more to the Greenie movement and Mother Earth than anything else. George Bush used to mockingly call him 'Ozone Man'.

Should Mr Clinton step out of line, there is always a back-up.

It is noticeable that, like other vice-presidents before him, he keeps a very low profile. One columnist wrote "A...l G.....e is so boring his secret service name is A....l G......e. Another wrote, that the only reason Clinton has not been shot is because the alternative could be worse."

Oh well. Such is life in politics. I'm sure they are both doing the best they can.

People, being people, unwisely tend to say nasty things about others whom they have not even met.

A Future Trojan Horse President

As we have made very clear throughout this book, our subject is not about personalities who are merely **pawns in the game**. This is why we do not print their full names of the small-time players for future generations to read. These people will all pass on having played their part in fulfilling the ancient prophecies.

Here today – gone tomorrow, yet, "He that doeth the will of God, abideth forever."

The two apparent contenders for the 1996 elections are:

a) Bill Clinton – Democrats
b) Bob Dole – Republicans – down in the polls during 1996 with Newt Gingrich – Republican adviser

Many voters feel Bob Dole is too old.

Many Americans fear House speaker Gingrich and his plans to follow New Zealand.

That leaves Bill Clinton who has a number of scandals to face, possibly after 5 November 1996. Next he could find himself:

a) In court
b) In his grave
c) Impeached (as was Richard Nixon before him)

History tells us, that even if a man is perceived to be less that honest, and even a rascal, people will often re-elect them. They say "He's cunning, audacious, and a stranger to the truth, yet he sure gets things done. Better the devil you know...."

However, the world at large is far more forgiving in this our day. They feel a sense of relief and can say "Our leaders can do it and get away with it so we need not feel guilty."

The same situation applies in Great Britain with certain members of the Royal Family kicking up 'bobsie di'!

We will watch the elections keenly and watch for the New World Order Trojan Horse President who will sell out his country.

Some believe that the 1996 elections could turn out to be the second to last, if not the last elections, Americans will ever see.

Very soon, we will see massive changes taking place in the U.S.A.

1. A crisis in some form i.e. possibly similar to the Oklahoma bombing, will irritate the Federal Government.
2. F.E.M.A. (Federal Emergency Management Act) will be introduced, giving the President all the executive powers of government.
3. A state of emergency will be declared.
4. **The U.S. Constitution must be suspended and revised**. The

New Columbia Constitution must therefore take precedence over the old one, and citizens must be made aware of this.

5. The U.S. will decline rapidly in power and undergo a massive tragedy as a nation. **The ancient prophecies describe a system called 'Mystery Babylon' as leading trade and religion**.

The religious base for the World Church is no doubt the city of the 7 hills – **Rome** – Mystery Babylon – Religion.

Note well!! – Within this area lies the sovereign state – **The Vatican**

[2]*"And here is the mind which hath wisdom. The seven heads are seven mountains on which the woman sitteth.*

And the woman which thou sawest is that great city, which reigneth over the kings of the earth." End quote.

"The city, as everybody knows, was built on seven hills. The highest of these, **the Capitoline**, has an elevation of only 194 feet, the lowest, **the Esquiline** is 100 feet high. These are called the Classic Seven."

We visited this area during 1996, and asked our tour guide to specifically point out these two hills.

6. **The world base for trade and economy** is another aspect to be investigated. Mystery Babylon will also head up world trade. The details are found in the writings of Jeremiah the Prophet, and the Apostle John in his book of Revelation.

Here are some of the characteristics:

Does this apply to the U.S.A.?

[3]a. The youngest of the nations – Jeremiah 50:12

b. Born from a mother country (which was Britain for the U.S.). Jeremiah 50:12.

c. A mighty military and political power – Jeremiah 50:23.

d. An arrogant, proud, and haughty nation – Jeremiah 50:31.

e. People of foreign descent – Jeremiah 50:37.

f. Covetousness reigns as the people live sumptuously, but want more while many in the world are starving – Jeremiah 50:38.

g. Nation with a Godly heritage – Jeremiah 51:7.

h. A nation of great wealth and prosperity – Jeremiah 51:13.

i. Great attainments – Jeremiah 51:53.

j. Space travellers – Jeremiah 51:53.

k. A home for the cults and occult practises – Revelation 18:2.

l. Worldwide immorality – Revelation 18:2.

m. Large in foreign aid – Revelation 18:3.

n. Large importers to satisfy the lust of the people – Revelation 18:3.

o. Centre of Christianity – Revelation 18:4.
p. Excessive crime, sexual permissiveness, homosexual freedom, decadence of marriage vows, etc – Revelation 18:5.
q. Proud and boastful people – Revelation 18:7.
r. Other countries' economic strength depends on her economic strength – Revelation 18:9-19.
s. World Trade Centre – Revelation 18:11-13.
t. Extravagant tastes – Revelation 18:14.
u. Nation of influential cities – Revelation 18:18.
v. Nation known for her music – Revelation 18:22.
w. Nation known for her crafts (manufacturing capabilities) – Revelation 18:22.
x. Nation known for her food production – Revelation 18:22.
y. Her businessmen and great corporations are known world-wide – Revelation 18:23.

LUCIFER'S EYE

Now it is obvious that this does not refer to Saddam Hussein's modern Iraq, which is built in the area of ancient Babylon in Mesopotamia between the Tigris and Euphrates rivers.

Clear thinking tells us that Mystery **Babylon's trading centre is the United States of America and Wall St in New York City in particular.**

Did you note that the numerics for New York are 666? The key – a=6, b=12, c=18 etc. Keep adding 6 then add numbers of each letter.

What are God's plans for this city.

[4]*"Alas, alas, that great city Babylon, that mighty city for in **one hour** is thy judgement come."* End quote. (Emphasis added.)

[5]*"Alas, alas, that great city.....for in **one hour** so great riches is come to nought."* End quote. (Emphasis added.)

[6]*"Thus with violence shall that great city Babylon be thrown down."* End quote.

[7]*"And there followed another angel saying Babylon is fallen, is fallen, that great city."* End quote.

It becomes clear to the reader why this must be the case, when you allow your country to be controlled by Satan. It is fruitless venting your anger at this stage on this author. He did not design the seals.

Are you considering emigrating to the U.S.A.? Perhaps you should reconsider your options.

VISIONS OF THE FUTURE OF AMERICA

Washington

In the year 1777, George Washington had a most significant visitation from a very beautiful being, who showed him three major crisis that must come upon America.

Commencing each time with the words *"Son of the Republic, look and learn"*, he was shown:

1. The American War of Independence
2. The Civil War, north versus south
3. The invasion of the United States by forces from Europe, Asia and Africa

We understand this to be the combined forces of the New World Order, under the auspices of the United Nations, who have their Trojan Horse building on Rockefeller donated land in New York city.

Washington, although a Freemason, certainly made it quite clear that he did not invent the scenarios. ('Prophecies of the Presidents' by Beckley and Crockett; Inner Light Publications, Box 753, New Brunswick, N.J. 08903, U.S.A.)

148

Duduman

From the Romanian pastor's book "Through the Fire", we quote in part – "The Heavenly messenger showed me all of California, Las Vegas, New York and Florida, and said, "This is Sodom and Gomorrah! All of this – in one day it will burn." End quote.

'Through the Fire Without Burning', by Dimitru Duduman; Hand of Help Inc, P.O. Box 3494, Fullerton, California 92634, U.S.A. Ph: (714) 447 1313.

We personally have met this very Godly old pastor and heard him tell his remarkable story. I highly recommend this book.

Wilkerson

"*America's cup of iniquity is full. The bear has prepared and is set to act. It is now only a matter of time.*

From over the North Pole, the deadly missiles will come. Fear, and some kind of supernatural impulse will cause the enemy to make the first strike."

"*For the spoilers shall come from the north", saith the Lord.*" Jeremiah 51:48. End quote.

'Set the Trumpet to Thy Mouth', by David Wilkerson; World Challenge Incorporated, P.O. Box 260, Lindale, Texas 75771, U.S.A.

There's more to come. Be of good cheer.

Prediction

In the U.S.A., Mr Bill Clinton has been chosen to continue on "for a season". (Predicted 25 April 1995.)

Any situation or person who could possibly halt Mr Clinton's winning a second term in the White House has been taken care of. **The United States of America, a comparatively young country, now moves into top gear to fulfil the purpose of its existence.**

Remember this purpose is 'peculiar' and 'particular' i.e. the positioning of Lucifer (Satan) to the leadership of the world.

However, should the World Government rulers decide to change horses in mid-stream, it would be very simple to raise one or two of the scandals, so well-known to all media watchers, and replace him with another puppet i.e. Al Gore.

Both Kennedy and Nixon knew all about the tightrope that they were walking as does Bill Clinton.

The American elections on 5 November 1996, could cause real problems on Wall St.

The President of a large institutional brokerage in Manhattan points out that Wall St is 'shuddering' at the prospect of the Democrats regaining control of Congress in the November elections.

He says "If the Republicans lose the House, the market will sell off. If they lose the House and the Senate, the market will crash."

Time will tell!

Footnotes

1   The Holy Bible; 1 Corinthians 2:9

2   The Holy Bible; Revelation 17:9&18

3   The Last Days in America by Bob Fraley; p247-248; published by Christian Life Services, P.O. Box 22134, Phoenix, Arizona 85028, U.S.A.

4   The Holy Bible; Revelation 18:10

5   The Holy Bible; Revelation 18:16-17

6   The Holy Bible; Revelation 18:21

7   The Holy Bible; Revelation 14:8

We also recommend that you purchase a copy of "**Operation Vampire Killer 2000**"; American Police action for stopping the programme for World Government rule, P.O. Box 8712, Phoenix, Arizona 85066, U.S.A.

CHAPTER TWENTY-TWO

SETTING THE STAGE FOR THE STRONG WORLD LEADER

Away back in 1957, Henri Spaak, Secretary General of Nato, made a very interesting comment along this line. *"We are tired of committees. **Send us a man, whether he be God or the devil, we will receive him**."* (Emphasis added.)

In a criticism of the European Union, some years ago, Dr Henry Kissinger pointed out that the Community lacked strong leadership. *"There is no strong leader with whom one can negotiate and speak for the group as a whole."*

'Evening Post', 26th June 1995 – *"Accusations of incompetence flow freely in a vacuum of Leadership.*

....Some observers blame the current difficulties on a lack of leadership and courage among world leaders...." End quote.

Plans for the Expanded European Union

France and Germany are tired of the lack of progress in the enlarged Community. They now propose a three tier structure.

a) Within the Central Circle it is proposed that 10 nations, keen on full political and monetary union should make all major decisions i.e. France, Germany, Belgium, Netherlands, Luxembourg and 5 others.
b) Tier two, those nations showing some promise of co-operation.
c) Tier three, the drifters or hangers on and not strong contributors to the Union as a whole.

'Evening Post', 25th February 1995 – *"Europe bets on a single currency.*

New Era Britain can stay out of monetary union if it wants, but by 1999, seven European countries are likely to be using ECUs rather than their own currencies.

...In the present loose union of 15 countries, the most important change will the creation of a single currency and of supranational political institutors to accompany it.

...France believes seven countries – Austria, Belgium, Finland, France, Germany, Luxembourg, and the Netherlands will be able to go ahead with monetary and political union. Some European Commission officials say Ireland is a likelier candidate than Finland."

From the 'Daily Telegraph', 16 December 1995, things continue to quickly progress.

"*John Major yesterday brought to light the economic complexities of introducing a single European Currency that would apply to only a small minority of the 15 strong E.U.*

..."*There is a danger of creating a privileged elite of countries inside a new single currency, hugely outnumbered as other countries join*", he said.

*...Europe's proposed single currency was named **the Euro** yesterday with the minimum of fanfare.*

*Mr Major argued that "**it seemed rather odd to name the baby before the pregnancy**.*" End quote.

No doubt, a clever little phrase, yet Mr Major must learn that this European Union is wrapped up inextricably with the

a) New World Order plan
b) A future world leader
c) A new world monetary system

It is therefore, also clear that opposition to any such innovations might be called 'political suicide'.

The rules of the New World Order are quite simple. "Go along with the plan. Don't rock the boat or you're out!"

On the same page in the 'Telegraph', we read – "*Snow had fallen in Madrid, snow on snow.*

In the bleak midwinter wise men come, mainly from the East to behold a wondrous thing.

They come to bear witness to the nativity of a single European currency, and they gave it a name...." End quote.

This article was headed "***Lo Its Name Shall be Called Euro***."

A Further Point of Interest

'Daily Telegraph', 16th December 1995 – "*The Deutschmark by another Name.*

*So farewell then franc. And lire, and peseta and guilder and krone. The one currency that may not disappear when and if the absurdly named Euro starts circulating (let us leave the pound out of this) is the **German mark**.*

*....In due time it will be called the **Euromark** then someone will drop the Euro prefix and the Euro will have what it has now, a currency system based on the German mark...*" End quote.

Actually, the writer was only half right. The world will have a currency system based on the **mark of the Beast**.

'International Express (Australian edition)', 18-24 October 1995 – *"Euro plan for "super Santer". Plans to create a powerful European presidency.*

The new Euro "head of state" would outrank all existing Brussels bureaucrats and have precedence over national premiers.

He would represent the E.U. on the international stage, and would attend summits with other national leaders like President Bill Clinton.

The six monthly summits, where vital decisions on Europe's future are taken would be headed by the new president whose term would run for three years.

....The idea will be put to the Maastricht Mk II summit next year." End quote.

15 years ago when I wrote my first book 'Warning', I did not realise just how popular the type of information would prove to be. We reprinted this book in 1981, 1982, 1983, 1984, 1985, 1986, 1987, 1989, 1991, 1992.

This book is now very up-to-date and gives the reader much information on the European Union and its future leader.

It was predicted in great detail by the prophets away back in 586 B.C. and then in 96 A.D. that the following points would be of significance.

a) In world history there would be 7 significant empires, the European Union being the last.

[1]*"And there are seven kings (empires), five are fallen (i.e. Chaldees, Egypt, Babylon, Medo Persia and Greece), one is (i.e. Rome at the time of the prophecy being given) and the other is not yet come (i.e. the European Union)..."*

b) This final empire will continue to bumble along until a strong leader is appointed. **Union without unity** is the initial state of this group. The inner ruling tier of 10 nations will finally submit to a strong leader.

Remembering that Daniel the prophet was living under the Babylonian captivity, therefore he viewed these seven empires as starting with Babylon.

Therefore, he numbers the world empires thus:

Country	Daniel 2	Daniel 7
1. **Babylon**	represented as gold	represented as a lion – kingly

2. **Medo-Persia**	represented as silver	represented as a bear – strong
3. **Greece**	represented as brass	represented as a leopard – swift
4. **Rome**	represented as iron	represented as a beast – cruel
5. **European Union**	represented as iron and clay	this comes out of no.4 – a mixture of weak and strong nations.

[2]*"And the ten horns (European Union) out of this kingdom (Rome) are ten kings that shall arise (the inner circle of decision makers) and another shall rise after them (the strong leader)."*

This future strong leader has 4 titles:

1) Antichrist
2) Beast
3) Man of Sin
4) **Son of Perdition**

This final title was previously applied to another man who played a prominent role in the betrayal of his Master i.e. Judas Iscariot.

Consider now, the following prophecy.

[3]*"And the beast that was* (i.e. the same spirit was in Judas Iscariot) *and is not* (i.e. **as John wrote this down in 96 A.D., he did not know the future world leader's identity**) *even he is the eighth* (i.e. **there are seven empires preceding his rise to power**) *and is of the seven* (i.e. **he is ultimately appointed leader of no.7**) *and goeth into perdition* (i.e. **the same place of judgement reserved for Judas Iscariot is also reserved for this future strong E.U. leader.**)

c) The European Union will only last for a very brief time *"....and the other is not yet come, and when he cometh, he must continue a 'short space'."*

d) The European Union will not exercise real power until a strong leader is appointed. This man's rule will last prophetically speaking for 'one hour'.

[4]*"And the ten horns which thou sawest are ten kings which have received no kingdom as yet, but receive power as kings one hour with the beast."*

How long a period of time does the 'one hour' represent?

[5]"*And there was given unto him a mouth speaking great things and blasphemies, and power was given unto him to continue forty and two months.*"

The 'one hour' leadership of this future strong man, will actually last for 42 months, which is only three and a half years if the Jewish calendar at 30 days to a month is used.

e) During the time of the strong leaders reign, Almighty God will personally see to it that His will is fulfilled as the ten decision makers in the central tier hand over their authority to this one man.

[6]"*These have one mind, and shall give their power and strength unto the beast.*"

f) It is obvious at this point, that this will require supernatural intervention, as the European Union countries have not previously been known for co-operation.

[7] – Initially therefore, "*....the kingdom shall be partly strong* *[8] – and partly broken....*" but wait, "*For God hath put in their hearts to fulfil His will and to agree, and give their kingdom unto the beast, until the words of God shall be fulfilled.*"

g) **The Lord Jesus Christ is likened in Scripture to a great stone or a rock.**

If that rock falls on you, it will crush you. If, however, you choose to build your life on that rock, you will live forever.

This great stone will collapse all earthly empires and set up His own at a certain time in history. This particular time in history can now be easily calculated once all power has been handed over to this future strong leader.

[9]"*Forasmuch as thou sawest that a stone was cut out of the mountain without hands, and that it break in pieces the iron, the brass, the clay, the silver and the gold....*"

Notice that in that day, the Lord Jesus Christ will not be in competition with any other.

h) God, through the Lord Jesus Christ will set up His own empire and rule the whole world.

[10]"*And in the days of these kings shall the God of Heaven set up a kingdom which shall never be destroyed.*"

[11]"*And the Lord shall be king over all the earth. In that day shall there be one Lord, and His Name one.*"

i) The information that you have read thus far is not 'hope so', 'could be', 'may be so', 'occultish', 'new age wishful thinking *12 - and supposition', "....*the dream is 'certain' and the interpretation thereof 'sure'*."

All that remains to complete the jigsaw is for us to now point out the future world strong man's characteristics and to identity him.

Summary

In identifying this future leader, we can now be sure that he will be involved in 3 main areas:

<u>A Man of Finance</u>

1) He will work along with another religious man called the 'False Prophet' to introduce the mark of the Beast i.e. a silicon chip or similar, placed under the flesh of every individual who wishes to buy or sell.

[13] *"And he causeth all, both small and great, rich and poor, free and bond, to receive a mark in their right hand, or in their foreheads: And that no man might buy or sell, save he that had the mark, or the name of the beast, or the number of his name.*
Here is wisdom. Let him that hath understanding count the number of the beast: for it is the number of a man: and his number is six hundred, threescore and six."

<u>A Man of Peace</u>

2) He will confirm a seven year comprehensive peace treaty in the Middle East and break it after three and a half years.
   This treaty must also include Syria and Lebanon.

[14]*"And he shall confirm the covenant with many of one week: and in the midst of the week he shall cause the sacrifice and the oblation to cease..."*

<u>A Future Strong World Leader</u>

3) This same man will control the up-dated European Union (E.U.).
   Once you've read this book, you will be able to watch world events in a new light.

[15] *"And the ten horns out of this kingdom, are ten kings that shall arise, and another shall rise after them..."*

This refers to the future strong man we are looking for.

Footnotes

1   Revelation 17:10; The Holy Bible
2   Daniel 7:24a; The Holy Bible
3   Revelation 17:11; The Holy Bible
4   Revelation 17:12; The Holy Bible
5   Revelation 13:5; The Holy Bible
6   Revelation 17:13; The Holy Bible
7   Daniel 2:42b; The Holy Bible
8   Revelation 17:17; The Holy Bible
9   Daniel 2:45a; The Holy Bible
10 Daniel 2:44a; The Holy Bible
11 Zechariah 14:9 – The Holy Bible
12 Daniel 2:45b; The Holy Bible
13 Revelation 13:16-18; The Holy Bible
14 Daniel 9:27a; The Holy Bible
15 Daniel 7:24a; The Holy Bible

Predictions

Great changes will occur in the European Union, and arguments and divisions will become more common.

One man will ultimately be given full authority and this will unite the previously divided countries.

Many times we hear the question, "If he is alive today, do you have any ideas as to his identity?

Read on!!

CHAPTER TWENTY-THREE

WHO IS HE?

Students of prophecy have endeavoured to identify him for centuries. Nero, Hitler, Mussolini, the Pope, Idi Amin, Sadat, King Juan Carlos of Spain and others have all been suggested. However, the timing needs to be a consideration. We are now living at the correct stage in history for the world leader to be revealed.

Remember, many little antichrists precede the main Antichrist at the time of the end.

Who is he?

I confess at this stage, I don't know, but I'm watching!!

The Scene – Jerusalem

Saturday night, November 4th. We in our tour party, along with the people of Israel, and friends of Israel world-wide, were in a state of shock.

At 11:15 p.m. the solemn words were announced over CNN, **"Yitzhak Rabin is dead**."

Sleep was the last thing on our minds. A number of thoughts chased through our heads.

What about Mrs Rabin and family? What about the possible repercussions of the shooting? Was an Arab responsible? If so, all out war was on the agenda. What about the peace process that was moving along so quickly to that point?

The CNN programme continued with an interview with Lawrence Eagleburger, ex-U.S. Secretary of State.

He said that the Middle East peace talks must not be allowed to founder, and that there was only one man with the clear thinking, astute mind of Rabin. He was referring of course to none other than **Dr Henry Kissinger**.

Let us examine some of this man's outstanding characteristics as a **possible example** of the great leader we are looking for.

WARNING!

Let us not fly to any instant conclusions. There are many other powerful men with qualifications which are most impressive. We will view Mr Kissinger as a "prototype" only.

To our very great surprise, the next interviewee on CNN was a sobbing Henry Kissinger. The man was so obviously moved that he was finding great difficulty in speaking. Between strong bouts of emotion which included tears, this ex-Secretary of State for the U.S.A. told us that the peace process must continue on.

I noted a key word which he used continually – **'balance'**. This word was taken from a phrase familiar to Kissinger and borrowed from former European negotiators.

Balance of Power

Some years ago, Kissinger, when explaining this phrase, pointed out that when conducting peace negotiations, you did not want any nation perfectly at peace, but at all times balanced on the edge of peace and war. **This left these nations insecure** and therefore able to be **easily manipulated** with subtle suggestions.

To establish this fact, look at the **peace** in Russia, Somalia, Bosnia, Vietnam, Korea, and Ireland.

It was now after midnight, Sunday, November 5th and Kissinger continued on to speak of his long association with Rabin and their combined hopes for peace in the area.

Political commentators give us some interesting insights into his past behaviour, which helps in our understanding of his methodology.

[1]Quote – "*When Kissinger returned from a trip....at the last stop before Washington, his aides always sent a cable like this one:*

1. *Would appreciate your arranging to have the following items available planeside upon arrival Andrews.*
2. *'Sunday Times' and 'Post'.*
3. ***Up-to-date-set of Rabin briefing books*** (*a second set for the secretary as well as a back-up set should be available in the Department by 0800 Monday.*
4. ....
5. ....

Kissinger
Limited Official Use." End quote. (Emphasis added).

This makes it abundantly clear that Rabin and Kissinger were working **hand in hand** on Middle Eastern affairs. No wonder he was weeping when his friend was blown away.

Rabin later made this comment to a biographer regarding Kissinger.

[2]*"He was a person of great talent. He really penetrated the problem. He knew the limitations, he knew the personalities, he knew the situation, he had a creative mind. It was a real pleasure to work with him."* End quote.

During his early days at diplomacy, Kissinger made sure he made friends and contacts of not only people in power at the time, but also **people who would later be in power**.

He obviously was aware of the concept, "**It's not what you know, but who you know**".

Syria

[3]*"On the Syrian side," he said, "Nobody wants to be the first Syrian to negotiate with the Israelis, especially when they don't know the outcome....the Syrians have no negotiating experience. they have a different concept of what a negotiation is. **They want me to do everything by myself**. I cannot seriously say what they are asking me to do."* End quote.

Note now that Rabin needed him, just as the Syrians needed him, over 20 years ago. The same man, although now a background figure, is still involved in **Middle Eastern matters**.

As we travel on the lecture trail, we hear the sentence regularly **"But he's too old now!"**

Is he?

Q. Where was Henry Kissinger in the year 1983, just prior to the setting up of EFT (Electronic Funds Transfer) systems, which lead on to the cashless society and the Mark of the Beast system?

A. In Australia holding discussions with the monetary and banking heads. He also visited some towns around Gloucester in New South Wales, and after giving a lecture or two, flew away.

How do I know? One of his bodyguards became a committed Christian and gave his life to Jesus at one of our gatherings.

Q. Where was Henry when the guinea pig country of New Zealand brought in G.S.T. (Goods and Services Tax)?

A. I received a call from the New Zealand Tax Department one morning with a voice saying, "Guess who's in here today? Henry Kissinger!"

Q. Where was Kissinger during the month of November 1995?

A. On a four day visit to India. He met Prime Minister Rao, and other officials but made his concepts quite clear in an interview[4] with "India Today", November 1995.

We quote in part herewith from this interview.

Q. *"So you aren't apprehensive about opposition to multinationals in India?"*

A. *"The fact is that if you want foreign capital, you have to get it from foreign capitalists. Governments don't have enough money any more to make a substantial contribution to economic development."* End quote.

What he is saying here in obviously veiled language is "Come on India. Hurry up. Get involved. Privatise – sell up your government departments and their assets to the World Government guys. Get ready to join the leaders of the world in **yielding up independence and sovereignty** to the New World Order leaders. Get ready to kiss India goodbye."

And again, from the same magazine, a reference to his firm, 'Kissinger Associates'.

Q. *"Is your firm 'Kissinger Associates taking up any offer to represent the Indian Government in the U.S.?"*

A. *"No, no, no. Let me make one thing absolutely clear. We do not take money from governments. We do not represent governments ever. We require any client of 'Kissinger Associates' **to sign a contract** that makes it clear that we do not intervene with the United States Government. So there is no possibility whatever that we will do anything of a financial nature with the Indian Government."* End quote.

Q. Why is this?

A. **National governments no longer matter**. They are all selling out their assets and power to shadowy overseas groups and characters with a maze of interlocking directorships.

Q. On the night Rabin was assassinated, where was Kissinger?

A. In China, and we make bold to say that had the murder not occurred, only a tiny minority of people would have known his whereabouts.

Q. What was he doing in China?

A. Helping them set the scene for the Communist takeover of Hong Kong in 1997, and to make sure that big business would be able to gradually buy their way into the political scene through a **restructuring scheme called 'privatisation'**.

Note well that governments, both capitalist, and communist, pose no problem to our restructuring front-man – Dr Henry Kissinger.

One author makes a fascinating observation.

[5]"*While he was still an academic, Kissinger wrote "**Men become myths, not by what they know, or even by what they achieve, but by the task they set for themselves**".*

The task he set for himself was the establishment of a New World Order whose organising principle would be international stability...."
End quote.

We left Israel, flew down to Rome, Bangkok and Sydney, and back to New Zealand via the Gold Coast, Australia.

Q. Where did we next hear the name Henry Kissinger?

[6]A."*Kissinger warns on World Stability.*"

Here he was again. This time in Sydney, Australia.

Please take note of his New Age phraseology, reported in this article.

Quote – "*Dr Kissinger said a "**fundamental change in human consciousness was occurring.**

...Addressing a lunch at Sydney's Regent Hotel, sponsored by the 'Australian Financial Review'.....*

China was sincere in wanting a one-country, two systems outcome when it took over Hong Kong in 1997, but it was uncertain whether Chinese officials could make the system work and whether Hong Kong people could learn to operate within a Chinese system.

*....He said it had never previously been the case that **the entire global system was up for restructuring**.*

National leaders now had to deal simultaneously with universal issues..." End quote.

Too old is he? He's talking about restructuring the world.

One author asks a very pertinent question.

[7]"*Will Mr Kissinger rise to head the world government he is preparing and promoting?*"

Recap of Necessary Qualifications for the Future World Leader

Away back in 1978, we wrote a list of prophetic qualifications in our book 'Warning'.

Prediction

1978 – **He will arise after the ten nations.**

Update 1995 – there are now 15 nations in the European Union. The **inner decision making tier** will comprise of ten nations.

Henry Kissinger appears to be well suited to ultimately control this group, as he has been a student of European political history for many years.

He examined and adapted many of his policies from the ideas of previous European movers and shakers of note – Bismark, Castlereagh and Metternich.

A Final Revelation

When Henry Kissinger wrote his Ph.D. study of **Metternich** and **Castlereagh**, many years ago, he did more than draw a remarkable portrait of the two statesmen who managed, in the upheaval of post-Napoleonic Europe, **to balance competing forces and thereby provide a period of relative peace**, at the same time, he unintentionally drew a portrait of himself.

[8]*"Both", wrote Kissinger, from 'A World Restored', "**dominated every negotiation** in which they participated: Castlereagh by the ability to reconcile conflicting points of view, and by the single-mindedness conferred by an empirical policy: **Metternich through an almost uncanny faculty of achieving a personal dominance over his adversaries** and the art of defining a moral framework which **made concessions appear, not as surrenders, but as sacrifices to the common cause.**"* End quote.

Prediction

1978 – Three of the Ten in the E.U. will be uprooted by him.

Update 1995 – With the zeal of Germany and France keepings things moving, it is easy to see how at least three nations would not go along with the plans **for full political and monetary union**.

It was because of her desire to hold on to the status quo in Great Britain that Margaret Thatcher lost her job.

[9]Mr Kissinger is a master manipulator. *"He was fond of saying that the successful conclusion of any negotiation would leave both sides dissatisfied. And he had no aversion to seeking refuge in ambiguity."*

[10]*Discussing a session in Damascus he said, "There's no attempt to fool the Syrians. Sometimes the art of diplomacy is to keep the obvious obscured...."* End quote.

Prediction

1978 – He will arise out of the nations – possibly German origins.

Update 1995 – On May 27th 1923, Heinz Alfred Kissinger was born in Furth, Germany.

Prediction

1978 – **One man – not a committee**.

Amongst the statements attributed to Henry is the one where he points out that he feels like the lone cowboy riding into town.

[11]Once at a Washington dinner, a man walked up and said *"Dr Kissinger, I want to thank you for saving the world."*

"You're welcome", he replied.

Update 1995 – Take note of the countries he has visited even during the course of last year. He once said, *"My success stems from the fact that I've always acted alone."*

Prediction

1978 – **He must be Jewish**.

[12]Update 1995 – In the month of December 1973, on a visit to Yad Vashem, the Holocaust museum, Henry Kissinger's Jewishness became very apparent.

The Administrator dug out a lot of material from Kissinger's birthplace of Furth, and in their records, the name Kissinger cropped up regularly as being victims of Hitler's murder squad. Henry bowed his head and was so silent that the biographer used the words 'almost paralysed'.

Yet, he apparently was deliberately sworn in as Secretary of State on the Sabbath day and took his oath on the King James Bible. His parents, both strongly Jewish, refused to ride in a car and, in contrast to their son's anti-religious activities, walked from their hotel to the White House.

Prediction

1978 – A man of boasting arrogance.

Update 1995 – When giving a speech at the Bohemian Grove, north of San Francisco, he was introduced in such a flowery manner that [13]he commenced by saying, *"**After that introduction, there is nothing left for me to do but walk on water**."*

Prediction

1978 – Something special about his eyes.

Update 1995 – Some commentators have observed that Kissinger has an owl-like stare.

An acquaintance of this author met Henry Kissinger on at least two occasions, and reported that so penetrating and strong was his stare, it was almost as if he was looking around the back of his head, right into his brain.

Prediction

1978 – Outstanding in his field – peace negotiations.

Update 1995 – Firstly, this man never seemed to suffer from jet lag. After a long trip which left his staff and media followers completely wrecked, Kissinger would spring out of bed and conduct full-scale negotiations.

[14]Mrs Golda Meir said, *"At this point (October 1973) the outstanding personality in the Middle East became not President Sadat, or President Assad, or King Faisal, or even Mrs Meir herself.*

*It was the U.S. Secretary of State, Dr Henry Kissinger, whose efforts on behalf of peace can only be described as **superhuman**.*

....I think that possibly one of the most impressive qualities is his fantastic capacity for dealing with the minutest details of whatever problems he undertakes to do...." End quote.

Prediction

1978 – Not to be trusted.

[15]Update 1995 – The Israelis did not always believe – or at least, they did not always believe everything. *"It's not that he lied",* said one prominent Israeli diplomat. *"He had a unique ability of explaining every situation in the manner most pleasing to the one who heard it. We trusted him",* the diplomate added, *"but with the necessary discount."* End quote.

[16]*"...Rabin recalled that "Kissinger had a Metternichian system of telling only half the truth. He didn't lie. He would have lost credibility. He didn't tell the whole truth. He stressed certain points he wanted out of proportion to the **proportions** of the parties."* End quote.

Metternich of Austria, one of Kissinger's heroes, was well known for **the art of ambiguity** – amounting at times to **deception**.

Prediction

1978 – Good people rely on him.

[17]Update 1995 – ....regardless of the fact that everyone knew he didn't tell the whole truth, he created a kind of intensive relationship that forced people to be in a way committed to him.

Shimon Peres remembered that *"if you didn't listen exactly word by word, you could be carried away by what he said. But if you listened word by word, he wasn't lying."*

Prediction

1978 – A party type or swinger.

[18]Update 1995 – Kissinger has dated some of the world's most beautiful women. A key Kissinger phrase reads thus, "*Power is the ultimate aphrodisiac.*"

Names such as Zsa Zsa Gabor, Judy Brown, Marlo Thomas, Gloria Steinem, and others, make interesting reading. After reading the many books written about him, there is no doubt left in our minds that this qualification certainly fits this man.

Some media reports list him as a **very successful swinger**.

Prediction

1978 – World traveller – Seeks world domination – He is a One Worlder.

[19]Update 1995 – One State Department official who travelled with him on an earlier trip to China remarked, "*He has an incredible psychological capability of not being bothered by space and time change.*" End quote.

[20]A reporter once estimated the cost of Kissinger's travel to be about $20,000 a day, particularly while he was involved in his Middle East shuttle diplomacy.

He was one of the first well-known diplomats to use the term "New World Order" in his speeches.

He had a **global perspective**, where small nations didn't count, and this concept, put together with the term **'balance of power'**, were terms borrowed from previous European visionaries who had similar aims, many years before Kissinger was born.

In 1973, he travelled 120,000 miles, which is about 5 times around the world, contacting the nations' leaders.

Prediction

1978 – Will consider changing times and laws.

Update 1995 – Newswatchers will probably be aware that during the year 1995, there was discussion in Europe about the synchronisation of all European Union countries into a common time zone.

This would initially cause great confusion as folk living in **Ireland** would have the same time system as those living out to the east, in such countries as **Greece**.

This in time would cause terrible confusion to countries to the south e.g. African nations etc.

Laws – Already discipline has been removed from the schools and also unfortunately many homes, leaving the younger generation out of control in society.

Men appear in many cases to be emasculated and effeminate, with women taking the leadership.

An ancient prophecy gives us **the world condition** just prior to this future world leader being revealed. How is this for an accurate prophecy given thousands of years ago, setting the scene for today's society?

[21]*"As for my people, children are their oppressors and women rule over them."*

[22]***"Therefore, the law is slacked, and judgement doth never go forth, for the wicked doth compass about the righteous, therefore wrong judgement proceedeth."***

Prediction

1978 – Will cause corruption and destruction.

Update 1995 – The Vietnam "peace" brought about by Kissinger and Le Duc Tho of Vietnam was so ambiguous that fighting continued on after Kissinger accepted the Nobel Peace Prize, and Le Duc Tho refused his.

After the signing, it was estimated that 50,000 North and South Vietnamese had been killed, which was more deaths than the Americans lost in 12 previous years of fighting.

Prediction

1978 – Will not work alone – has a counterpart in religion.

Update 1995 – Readers please note that owing to a very old pact between the **Vatican** and the **Moslems**, the papacy would not recognise the State of Israel, until the Palestinians regained a foothold in the land.

Notice, that as soon as the PLO and Israel signed their peace agreement, the Vatican again recognised the State of Israel.

At the conclusion of 1995, the media presented a graphic headline – *"Holy 2000. Israel and the Vatican are working together to boost tourism.*

*One year after the Vatican and Israel normalised their diplomatic relations, the two are engaged in a joint campaign to bring turn of the century pilgrims to **Rome and Jerusalem**.*

...This is being encouraged by none other than Pope John Paul the 2nd himself.

In fact, one of the Pope's most cherished projects for the Grand Jubilee, Year 2000, is to hold a summit of representatives of the three Abrahamic faiths at Mount Sinai.

The Pope has said, the Jubilee should "stress the relationship with our Jewish brothers whose presence in Rome is more ancient than that of Christians, so that celebrations in Rome adequately correspond to those in the Holy Land." End quote.

What is it called again?

The Jerusalem 2000 Celebrations.

A fascinating prophecy dated from the crucifixion of the Lord, should be taken note of. Remember the rule –

[22]**"One day with the Lord is as a thousand years, and a thousand years as one day."**

[23]"*Come and let us return unto the Lord, for He hath torn and He will heal us, He hath smitten and He will bind us up.*

After two days, He will revive us.
In the third day He will raise us up.
And we shall live in His sight."

A Simple Calculation

Working on the basis of one day being equal to 1000 years – two days (as specified in the previous verse) = 2000 years of history. From Christ until today = 1996 years have elapsed.

$$\begin{array}{r} 2000 \\ -1996 \\ \hline 4 \end{array}$$ years remain until the 'two days' are over.

Note – This is **an approximation only**, as there are some variations in the world dating systems.

Prediction

1978 – Outwardly peaceful and a flatterer.

[24]Update 1995 – "*It has always been Kissinger's special style to flatter and charm an adversary*" says one author in a Kissinger biography e.g. "*While visiting the great pyramid of Cheops, an Egyptian reporter asked this Jewish diplomat, "Do you know much about our history, Dr Kissinger?"*

He replied very diplomatically, "I've always been fascinated by Egyptian history – its sense of permanence." End quote.

When negotiating with Sadat during the 1973 war, he said "*Sadat showed great wisdom. You have to give him a lot of credit.*"

Prediction

1978 – Will allow his image to be installed in Jewish Holy Place.

Update 1995 – The media has now clarified a former stumbling block in our search for this great world leader.

The Messiah they seek **does not necessarily need to be a religious character. A secular leader** who can bring a satisfactory peace to the area could well be regarded as a Messiah-like figure, as Israel today is largely a secular country.

Never forget that '**total power corrupts totally**' and with the whole world gasping at your every word, laughing, even at your hopelessly weak jokes, the final stage of accepting the worship of people, shouldn't be considered too outrageous.

[25]As one top official said, "***Henry adores power, absolutely adores it.***"

When asked by a reporter as to how he should now be addressed [26]after becoming Secretary of State, he replied, "***Oh I don't stand on protocol. If you will just call me Excellency, it will be okay.***"

Prediction

1978 – Will confirm a seven year treaty.

Update 1995 – With the **enlarged peace talks** getting underway at the end of the year 1995, it is simply a matter of **SIT BACK – WATCH AND SEE**.

Remember the three main qualities –
a) It must be confirmed by a well-respected Jewish leader.
b) It must include the vast majority of Arab countries, including Syria and Lebanon, together with Israel (many).
c) It must be for an initial 7 year period.

Unless all three points apply, this is not the treaty that we are looking for.

[27]Remember the original prophecy – "*And he shall confirm the covenant with many, for one week, and in the midst of the week, he shall cause the sacrifice and the oblation to cease....*"

Meaning – **The comprehensive peace treaty will be confirmed for an initial period of 7 years. The one who confirms it will be a** non-religious Jew. Halfway through this seven year period, after three and a half years, this man will stop the Jewish sacrificial system. This will be the very system that he assisted them to set up on the temple mound.

Note – The new P.M. in Israel will fit in with the U.S. State Department plans for the Middle East peace. If not, we will all repeat together, "Goodbye Mr Netanyahu".

Prediction

1978 – This great future world leader will be destroyed by Christ at His public coming.

Update 1995 – To this man who is so bereft of language skills that he enjoys blaspheming, and using the Name of the Lord as a curse, his day will come.

Kissinger has been known to link the revival of the nation of Israel, to the coming together of the prophet **Ezekiel's dry bones**. When questioned on this, he answered good humouredly,[28] – "*I do it sarcastically*."

When once questioned as to the accuracy of a President Nixon[29] – statement he exploded, "*No. The President of the United States doesn't know what the ..... he's talking about. ...., I thought you would never ask*."

The prophet had this to say about the future world leader, whoever he happens to be.

[30]"*And then shall that wicked be revealed, who the Lord shall consume with the spirit of his mouth, and shall destroy with the brightness of his coming*." End quote.

Because the Almighty God is light and the Lord Jesus Christ is this light hidden and veiled in human flesh, this would explain why we need to approach God, only through our Lord Jesus Christ.

No-one else!

God has ordained that there are not many ways into His presence. Just One.

Don't miss out.

Listen - learn - act!

At the conclusion of 1995, we read "*President of Europe proposed. German and French parliamentarians called yesterday for the E.U. to name its own president for a three year term, in reforms they want to see from a Maastricht Treaty review starting next year.*

*...They said, this president would head the **European***

Council*....This office holder would represent the E.U. to the outside* world, and be above the European Commission President..." End quote.

The World Leader's Name Must Add Up To 666

[31] *"Here is wisdom. Let him that hath understanding count the number of the beast for it is the number of a man and his number is six hundred, threescore and six."*

	Greek	**Meaning**
Six hundred	Chi	To prick and mark
threescore and	Xi	in recognition of
six	Sigma	ownership

Here is a beautiful description of a silicon chip being inserted under human flesh. This will be done much in the same way that animals are now being injected with identifying chips.

Now, if we have wisdom, we have God's permission to count and to identify our future world leader. There are various codes available, but the most simple would be the following.

Take 6, the number applied to man and write down the alphabet from A-Z and keep adding 6 all the way through.

A - 6	G - 42	M - 78	S = 114	Y = 150
B - 12	H - 48	N = 84	T = 120	Z = 156
C - 18	I - 54	O = 90	U = 126	
D - 24	J - 60	P = 96	V = 132	
E - 30	K - 66	Q - 102	W = 138	
F - 36	L - 72	R = 108	X = 144	

Let us try this name -	**and this -**	**and this -**
K – 66	W – 138	N – 84
I – 54	I – 54	E – 30
S – 114	T – 120	T – 120
S – 114	C – 18	A – 6
I – 54	H – 48	N – 84
N – 84	C – 18	Y – 150
G – 42	R – 108	A – 6
E – 30	A – 6	H – 48
R – 108	F – 36	U – 126
666	T – 120	654
	666	(Not quite)

171

and this –	and this –
C – 18	N – 84
O – 90	E – 30
M – 78	W – 138
P – 96	
U – 126	Y – 150
T – 120	O – 90
E – 30	R – 108
R – 108	K – 66
666	666

Remember, the number of perfection or God's number is 777.

Finally – Is Kissinger the man who will lead the world for three and a half years or do we look for another?

To us, he is merely a prototype as we scan the media columns for a possible candidate.

Time will tell! (Remember, your own name may add up to 666!)

Footnotes

1, 2, 3, 5, 9, 10, 12, 13, 15, 16, 17, 19, 20, 28, 29 – Travels with Henry by Richard Valeriani

4   India Today; page 5

6   Australian Financial Review; 14 November 1995

7   Henry Kissinger Soviet Agent by Frank Capell; page 5

8   A World Restored by Henry Kissinger

11   Kissinger by Marvin Kalb and Bernard Kalb; page 73

14   My Life by Golda Meir

18   Kissinger – The Adventures of Super Kraut by Charles Ashman

21   The Holy Bible; Isaiah 3:12

22   The Holy Bible; Habakkuk 1:4

23   The Holy Bible; Hosea 5:1-2

24   Kissinger by Marvin Kalb and Bernard Kalb; pages 576-577

25   Kissinger by Marvin Kalb and Bernard Kalb; page 232

26   Kissinger by Gary Allen; page 24

27   The Holy Bible; Daniel 9:27

30   The Holy Bible; II Thessalonians 2:8

31   The Holy Bible; Revelation 13:18

Recommended Reading

Kissinger by Marvin Kalb and Bernard Kalb; published by Dell Publishing Co. Inc; 1 Dag Hammarskjold Plaza, New York 10017, U.S.A.

Kissinger by Gary allen; published by 76 Press; P.O. Box 2686, Seal Beach, California 90740 U.S.A.

Kissinger – Man of Peace by Salem Kirban; Kent Rd, Huntingdon Valley, Pennsylvania 19606, U.S.A.

Travels with Henry by Richard Valeriani; printed by Houghton Mifflin Company; 2 Park St, Boston, Massachusetts 02107, U.S.A.

Henry Kissinger – Soviet Agent by Frank Capell; published by Herald of Freedom; Zarephath, New Jersey 08890, U.S.A.

Kissinger – The Adventures of Super Kraut by Charles R. Ashman; published by Dell Publishing Co. Inc; 1 Dag Hammarskjold Plaza, New York, 10017, U.S.A.

Prediction

Watch for a future world leader's involvement in Middle East Peace negotiations whoever he may happen to be.

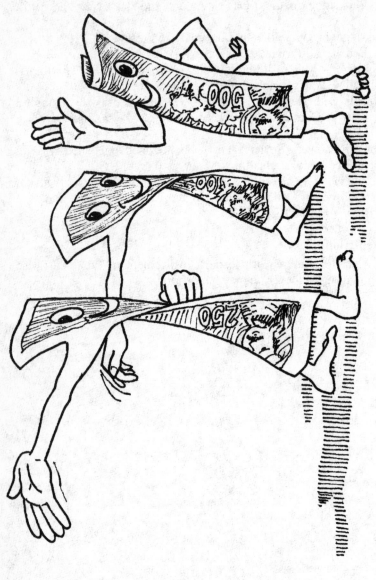

CHAPTER TWENTY-FOUR

FAREWELL TO CASH

FAREWELL TO CASH UPDATE

My friends used to laugh and harass me in a jocular manner. "There goes old Smithy playing on his one stringed violin again – money crash – New World Order – Mark of the beast etc."

Both George Bush and Jimmy Carter had something in mind however when they referred to:

a) A New World Order
b) A Thousand Points of Light
c) Global 2000

In other words, **as we approach the year 2000, the smiles seem to have disappeared from my friends' faces** and have been replaced by looks of concern and alarm.

I took all the laughing and chafing with a smile – life was meant to be enjoyable so why not?

Now, it is time to face the facts.

Cash is about to make its exit from the world scene.

Our four other books make all this very clear, so we herewith merely insert an update on latest information.

Order of Future Events

1. World-wide money crash, possibly starting in Japan.

'Herald Sun Business', 10 April 1992 – "*Collapse of Japan will bring the New World Order*". Thus reads the news clipping in front of me.

A scientist friend of mine tells me that ocean temperatures are heating up particularly in the areas of Japan and California.

Is this earthquake material or isn't it?

a) A Kobe-type earthquake in Tokyo could shake the reclaimed waterfront area into the sea, bringing down Japan's most valuable real-estate. This real estate, with its highly inflated values, would then collapse into the Tokyo harbour.

2. That was the good news. Now for the bad news, comparatively speaking.

The Japanese economy, which is based upon the real-estate value of the country would immediately collapse. The government of that country could then issue a decree that **overseas investment money**

must be immediately brought back to that country to help rebuild its shattered economy.

This in time would collapse each and every country where the Japanese have invested e.g. The Gold Coast, Queensland, Australia, the pine forests of New Zealand, the U.S.A., Canada, and Great Britain.

A big earthquake in California could also usher in the demise of cash as we know it today.

3. **An all-embracing smart card** will be issued to each citizen. The chip built into the card can hold masses of information on each individual owner. **This has already commenced in Swindon, England**. Called the Mondex card, it is a trial run for wider distribution. Mondex is from the French 'Le Monde', meaning 'the world'.

In 1997, it will make its debut in New Zealand, the guinea pig country, going on to Australia, to South Africa, then to the rest of the world.

The laser card has been introduced in certain parts of the U.S.A.

The 6.6 megabyte card is the highest data capacity of any credit card format. This can store 4.2 megabytes of user data, allowing up to 2,000 pages of text information.

The medical information card can hold the following information.

a) 1,000 pages of text
b) 35 medical x-rays
c) 50 scanned documents
d) 10 high resolution photographs
e) 5 minutes of digital voice recording
f) 10 digital fingerprints
g) 2 hand geometry scans
h) 1 dynamic signature

All on one 6.6 megabyte card.

4. The plastic card has a number of problems, which we have outlined in previous books. **They can be lost, stolen, wiped, bent, carbon copies can be used illegally, or the plastic cards can be broken or duplicated**.

All this leads on in a natural progression to the final stage that has been outlined very clearly in the prophecies – dated 96 A.D.

5. Johannesburg, South Africa, 'Sunday Star', May 17th 1992 – Notice the front page article along with the illustration. "*Take*

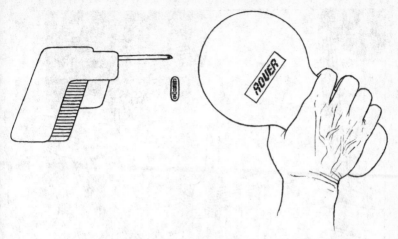

INJECTOR, SILICON IDENTIFICATION CHIP,
AND SCANNER FOR ANIMALS

*the advantage – **New concept implants chip in your body for
easy access to a world of benefits**.*"

We then turn the page in this same newspaper, one of the country's
most well-known, and read the following – "***Chips that get under
your skin***.

[1]***And he causes all..... to receive a mark on their right arm or
their foreheads***....

*In this modern day and age, the text (Revelation 13:16) has led cynical
observers to explore the reality of Orewellian total control*...." End quote.

Another heading on the same page reads "***Why carry cards when
an implant will do the trick***?"

As we go ahead and explain the inevitability of all this taking
place, some listeners or readers smugly comment "Oh, but that
article was written away back in 1992, probably by somebody
with a bent for science fiction."

Our next article is from Johannesburg "Sunday Star", 27th May
1995 – "*Your next computer may be your last.*

Scientists want to insert electronic chips in our heads *so we
can plug directly into the information super highway.*

*....The theoretical work on which "chip grafting" is based has been
carried out by a group led by G....g K....S, professor of electrical
engineering at Stanford University in California*...." End quote.

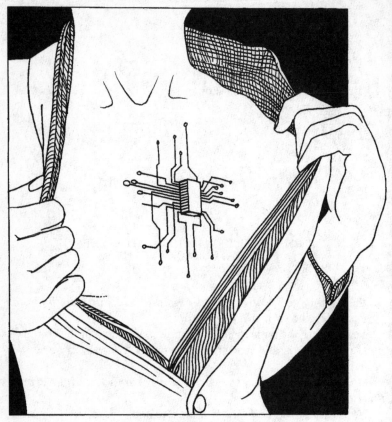

CHIPS BUILT INTO MAN'S CHEST

Excuse me for suggesting such a thing, but is there any possibility that the A.D. 96 prophecy is getting ready to happen fairly shortly? – possibly even before the year 2,000?

Why not chips for humans? They are using them already to identify animals.

[2]Perhaps I'm just being paranoid. However, the prophecies tell us that a great world leader will arise and will ultimately force the silicon chip on every individual to use for such normal tasks as buying and selling.

But wait – I've found another item of interest. Johannesburg 'Star', 31st May 1995 – "*Another silicon implant in mind*.

The human brain may be connected directly to computers....scientists will start to develop ways to link powerful silicon chips directly to the brain, possibly by growing nerve cells on the chip..." End quote.

Hey, Nostradamus missed out on this one.

The information to this point has been fairly mild. Let us proceed to deeper issues.

Footnotes

1   Revelation 13:16; The Holy Bible.

2   Revelation 13:16-18; The Holy Bible.

Recommended Reading

The Mark of the New World Order by Terry Cook; World Distribution Center, 1825 S. Franklin Rd, Indianapolis, IN 46239, U.S.A. Ph: (317) 359 1900 or 1-800-9-VIRTUE if living in the U.S.

Predictions

The world monetary system will be brought to a sudden halt – there will be no warning.

Sunday is a good day to make it happen, as the banks are shut.

Psychologists have been employed to advertise the "**smart cards**" showing only the benefits.

The silicon chip will be used in a test run on such 'at risk' groups as:

a) street kids

b) alzheimer's patients

c) prisoners

d) military forces

e) the general public

N.B. A DNA register will be linked to the chip for fool-proof surveillance and tracking.

CHAPTER TWENTY-FIVE

GLOBAL 2000 – WHAT FUN!

"Barbara and I will meet you at the Great Pyramid of Gizeh in the year 2000."

Ex-President of the U.S., George Bush, is obviously no stranger to the importance of the new millenium.

His links to **the Order** and **the Skull and Bones** secret society at Yale University, make him quite an influential figure as we approach this most important date.

New Zealand, the role model country for the New World Order, will be the first country of importance to usher in the 1.1.2000. Many hotels in this country are already pre-booked with masses of visitors planning to be "on the spot".

The next day, a lot of these visitors plan to fly east across the date-line to Western Samoa to celebrate the demise of 1999.

Many of the hotels in that country are also booked out.

Exciting isn't it?

But wait – don't become too excited until you read the next astounding piece of information.

CHAPTER TWENTY-SIX

GLOBAL CHAOS

Did he fall, or was he pushed?

The eternal question confronts us again.

The designers of the world's computers apparently did a very foolish thing. When designing these machines, they used a binary system for recording the date.

e.g.   1920 = 20
       1933 = 33
       1999 = 99

Unfortunately therefore, when the new millenium commences at one minute after midnight on the 1.1.2000, the binary date will then read 00. Horror of all horrors – does the computer mean 1900 or 2000? Confusion!

The 'Sunday Times' in England published a very detailed article which was picked up and recorded by the 'Australian' newspaper, (25 June 1996) regarding a British Telecom worker's shattering experience – "*Countdown to Armageddon.*

....returned to work from maternity leave...

When she was asked to assess how the millenium would affect her company's computers, it seemed just a job.

Ms ...... reached the startling conclusion that the millenium confronted her employer B.T. (British Telecom) with one of its biggest problems, a challenge of greater complexity than changing every telephone code in Britain.

The cost of solving it would be huge....

By coincidence, the computers at B.T. were already beginning to fail. When contracts running into 2000 were drawn up, the system seemed unable to cope....

The crisis does not just face B.T. It threatens almost every computer in the world.

....A United States' study suggests that preventing a global millenium meltdown may cost $400 billion....Many computers can tell the date only in terms of two digits.

But the year 2000 will be 00 and countless computers will remain stuck in the 20th century, thinking it is 1900 and act accordingly. Result: incalculable chaos.

...may be the biggest, most costly and absurd mistake in the history of the industrialised world.

...thousands of legal actions could be struck out... and a hundred years of interest could be added to credit card balances.

A computer scientist...who represented Britain on an international committee that standardised such programs said, "We did not really understand or anticipate that the programs people were using many years ago would still be in use now.

The consequence is that at midnight on December 31st 1999, many computers detecting the arrival of the year 00 will assume an error and shut down.

Others will carry on as if time has gone into reverse.

Experts speak of chaos enveloping New Zealand, where the millenium dawns first, then advancing like a wave across the world.

....45000 main-frame computers will crash, paralysing whole societies.

For instance, the Jeremiahs say everything from lifts to aircraft will cease to function because computers will tell them they have not been serviced for a hundred years. Children will receive pensions.

....In the United States, the Government has been warned that it faces a bill of $US20 billion to adapt its computers.

...The Internal Revenue envisages taking 300 man years to defeat the "new millenium bug". (Author's note - this is the only positive result we can report.)

....Personal computers that will not function properly after 2000 without modifications were widely sold until as recently as last year.

A consultant with IBM .... said that the company's p.c's had been "millenium-friendly" since 1995....

"The problem is too big for a miracle cure to be found in the next few years," the director of computers at one company said.

"Companies must not wait."

"If nobody does anything about this, then the economy as we know it will cease to function." End quote. (Emphasis added).

A computer expert has made the observation that if you are speaking on the phone as the year changes from 1999 to 2000, you could end up with a phone charge for 100 years.

Some computer buffs of course, may argue the point about this information, and say that the whole issue is based on media hype which produces paranoia.

Let us wait and see shall we?

To check your own computer, set the timing programme for 11:59 p.m. on 31st December and see what happens. If after a minute it reverts to 1980, you may require specialist assistance.

Prediction

This strange phenomena is certainly not an accident, but a carefully planned scenario.

Prior to the year 2000 the New World Order advocates will come up with an answer to the problem.

This is in keeping with the Hegelian Dialectic along which lines they operate.

a) Create the problem

b) Solve the problem to their advantage

The Media will be employed to bombard us with the seriousness of the problem. The suggestion will then be made that help is available. Simply transfer your information and data on to a government-backed "millenium-friendly" computer, and you can collect it back again at a later date when you are in a position to do so.

Personal privacy is to be a privilege of the past, and domination from the cradle to the grave is to be our inheritance from our benevolent new masters.

Don't give up however.

Help is on the way.

THE SECRET IRON MOUNTAIN MEETING

CHAPTER TWENTY-SEVEN

THE REPORT FROM
IRON MOUNTAIN

Over a period of 24 years, we have been putting all this information together. We have endured laughter, cynicism, mocking, and threats. At the same time, we have enjoyed sharing this larger picture with audiences world-wide, and as a result, seen the wonderment on our listeners' faces as doubt and scepticism turn to shock, serious consideration then belief.

One of New Zealand's ex-Prime Ministers was asked by a listener on a talk-back radio programme, his opinion of our information. His reply was, "Oh, that Barry Smith. He's just a prophet of doom!"

On the 24th February 1996, whilst lecturing in the Kalamunda Hills area of Perth, Western Australia, I was handed two videos which really put together into a neat package, what I have been pointing out for so many years.

Their titles: "Report From Iron Mountain"
                "America Under Siege"

Doubt No Longer

The needed proof is here. A brief precis of the information contained in these two tapes will suffice. You may then purchase the videos yourself and enlighten your friends, and if possible any government members and politicians you can reach.

Blueprint for Tyranny

a) During the year 1961, President Kennedy commissioned 15 experts to prepare this highly secret document. The plan continued on until the year 1966, as this panel of chosen experts put this diabolical document together.

President Johnson made it clear that this report must never be released to the public.

However, one of the men in the study group released it, and some large libraries have copies of it to this day.

The rogues who ordered this commission were then bound to deny its authenticity, yet, in the light of today's events, we know that it is **extremely accurate**.

"THE PLAN"

TOWARDS 2000

NATIONS HELD TOGETHER THROUGH COMMON PROBLEM.

WAR IS THE GLUE.

THE YEAR 2000

BEYOND 2000

NATIONS HELD TOGETHER THROUGH A FALSE, CONTRIVED PROBLEM.

THE ENVIRONMENTAL MOVEMENT IS THE GLUE.

If you have the facility to do so, check this out on the Internet, and notice the disclaimers. Note also, that it has been removed from the Net. "Why?" we ask. Has somebody received threats?

b) A number of background planners have an agenda. George Bush referred to these planners in his Gulf War speech. he used the phrase "a thousand points of light". There is **no morality**; there are **no ethics** in this plan. Humanity is looked upon as a herd of animals with no rights whatsoever. The report is clear – *"**Disregard all moral assumptions**."*

c) The Iron Mountain Committee were commissioned to solve *"**A problem facing the U.S. if War gave way to Peace by the year 2000**."*

 1) This peace would be under the full control of the United Nations.

 2) The U.S. would have to give up its Constitution along with its Civil Rights.

 3) The U.S. would then link up with the United Nations.

 4) A world government constitution would then be drafted. The report says *"**The age of nations must end.**

 ***The age of humanity must begin**."*

 5) A world police force will enforce peace.

It should be stated at this stage that over 1400 years ago, the ancient prophecies told us that a Luciferian, satanic, world leader would arise.

[1]*"And through his policy also he shall cause craft to prosper in his hand, and he shall magnify himself in his heart, **and by peace shall destroy many**. He shall also stand up against the Prince of princes, but he shall be broken without hand."*

Again, another prophecy from the year 96 A.D., (1900 years ago at the time this book went to print.)

[2]*"And it was given unto him to make war with the saints, and to overcome them, **and power was given him over all kindreds, tongues and nations**."*

Obviously a clear reference to a world dominating force such as the United Nations.

d) The Iron Mountain report reveals the true functions of war.

 1) War is the basic social system. The capacity to make war is the greatest social power it can exercise...It is a matter of life and death.

 2) War is the glue which holds a nation together.

3) War is a necessary economic waste, and works outside the normal supply and demand system. It creates an artificial demand.

4) It acts as a counterbalance to destroy and then rebuild. An excellent example was provided for us during our annual tour of Great Britain, April 1996.

London 'Times', 6th April 1996 – "*Clinton Approved Iran's Secret Arms Deals with Bosnia.*" The Los Angeles 'Times' initially reported the information. "*...The White House offered a curt statement last night which did little to refute the allegations...*" End quote.

'Sunday Telegraph', 7th April 1996 – "*President Clinton sailed into another political storm this weekend over claims that he gave his personal approval for Iran to supply arms to Bosnia in direct contradiction of United Nations' policy...*" End quote.

We then learned that Mr Ron Brown of the Clinton administration was on his way to Bosnia when his plane went down. Why was he travelling to that country?

To assess the costs and needs for rebuilding that country. Clear isn't it?

By the way, the plane had no black box flight recorder. Strange, don't you agree?

5) War spurs technological advances.

6) A nation has to have a common goal and a common identity.

7) It gives strength to its ability to deal with other nations. This is termed – foreign affairs.

8) War is the defining fact in foreign policy.

9) **The elimination of war brings us World Government** as a nation's authority rests in its war footing.

A Substitute For War

1) Something else needed to be phased in to control the people and bring stability to the system.

2) Until the new threat is fully set up, wars will continue otherwise the world's leaders lose power.

3) **The new problem** must be of **credible quality**.
   Key phrase
   Such a threat will have to be INVENTED!
   It has been invented. It is called **the environmental movement!**

4) Selectively produce pollution. Encourage governments to be slow on Pollution Control.

5) Ozone thinning, worse in winter would cause C.F.C.'s to be blamed. They would research a replacement for C.F.C.'s.
6) Earth's Resource Management will be made important.
7) All land should be taken over by Wilderness Groups.
8) Ultimately the land will be controlled by the World Environmental Bank.

United Nations' Charters, plus the signing over of "Wilderness areas" to "World Heritage" groups will see to this.

The prophecies given over 1400 years ago told us that this is exactly what this great world leader will do.

[3]*"...and he shall cause them to rule over many, and shall divide the land for gain."*

9) The Iron Mountain Agenda involves the nations **continually signing new treaties**, and forming International Agencies.

Agenda 21 is an 800 page Action Plan, which includes **controlling gases and endangered species**, along with **observing the impact economic development has on a nation's forests**.

This is of special interest to New Zealanders and citizens of Chile. Pinus Radiata grows more quickly in these two countries than anywhere else in the world.

Sickening isn't it?

So you thought there was a real environmental problem did you?

Iron Mountain makes it absolutely clear that we were correct in our previous books when we spoke of these **scams**. (See Final Notice, page 91 onwards.)

The Global Warming Scam

During the months of June and July 1996, the citizens of New Zealand and South Africa, went through some of the coldest weather that these two countries had ever experienced. (**Please don't bring your global warming message to either of these two countries or you take the risk of being laughed off the platform**.)

We observed a so-called scientist, who had recently attended a large global warming conference, being asked how he explained this phenomena.

He smiled in a knowing, patronising, manner (as teachers sometimes do when explaining simple problems to their pupils).

"So much greenhouse gas in the atmosphere has upset the world weather patterns." He then went on to explain that a "carbon tax" was part of the answer.

We are not surprised as they need to finance their global warming conferences, discussing problems that do not exist.

Please note – Carbon dioxide (CO2) is not a pollutant. It is this gas which keeps the earth's plant life alive. When there is a lot of it, plants grow faster and really take off. We in turn benefit from the additional oxygen made by the plants.

Some years ago, a "global warming _expert_" was asked on a B.B.C. programme, "If all the carbon fell out of the atmosphere like black snow, how deep would it be?

His answer was "Tens of metres."

The correct answer should have been 1-2 millimetres. As a writer to the editor of the Weekend Australian newspaper points out, "_CO2 is not building up like a lake, it is flowing like a river._"

How is this for a piece of mis-information?

'Weekend Australian', 8/9 June 1996 – "_Island Evacuation, a greenhouse solution...._

An evacuation by small island nations threatened by rising sea levels, might be more efficient than forcing industrialised countries to cut greenhouse emissions...." End quote.

'Sunday Times', U.K., 11 September 1994 – "_Met Office says global warming is just a myth._

A unique study by British scientists has cast doubt over the severity of global warming, a phenomenon seen by many environmentalists as the greatest threat to both human and natural worlds.

_Experts at the Meteorological Office in Bracknell, Berkshire, revealed last week that the rate of warming could be as slow as 0.15c per decade – half the best estimate endorsed by 400 scientists in a 1990 United Nation's report that prompted research costing billions of pounds, a climate treaty signed by World leaders at the Earth Summit in Rio and Brussel's demands for _energy taxes_ to curb pollution._

...At the Met. Office, a three month simulation of climatic change by one of the world's most powerful computers found that **sulphate aerosols offset the impact of a buildup in greenhouse gases, such as carbon dioxide.**

**In effect, one form of pollution largely cancels out the other.**

...regions in which sulphur pollution was increasing could actually cool.

...Such statements contradict repeated claims by environmental groups and eminent scientists that the earth is heading for disaster, with low-lying cities flooded by an expanding sea and millions of environmental refugees." End quote. (Emphasis added).

Again – 'Daily Telegraph', Great Britain, 10 March 1990 – "*No signs of a warmer globe after 10 year space study.*
A 10 year satellite study of world temperatures has found **no evidence of global warming** *predicted by many scientists...*" End quote. (Emphasis added).

'Dominion', 1 December 1992 – "*Holes poked in the ozone scare.
...all this doomsday stuff about the ozone layer, the panic over skin cancers, cataracts and break-down of the immune system...Is it true? Or is it all a tall tale? Peter Toynbee, a retired Wellington scientist says "That's exactly what it is."*

For years he has insisted that the ozone hole over Antarctica is not caused by man-made chemicals but is a **natural and short-lived annual phenomenon supported by scientific evidence ignored by an environmentalist "industry" bankrolled by an international chemicals cartel**.*" End quote.

'Sunday Times', 13th November 1994 – "*Don't throw away your fridge:* **the hole in the southern sky is caused by nature**.

"The Great Ozone Hoax"...

The Greens need environmental scares as much as arms manufacturers need wars..." End quote.

One man who has studied this subject is a Mr Harry Alcock, from Hamilton, New Zealand.

His views, although different to the established meteorological theories, are well worth investigation.

In an article published in 'This Week', 25th July 1996, he says that "*government moves to introduce a carbon tax on industrialists that 'pollute' the air with carbon gases beyond a set amount, is little more than a 'scam'...*

He describes the government advisers' so called experts who know 'little or nothing of the real causes of climatic change."

Harry says the only rise in CO2 levels in the last hundred years has been a "virtually insignificant .01%.....

"The truth is that **the earth was set up as a self-regulating system that absorbs all sorts of changes**, *including fluctuating C02 levels. After all, trees live on carbon dioxide, turning it into more oxygen. So the more C02 there is, the more trees grow," he says.*

Harry maintains arguers for global warming and the greenhouse effect forget how moon and earth orbits determine global temperatures.

"Far from global warming, we are in fact headed for colder

weather as the moon's orbit shifts further away from the equator towards the poles. That is why right now there is more snow in the South Island, and in the U.K. and in the U.S. in fact we are in a repeat ice age like the one scientists talked about in the 1970's...."

"It is accepted scientific fact that the moon not only causes the seas to ebb and flow, but also creates 'atmospheric tides', spilling huge quantities of warm air from the tropics into colder regions...", he says.

When some global warming does occur in the moon's next beneficial phase, Pacific Islanders need not fear rising sea levels will swamp their atoll homes, Harry says, "despite warmer temperatures, the poles will stay frozen."

And even if more ice did melt it would not mean rising seas flooding low lying Pacific atolls. ***Those who suggest that should know better. Ice occupies a much greater volume than water. So if it melts, it will take up less volume, not more...***

He dubs it "absurd" to blame refrigerant and aerosol gases for ozone layer depletion. Freon, for example, is an inert gas. it doesn't act upon anything, so how could it destroy ozone he asks.

A study of almanacs lead to his conclusion that these and virtually all major weather changes were caused by the moon....

Ruapehu's recent eruption began as it did last year on the New Moon, Harry points out...

"I was totally rubbished when I began putting out forecasts twelve months in advance. ***Yet today my book 'The Lunar Effect' is required reading for all budding meteorologists", he says.*** End quote. (Emphasis added.)

All this global warming and ozone depletion is a serious deception and fortunately, you are now aware of it.

Unfortunately however, this is not all.

2nd Scam – U.F.O. Phenomenon

Please refrain from laughter at this point.

These Iron Mountain people were deadly serious when they chose this subject as Scam no.2.

There are far more people than you possibly realise who are concerned to know the truth about these things and yet are nervous about bringing the subject up for fear of ridicule.

Sometime ago, the Australian Broadcasting Corporation sent a full television crew across to New Zealand to video these UFO's flying up the Kaikoura Coast.

London 'Times', 2nd February 1996 – "*UFO "Buzzed" Airliner at Manchester Airport.*

A British Airways passenger jet had a close encounter with an unidentified flying object, while landing at Manchester airport, an official report disclosed last night.

The Boeing 737 with 60 people on board was over-taken at high speed by a wedge-shaped craft as the plane descended through 4,000 ft on the final stages of a journey from Milan...the U.F.O. which was emblazoned with small white lights and possibly a black stripe down its side, flashed silently down the side of the jet, so close that his co-pilot....involuntarily ducked as it went by..." End quote.

Crop Circles

These are 'cropping' up in various places in the south of England. The British media recently reported the following:

"*Farmer Phillip Sandell is cashing in on one of the most elaborate crop circle patterns ever seen in Britain.*

He is charging visitors from around the world 2 pounds a head to go into his wheat field on Salisbury Plain and marvel at the 900ft by 500ft formation containing 151 different circles.

Now researchers at Yale University are set to probe deeper into the baffling phenomenon.

The amazingly sophisticated arrangement appeared in broad daylight about 300 yards from Stonehenge within a quarter of an hour, Phillip, aged 25, said yesterday.

"There was nothing there when a pilot flying from Exeter to Thruxton flew over the site and looked down on the field," he said. "But on the return journey 15 minutes later he spotted it."...

"We've got our own web site on the Internet and I'm told three groups of Americans are flying in next week specially to see it."...

Colin Andrews, who claims to be the world's only full-time crop circle investigator, said the pattern was the most startling he had ever seen in 13 years of investigation.

"We're looking at 150 circles neatly and accurately positioned in a way that could fit a mathematical model."

"And all this in a place that never stops pumping traffic day and night.

I've checked with the security guards who are at Stonehenge 24 hours a day and not one of them saw anything." End quote.

To any sceptic who is interested in debating the question, we would

simply ask "Who was responsible for these strange markings and how come they were done in such a short time in broad daylight?"

The information we have to hand is that there are definitely Unidentified Flying Objects. However, we do not subscribe to the theory of little green men flying around the Universe with the intention of conquering other galaxies....

I believe that the UFO's of today are from two sources –
1. Man-made
2. Demonic

At this present time, the public are being sporadically bombarded with movies, radio, television, and advertising, depicting both good and bad aspects of the alien presence. All this is to prepare the people of the world for an apparent meeting with these 'beings' and to use it as a plausible excuse for when a great number of people disappear i.e. **the return of our Lord Jesus Christ**.

You do realise that He is returning shortly don't you? Millions will suddenly go missing. The New World Order guys desperately need an answer.

"For the Lord Himself shall descend from Heaven with a shout, with the voice of the archangel, and the trump of God: and the dead in Christ shall rise first:

Then we which are alive and remain shall be caught up together with them in the clouds, to meet the Lord in the air: and so shall we ever be with the Lord.

Wherefore comfort one another with these words."

1 Thessalonians 4:16-18.

We have information that tells us that the man-made UFOs have actually been created by the U.S. government using anti-gravity technology.

For those readers who are sceptical of demonic activity, please book yourself a flight to Haiti and interview Haitians who have been released from voodoo and the occult. This deliverance can only take place through the power of the Lord Jesus Christ. If you know any other way, please let me know. (You will need to find released Haitians because none of the bound ones will talk to you about it.)

It was the Lord Jesus Christ Himself who gave us fair warning nearly 2000 years ago.

"And as it was in the days of Noe, so shall it also be in the days of the Son of man."

195

Now what was it like in the days of Noah? What evil was it that brought on the flood?

[5]"And it came to pass, when men began to multiply on the face of the earth, and daughters were born unto them,

That the sons of God saw the daughters of men, that they were fair and they took them wives of all which they chose.

And the Lord said, My Spirit shall not always strive with man, for that he also is flesh, yet his days shall be an hundred and twenty years.

There were giants in the earth in those days, and also after that, when the sons of God came in unto the daughters of men and they bare children to them, the same became mighty men which were of old, men of renown.

And God saw the wickedness of man was great in the earth, and that every imagination of the thoughts of his heart was evil continually.

And it repented the Lord that he had made man on the earth, and it grieved Him at His heart.

And the Lord said, I will destroy man whom I have created from the face of the earth...."

The majority of occult books that speak of the future New Age of peace, speak of **the return of the Son's of God**, not realising who these creatures really are.

Let us now go through this passage carefully and clearly link it with the days in which we live.

Facts

The oldest man who ever lived was Methuselah. His name had a meaning – **"When he dies, it will come."** ("It" was referring to the flood which subsequently destroyed everything in the world except for Noah and his family.)

This old man lived to the age of 969 years, almost 1,000 years old.

Whilst living he could have said to his wife – "Honey, do you remember that birthday party we went to 700 years ago?"

Methuselah had a son called Lamech, who is turn had a son called Noah.

The reason Methuselah lived so long was to show the world how much God loves people and to give them as much opportunity as possible to be saved.

⁶It is written *"**The Lord is not slack** concerning His promises but is longsuffering to usward, not willing that any should perish, but that all should come to repentance."*

Recap

When Lucifer, who is now called Satan, was tossed out of heaven, the rebels who chose to stay with their master were also thrown out.

⁷*"And the angels which kept not their first estate, but left their own habitation, he hath reserved in everlasting chains under darkness unto the judgement of the great day."*

It is clear that although these angels were thrown out of heaven, **for a brief period of time, these so-called sons of God** will be allowed to return and as they did before the flood, even in our lifetime, have sexual relations with earth women, and bear children who appear to be human, yet have demonic natures and personalities.

Thus, as it was in the days of Noah, Jesus was correct once again, the world is completely out of control.

God's Word, the Bible, is scorned by the majority. It is under attack continuously by liberal theologians who only have themselves to blame as they choose the lake of fire as their future home.

Therefore, using the Jewish term, **Midrash**, we clearly see a repeat performance in this our day, of the scenes before the flood.

The demons will return, posing as space travellers.

A belief in evolution is essential when dealing with this subject i.e. we will be told that both space travellers and human beings are evolving at a different rate, yet we must unite to save both our civilisations.

From the moment of birth, it is obvious that a human being must have all organs in place i.e. can the reader visualise a person with no kidneys and no liver eating a meal at McDonalds whilst awaiting the arrival of these organs through the evolutionary process?

Can we not hear him cry out in anguish, "My word, I feel a bilious attack coming on".

Therefore, it is clear that a human being once born, would of necessity, have to come into existence completely formed.

Evolution, by the way, is the ultimate insult to the Creator God. He had all eternity to plan and design His creation down to the tiniest detail. He then spoke all things into existence.

Then, some upstart, who lives maybe 60-80 years on this earth, has the audacity to challenge God's role of designer and Creator.

198

Although this is an incredible scenario, it is no more incredible than the sad fact that the demons, Antichrist, World Government advocates, Lucifer, and all who ignore God and His beautiful plan of salvation, will all end up in the place that God calls Hell -originally designed only for the devil and his angels (demons).

[8]*"For if God spared not the angels that sinned, but cast them down to hell, and delivered them into chains of darkness to be reserved unto judgement,*

*And spared not the old world **but saved Noah**, the eighth person, a preacher of righteousness, **bringing in the flood upon the world of the ungodly**..."*

How long did Noah preach and warn the people?

120 years.

How many converts did he get?

7 + himself.

Where was the place of safety?

In the ark.

When the full number of people and animals were inside, who shut the door?

God did!

Why?

Noah may have weakened and let some of his ungodly neighbours in.

Did the people laugh at Noah?

Yes.

Why?

It had never rained before up to that point. A daily mist watered the earth.

Midrash

This means, it happened once, it will happen again.

God is so honourable, He never acts without an initial fair warning. Hence the title of one of our books – not 'Discussion' but 'Warning'.

Do the same circumstances apply today as in the days of Noah?

Yes, they do.

Was Jesus therefore correct in His predictions?

Yes, He was.

Are these devilish angels co-habiting with some of earth's women?

Yes. Just ask any witch who is willing to tell the truth for a change.

Two words for you to investigate are '**incubus**' and '**succubus**'.

Incubus – a demon in male form who visits women in the night.

Succubus – a demon in female form who visits men in the night.

Are there many genuine preachers of righteousness today who are out and about preaching as modern day Noahs?

A few, but not many. The old time preachers taught us from the Scriptures to confess our sins. Sadly, many modern preachers call upon us to confess our rights.

Are the majority of people on earth glad to receive their warnings?

No, only a few.

How many did Jesus say would be saved as they trod the narrow road?

A few.

How many did Jesus say would be lost in hell, as they trod the broad road?

Many.

When you preach your message in the western world, what do the majority do?

Stay at home feeding on a diet of television, and laughing at those who attend our conventions.

What do the minority do?

Repent, and turn towards Almighty God, through faith in His Son, the Lord Jesus Christ.

Believe me, the demonic, so-called, sons of God are returning as you will shortly find out.

A word of wisdom.

Get on board the ark.

Who is the ark today?

Where is a place of safety?

The Lord Jesus Christ.

Go immediately to the back of this book and pray the sinner's prayer.

A final question to all mockers, borrowed from Noah, the preacher of righteousness.

How long can you tread water? (see picture on p 194.)

Footnotes

1   Daniel 8:25; The Holy Bible

2   Revelation 13:7; The Holy Bible

3   Daniel 11:39; The Holy Bible

4   Luke 17:26; The Holy Bible
5   Genesis 6:1-7a; The Holy Bible
6   II Peter 3:9; The Holy Bible
7   Jude 1:6; The Holy Bible

Videos available from these addresses:

"*The Report from Iron Mountain*" and "*America Under Siege*".
*Best Video Productions, P.O. Box 69, Wheeler, Wi 54772, U.S.A.
*Countdown Videos, P.O. Box 125, Landsborough 4550, Qld, Australia. Ph: 074 941 596.

Recommended Reading

The Lunar Effect by Harry Alcock; 1 Amanda Avenue, Hamilton, NEW ZEALAND.
The Holy Bible.

Check the Internet for: **The Report from Iron Mountain.**

If it is a spoof as some on the Internet claim, we wish to ask the following questions:

1. Why is the information in line with events which are taking place in the world today.

2. Who was threatened to such a degree that the information had to be removed from the Net? Why was this necessary as the Internet is packed with both real and false information side by side? – Could somebody have been worried?

3. Net subscribers will help any interested parties to obtain a copy of this report as it is now available in book form.

CHAPTER TWENTY-EIGHT

HI MOTHER EARTH

Definition of an ecologist – "A voice crying over the wilderness."

In the light of the preceding chapter on the Report from Iron Mountain, this chapter will now make much more sense.

Near the end of 1995, we concluded our annual Great Britain lecture tour. Our luggage weight limit was well over, and therefore, when a friend brought me a large heavy book as a gift, I wondered whether it was worthwhile taking it home, all the way back to New Zealand.

The title of the book was "**The Gaia Peace Atlas – Survival into the Third Millennium**". Foreword by Javier Perez de Cuellar, Secretary General to the United Nations. (Published by Pan Books Ltd, Cavaye Place, London SW109PG, ISBN 0-330-30151-9).

I'm so glad that I did decide to bring it home and the reason is that almost everything you have read in this book can now be established as fact.

Have you noticed how all the environmental groups have suddenly become so prominent? They are called 'Greenies'.

If you are a politician and you **wish to gain votes**, what do you do?

Become an instant greeny!

Q. Why are so many embracing the environmental movement?

A. **Without a personal relationship with God, they have no future**.
All they have is a past and a present. No wonder the masses spend time reminiscing about the old days – looking up photo albums, talking continuously about how life was years ago and joining clubs and Lodges of like-minded persons.

Has it ever occurred to you that the greeny movement of the world today, sometimes labelled the '**environmental movement**', has become so strong that many politicians are riding on the bandwagon in hopes of gaining further votes in their favour.

In the year 1987 in Colorado, a massive convention was held by powerful men of our generation such as Edmund Rothschild, David Rockefeller, Michael Sweatman, Maurice Strong and others. (Many who attended this conference can be linked to the vast number of Illuminati conspiratorial groups.)

A friend of this writer was in attendance at this convention as a worker and not a participant. Mr G....e H..t, a very courageous man subsequently exposed the activities of this convention and has much proof to substantiate the true nature of what went on there.

The name of the convention held in 1987 was the Fourth World Wilderness Convention. **The word 'wilderness' in the title is in reference to the mother earth concept of the occult**.

What started in Colorado, the holy land of the **Gaia Movement**, now continues on very quickly. Some time ago, even the Pope visited that so-called sacred land of Colorado.

During a recent visit to Australia, I learned that a childrens' programme called "Captain Planet" is being shown there on t.v. and upon our return to New Zealand, discovered that the same programme is also being aired here. The female heroine is called....**Gaia**.

[1]We read in the ancient prophecies – "*He carried me away in the Spirit **into the wilderness** and I saw a woman sit upon a scarlet coloured beast full of the names of blasphemy having seven heads and ten horns*."

From the above information, we can see that the spiritual habitat of the end time world may be referred to as a 'wilderness'. **Strangely enough, the hierarchy of the Illuminati and all of their subordinate witches and occultists also refer to their new age of Aquarius as a wilderness**. This is a spiritual place within the embrace of Mother Earth where all people can be absorbed in collective thought and blend as one people without individuality in a blissful state of the lostness of the mind.

These people are not to be immediately classed as intellectually challenged (or nutters), but many of them are apparently intelligent yet completely deceived. Mind you, if you miss out on a personal relationship with Almighty God, through the Lord Jesus Christ, of course you are open to deception. If we miss the Truth (Jesus), all that remains is lies (the devil).

This Convention, held in September 1995, had as one of its objectives to make nature worship a state religion. **These ideas were only points for informal discussion at this stage**, but once they are ratified by the government of the day they could become treaties carrying the full force of the law.

There are 9 proposed objectives:

1. *To make nature the central organising principal and develop a policy that accounts for ecological values equally with economic values.*

2. *To establish a legal regime that will utilise international treaties to control all policies. The New World Order must unite us all in global partnership which recognises the transcending sovereignty of nature of our only one earth.*
3. *To make the use of natural resources a cost.*
4. *To promote the precautionary principle that scientific evidence is not necessary to implement radical environmental policies.*
5. *To inventory natural and human resources.*
6. *To make man equal to all other species.*
7. *To classify people as the enemy.*
8. *To create areas devoid of human presence.*
9. *To make nature worship a state religion.*

(Number six has begun already. The 'Australian' newspaper, 3rd May 1996: "*Now,* **It's Homo Gorillas**.
A team of Australian and New Zealand scientists has proposed that gorillas and chimpanzees be taken into the human family and reclassified as genus homo...." End quote.)

What type of people could consider putting forward such weird proposals? Oh well – it's a weird old world isn't it?

These nine objectives speak for themselves. Dr Adam Weishaupt's original Illuminati blueprint was based on the word Illuminati because, he said, it is derived from the word Lucifer which means bearer of the light.

All people are to be inventoried like livestock. Objective number 6 makes lots of people angry, including this author, for it grants to both animals and humans the same status.

Objective number 8 would force some people from their homes when, at the discretion of the United Nations, certain areas will be declared 'void of human presence'.

Objective number 9 is the most shocking of all however, for it makes the worship of nature a state religion because witchcraft is nature worship.

A sad critique of the environmental movement is that these dear people go to great lengths to protect the environment around them and then go out of their way to ignore the marvellous designer and Creator of all things they endeavour to protect! That designer's Name? **Almighty God!**

It is fascinating to notice uninformed people getting involved in this movement where they worship the creation rather than the Creator. A facetious sign on the back of a truck that we saw in Sydney revealed one person's opinion: "**The only true wilderness is the space between a Greenie's ears!**"

However, I must confess that I'm excited at the thought of collecting family support for 2 cows and a cat.

An article from the 'Edmonton Journal', 20th May 1994, should prove to be of interest.

"*Maurice Strong, who's encountered many hazards as chairman of Ontario Hydro, wasn't about to let a Costa Rican jungle throw him.*

The millionaire jet setter didn't budge this week when critics used words like 'crazy' and 'astounding' to describe his proposal to buy part of a Central American rain forest to offset air pollution.

....sources indicate Strong's jungle fever likely won't get past the proposal stage...

Strong was courted by an old family friend.....for the top job at Ontario Hydro.

It was considered a coup that Strong accepted after heading the 1992 United Nations Earth Summit in Brazil.

*...Strong enjoys easy access to powerful and influential people. He counts U.S. vice president, **Al Gore**, and actress, Shirley McLaine, among his friends.*" End quote. (Emphasis added.)

NOW A QUOTE FROM THE PEACE ATLAS

Under the heading "*The meaning of Gaia*", we read in part:

The scientist James Lovelock, believing that life on other planets could be detected by its impact on atmospheric chemistry, turned his attention to Earth and found its atmosphere so "improbable" in geochemical terms that only some regulatory process could explain it.

*The "**regulator**" he proposed was life as a whole self-regulating organism. **He named this entity Gaia after the ancient Greek goddess of the earth**.*" End quote. (Emphasis added.)

Evolution

It has now become obvious to all thinking people that the theory of evolution has run its course.

Not only does it fly in the face of the "**second law of thermodynamics**" that "**things always deteriorate and nothing ever improves of itself**", but it made its author, Charles Darwin, a very sick man.

The 'Australian' newspaper on the 18th March 1992, printed a very interesting article entitled "*Revealing the Enigma of Darwin, a Man Sickened by His Vision.*"

We quote herewith in part – "*For Dr Moore, the most illuminating discovery he made during his research was the extent to which Darwin suffered illness, most of his life, a fact not realised by even the best informed scholars.*

"*He was continually sick, and in a constant state of anxiety throughout most of his career," Dr Moore said.*

Anxiety would erupt at any moment. He would vomit, tremble uncontrollably, break out with eczema, or cry hysterically, that is, until he stopped his heavy theorising about evolution.

He literally made himself sick agonising over his theory....

His refusal to publish quickly, together with his perpetual state of anxiety are understandable when it is recalled that he was accused of trying to dethrone God at a time when people believed every word of the Bible..." End quote. (Emphasis added).

Comment – what a sad article.

These dear, deluded folk are so determined not to say the dreaded three letter word G-O-D, that they pretend to be satisfied with a very unscientific approach which suggests that life appeared from nowhere, picked itself up by the bootstraps, and then became the great self-regulator named Gaia or Mother Earth. Three words seem to sum this type of thinking up – "Gobble de Gook".

Oh, how we 'normal' people appreciate the Word of God, the Bible, and its simple definite, and authoritative statements.

Take for example Genesis 1:1 – in the original 7 Hebrew words, we receive our translation in English thus – "***In the beginning God created the heaven and the earth.***"

[2]Then again, "***All things were made by Him, and without Him, was not anything made that was made.***"

Choice – we now have to choose.

a) **The great eternal God who lives in the eternal present, tells us that He created everything in this beautiful world of design**.

b) **Life itself, obviously a mindless system described as a self-regulatory organism designed everything**, including the fantastic design found on birds' wings and hairs on animals' bodies.

In other words, the godless education curriculum is now so warped that they have the audacity to teach intelligent children that "Nothing created nothing."

If nothing creates nothing, we can wisely presume that nothing was created.

I guess if you wish to exclude any thoughts of God from your life, you will tend to scratch around in the mud looking for an alternative explanation.

There is no call for any emotional outbursts at this time, however, the repercussions of these choices last forever and ever.

Choice a – folk have nothing to lose either way.

Choice b – folk miss out here and throughout all eternity.

We live in a very beautiful New Zealand valley in the Pelorus area. When we need to exercise, it is our custom to climb a nearby hill and triumphantly shout some Scriptures out over the valley.

[3]*"In the beginning was the Word, and the Word was with God, and the Word was God.*

The same was in the beginning with God.

All things were made by Him, and without Him was not any thing made that was made.

In Him was life; and the life was the light of men."

What a feeling of joy and fulfilment. This explanation does great spiritual good to a person who acknowledges God as all in all.

Choice b – folk do incalculable **harm** to their own **intelligence**.

Choice b – folk do incalculable **harm** to their **consciences**.

Choice b – folk do incalculable **harm** to **their listeners** also who struggle not to laugh out loud at their obviously inadequate explanations.

Come on. Be daring. Call Him God. Forget evolution and nature, and even the "**regulatory organism**".

6. You are too intelligent for this type of thinking.

Some years ago, we had a visitor walk around the side of our house. We watched him through the front window and to my surprise, we saw him hugging a giant tree. Now, don't get me wrong. I love trees too, but I certainly don't hug them.

This dear man had been reading my books and came over for further explanation. I told him clearly how to find **peace with God, through a born again relationship**.

Sadly, he decided against this, and ultimately the environment's destruction so upset him that he took his own life.

Bad News

To all readers, both greenies and non-greenies, the prophecies tell us that in the end **the saving of this environment will prove to be an utter waste of time**, as it is all to be burned up with fire which looks suspiciously like a nuclear blast.

[4]"*But the day of the Lord will come as a thief in the night, in which the heavens will pass away with a great noise, and the elements will melt with fervent heat; **both the earth and the works that are in it will be burned up**.*

Therefore, since all these things will be dissolved, what manner of persons ought you to be in holy conduct and godliness.

Looking for and hastening the coming of the day of God, because of which the heavens will be dissolved, being on fire, and the elements will melt with fervent heat?"

7. The 'Save the Whales' folk, 'Save the Krill' folk, 'Save the Spotted Owl' folk, 'Save the Texas Butterfly' folk, etc, etc, I'm sorry, but they are all going to be burnt.

Don't be dismayed however.

Good News

The Lord is going to recreate everything.

[5]"*Looking for and hasting unto the coming of the day of God, wherein the heavens being on fire shall be dissolved, and the elements shall melt with fervent heat?*

Nevertheless, we according to his promise, look for new heavens and a new earth, wherein dwelleth righteousness.

Wherefore, beloved, seeing that ye look for such things, be diligent that ye may be found of him in peace, without spot, and blameless."

Our task then is to walk in peace and harmony with Him, and later to enjoy this glorious new creation.

Exciting information you will agree.

Goodbye Gaia. Design and build for yourself an asbestos suit. You'll be needing it!

Footnotes

1 Revelation 17:3; The Holy Bible
2 John 1:3; The Holy Bible
3 John 1:1-4; The Holy Bible
4 II Peter 3:10-12; The Holy Bible
5 II Peter 3:12-14; The Holy Bible

208

CHAPTER TWENTY-NINE

ISRAEL – THE GEOGRAPHICAL CENTRE

News Flash – "*Prime Minister Yitshak Rabin has been shot*".

We were there in Jerusalem, on our 1995 tour of the Holy Land. And then, the terrible shock. It was 11:15 p.m. when the announcer on the CNN news channel stated "**Prime Minister, Yikshak Rabin is dead!**"

The spirit of death swept the land like an invisible phantom, the news causing deep sobs from formerly apparently unconcerned citizens.

We were stunned. To read it in the paper was amazing, but for us to join the tens of thousands the next day as we crept along towards the Knesset (Israeli Parliament) where his coffin lay in state, draped with the blue and white Israeli flag was a never to be forgotten experience.

Candles in little tin cans littered the footpaths in all directions. I made the remark later that these people were well-named "the **Children of Israel**". Like a giant family in times of 'crisis', there was something there in that land that drew them together. The former political bickering was now subdued to a minimum. I thought of my country, over 10,000 miles away and wondered what the reaction would have been there had a similar tragedy occurred. Nothing like this, believe me!

Just the year before in October 1994, we marched though Jerusalem with born again believers from all over the world.

This was to show our solidarity and respect for this very important land.

A Jewish woman rushed up to us and handed us a flyer written in Hebrew and also in English.

I have it on the desk before me as I write.

"***JERUSALEM IS IN DANGER!***

Rabin signed an agreement with the mass-murderer, Arafat.
The Oslo Accords bring us back to the pre-1967 borders.
In 1967 and 1973, thousands of our beloved sons died and thousands were wounded regaining and defending our historic land, the Golan, Judea and Samaria and Jerusalem.
Now Rabin is giving our land away to our arch enemies.

WAS OUR SACRIFICE IN VAIN?

P.O.B. 7352 Jerusalem.
Tel. 02 249 887
Fax. 02 245 380
Registration no. 58 023120-7"

The look of anguish on the lady's face was something to behold. As one Jew once said to me **"You folk come from all over the world, explain prophecy and then return home. In our case, it is different. We have to live here."**

I heard very clearly what this man was saying.

Already Israel has signed peace with Egypt, with the PLO and with Jordan. The city of Jerusalem is indeed being surrounded.

Zechariah the prophet tells us that the final battles will be fought over the city of Jerusalem.

[1]*"And in that day will I make Jerusalem a burdensome stone for all people: all that burden themselves with it shall be cut in pieces, though all the people of the earth be gathered together against it."*

a) The Israelis want it
b) The Palestinians want it
c) The Orthodox Church wants it
d) The Vatican wants it

The PLO – Palestine Liberation Organisation made their aims very clear.

It is a strange feeling nowadays to leave Jerusalem, go down the hill to Jericho and move into PLO territory.

The colours of the army uniforms, flags etc, change at the border. It gives you an uneasy feeling that all is not as it should be.

'Press', 5th December 1994 – *"Palestinian Police begin Bethlehem changeover.*

Jubilant Arabs chanted "We don't want to see the Zionists any more", as they welcomed a first unit of Palestinian police to the Bethlehem area yesterday in advance of an Israeli pullout this month.

....Bethlehem, the traditional birthplace of Jesus Christ, was captured along with the rest of the West Bank by Israel in the 1967 Middle East war.

Israeli soldiers are due to quit the city on December 18th...

...Israel agreed under a West Bank self-rule deal signed in September with the Palestinian Liberation Organisation to pull its

troops out of six Palestinian towns and dozens of villages by the end of the year...." End quote.

'Press', 26th December 1995 – "*Freedom marks Bethlehem Christmas.*

Palestinian Liberation Organisation chairman, Yasser Arafat, sat in the front row of the Church of the Nativity with his wife, Sula, and several members of his self-rule Palestinian Authority in places occupied in previous years by Israeli officials. A tourism official in Bethlehem said Mr Arafat, a Muslim, was the first Arab leader to attend a Christmas midnight Mass at the church..." End quote.

Actually, Yasser got a little bit carried away at this stage, and it was reported world-wide that **he stated that "Jesus was a Palestinian**." This would be similar to making the statement many years ago that King David was a Philistine. The remark did not go down well at all as you can imagine. **We can only hope that his young wife told him off when they arrived home**.

THE MESSIAH IS COMING

During the early 1990's, a group of orthodox Jews in New York, claimed that they had found their Messiah in an old man called Rabbi Schneerson. Unfortunately, the old man passed away before the decade finished, thus dashing the believers' hopes.

Many Christians also believe that the Messiah is coming back, and one enthusiastic American author wrote a book entitled "88 Reasons Why Christ Must Return in 1988". **This book is not selling very well at present**.

P.M. Netanyahu

Where does the new Prime Minister of Israel fit into all this?

When Benjamin Netanyahu was elected by a thin majority in the 1996 election, many Jews living in occupied areas rejoiced as they hopefully thought that the 'land for peace' deals were going to stop.

I regret to announce that, like politicians world-wide, their power has been stripped from them, and they must do what they are told.

Netanyahu can keep up the charade of supposed power for only a season, and then the U.S. State Department will step in.

The Arabs, in the meantime, were dismayed at this man being chosen, as they felt Peres was on their side, and Netanyahu was not.

The whole political situation world-wide is now a giant puppet show with the 'goodies' and the 'baddies' in apparent conflict (i.e.

the German philosopher **Hegel's dialectic** – thesis versus antithesis) and then at the correct time in history, the negotiators with the real power step in and resolve the apparent conflict (i.e. This was called by Hegel – synthesis).

The one who must step in, is waiting in the wings even as you read.

The ancient prophets call him – Antichrist.

Meanwhile, as the game continues on, we are allowed to chuckle a little at the Arabic mastery of words, as Mr Netanyahu visited Egypt on a goodwill mission, soon after the election.

The editor of the anti-Zionist daily "Al Ahrar" wrote – "O you rotten one, you are soiling our land. You are a hated and abominable guest, and people curse you in the street. Our pure earth is nauseated by your polluted footsteps. The trees sway in anger, and the birds fly away to avoid smelling your hated fragrance!" Christchurch 'Press', 19 July 1996.

Who needs enemies with friends like these?

The information you are now about to read is vital to an understanding of the times in which we live.

A Foundation Statement

[2]*"Verily I say unto you, This generation shall not pass, till all these things be fulfilled."* (The Lord Jesus Christ said this.)

In simple English, it reads like this.

"If you see the beginning of the generation it is highly likely you will see the end."

Many Christian believers, along with many Jewish rabbis, agree that the beginning of this generation was 1948 when Israel became a nation on May 14th. Many also believe that the length of the generation is the length of a Jewish period called a Jubilee, or 50 years.

$$\begin{array}{r} 1948 \\ + 50 \\ \hline 1998 \end{array}$$

Another school of thought is that the generation commenced in 1967 during the 6 day war, during which time the whole city of Jerusalem passed back into Israeli hands for the first time in 2500 years. The general belief here is that the length of a generation is 40 years.

$$1967$$
$$+\ 40$$
$$2007$$

Jesus' words in Luke 21:24b is an important Scripture in this case. *"...and Jerusalem shall be trodden down of the Gentiles, until the times of the Gentiles be fulfilled."*

Whether it is 1998, 2007, give or take a year or two, there are many who believe that ours is the generation that will see the Lord's return.

Again, Daniel the prophet (approx 625 B.C.) has left for us a fascinating set of dates to consider.

Main points of the Daniel 8 prophecy

v13 – How long will non-Jews be allowed to defile this Temple area?

v14 – The answer is given as 2300 days.

In prophecy, days normally equal years therefore, within a certain time frame, the Temple area will be returned to the Jews as they await their Messiah!

Rule – In order to find out the date for the cleansing of the Temple area on Mount Moriah, we need first to establish the dates for the beginning of Daniel's vision.

Details

v3&4 – mentions a ram with two horns.

v5-7 – tells us of a he-goat with a conspicuous horn. This he-goat defeats the ram with two horns.

Interpretation

v20 – The ram with two horns represents the Medes and the Persians.

v21 – The he-goat with the conspicuous horn represents Alexander the Great of Greece.

The problem to be solved.

If we can establish the B.C. dates when Alexander of Greece defeated the Medes and the Persians, we can then subtract those B.C. dates from 2300 years.

The answers will then tell us the A.D. dates when the Temple

area on Mount Moriah will return into Jewish hands. This is necessary preparation for the coming of the Messiah.

The answer to the problem

The history books tell us that Alexander the Great of Greece fought all his battles between 334 B.C. and 323 B.C. (Remember, that with the B.C. dates, they must all be calculated back to front.)

We now do two sums. We subtract the B.C. dates from the 2300 years –

2300	2300
-334 BC	-323 BC
1966 AD –	**1977 AD**

Therefore, this Temple area on Mount Moriah must go back into Jewish hands during this time period.

It did of course, during the six day war of June 1967. Israel now controls the whole city of Jerusalem, although as we already know, there are many who are out to change all this if they possibly can.

Further exciting prophecy

We can now prove from the Jewish Scriptures that the Jewish carpenter named Yeshua ben Joseph, (Jesus, son of Joseph – the suffering servant) is about to return shortly as Yeshua ben David, (Jesus, son of David – the reigning king).

Therefore, any Jewish person reading this book can be confident that the author is a friend of Israel who has irrefutable proof that will help you identify your Messiah using only your own Scriptures.

When will Messiah come?

Paraphrase of Daniel 9:25 -

"The Messiah will come 483 years after the commandment to restore and rebuild Jerusalem."

Dr Ivan Panin, a Russian atheistic mathematician, set himself to the task of proving the Bible not to be the Word of God, and then discovered that through a series of mathematical formulae, he could prove conclusively that the Bible was the Word of God.

He put out a number of books, and from his book "Bible Chronology", he tell us that regarding Persian history, Biblical dates are far more reliable than secular dates.

Panin clarifies for us the answer to some important questions.

Q. Who gave the vital commandment to rebuild Jerusalem?

A. **Cyrus the Great of Persia**. (Note – Artaxerxes Longimus merely gave permission.)

Q. What was the date of the Commandment?

A. **486 B.C**.

Q. What date was Messiah revealed?

A. **4 B.C.**

Remember the angel Gabriel came to Mary in the sixth month.

Q. How long does it take for a baby to form in the womb?

A. Forty weeks.

Therefore, Yeshua (Jesus of Nazareth), was announced to be the Messiah at His conception.

[3]*"And behold, thou shalt conceive in thy womb, and bring forth a son, and shalt call His name Jesus."*

[4]*"He shall be great"* – that's Messiah;

"And shall be called the Son of the Highest" – that's Messiah;

"And the Lord God shall give unto Him, the throne of His father David" – that's Messiah;

"And He shall reign over the house of Jacob forever" – that's Messiah;

"And of His kingdom there shall be no end" – that's Messiah.

Challenge – He was conceived in 4 B.C.

He was born in 3 B.C.

i.e. 486
  - 483
    3 B.C.

Q. How did the wise men know to come from the East?

A. **The Daniel 9 prophecy**.

Q. Why did Herod seek for Jesus' death at that time?

A. **The Daniel 9 prophecy**.

Q. Why were Simeon and Anna the prophetess waiting around the Temple area at that time?

A. **The Daniel 9 prophecy**.

Where will Messiah be born?

[5]*"But thou, Bethlehem Ephra-tah, though thou be little among the thousands of Judah, yet out of thee, shall He come forth unto Me, that is going to be rule in Israel, Whose goings forth have been from of old, from everlasting."*

In the little guinea-pig country of New Zealand, we also have a Bethlehem. Folk from the U.S.A., Switzerland, and Australia, have told me that they also have a Bethlehem in their respective countries.

Whilst on the 1995 Israel tour, I enquired as to the meaning of Bethlehem Ephra-tah. The words mean "**Bethlehem on the way to Ephrat**."

To this point in our study, we have established:

a) The Messiah will be born in 3 B.C.

b) He will not be born anywhere in the world but Bethlehem on the way to Ephrat.

What will be His mission?

[6]*"But this shall be the covenant that I will make with the house of Israel: After those days saith the Lord.*

I will put my law in their inward parts, and write it in their hearts, and will be their God, and they shall be my people.

...for I will forgive their iniquity, and remember their sin no more."

In simple English, the Messiah will establish a new covenant or agreement, far better than the law of Moses. This covenant we now understand was initiated though the precious, perfect, God-created, sinless, blood of Yeshua (Jesus Christ of Nazareth) when He hung on the cross once and for all, for each of us individually.

Thank you Jeremiah, for clarifying this point.

We have now established:

a) The Messiah will be born in 3 B.C.

b) He will be born in Bethlehem on the way to Ephrat.

c) He will establish a new covenant agreement between God and man.

Will Messiah be God?

[7]*"For unto us a child is born, unto us a son is given: and the government shall be upon His shoulder: and His name shall be called Wonderful, Counsellor, **The mighty God**, **The everlasting Father**, the Prince of Peace."*

We have now established:

a) The Messiah will be born in 3 B.C.

b) He will be born in Bethlehem on the way to Ephrat.

c) He will establish a new covenant agreement between God and man.

d) He will be born a child and a son, and ultimately, this Son will be identified as the mighty God and the everlasting Father. The new covenant will involve his wounding, beating and death for us.

[8]*"All we like sheep have gone astray; we have turned every one to his own way; and the Lord hath laid on him the iniquity of us all."*

[9]*"And His feet shall stand in that day upon the mount of Olives which is before Jerusalem on the east..."*

We have now established:

a) The Messiah will be born in 3 B.C.

b) He will be born in Bethlehem on the way to Ephrat.

c) He will establish a new covenant agreement between God and man.

d) He will be born a child and a son, and ultimately, this Son will be identified as the mighty God and the everlasting Father. The new covenant will involve his wounding, beating and death for us.

e) He will place both feet on the Mount of Olives.

f) He will reign as king over the whole earth.

Who could possibly fulfil all these qualifications?

Jesus Christ the Lord, sometimes call Jesus of Nazareth, or Yeshua Ha Moshiach.

There are masses of prophecies to prove that we are on the right track, but these six qualifications should suffice.

GAP

We are living in this period right now. It lasts for about 2000 years of which **1996** have already passed.

Superfluous Information

At this point, I must be quite frank. I did not intend to write a fifth book until we reached a certain point in history. I believe we are almost there.

The end of the Daniel 9 prophecy

In chapter 9 of Daniel, the prophet is given the future history of Israel from his own day. The full period given supernaturally to him by an angel was to last for 490 years.

We now understand that from Cyrus' commandment until the Lord Jesus Christ, the Jewish Messiah, and our Saviour, 483 years of this period have already passed. The prophetic clock stopped for a period of about 2000 years.

This **gap period** is called "The Times of the Gentiles".

217

a) **It lasts for about 2,000 years**.
b) It is God's opportunity for non-Jews to get into God's family through a personal encounter with the Lord Jesus Christ.
c) 'Born again' is the name of this experience. This is a very special privilege extended, yet the majority of Gentiles (or non-Jews) do not appear to give God or Jesus a thought, until it is too late.

Now – notice   490 years is the full period promised

                            <u>483</u> years have already passed into history

                          GAP – 2000 years long Gentiles' opportunity

7 years final countdown leads to
a) the secret coming of Christ to pick up His people
b) the public coming of Christ to reign

The final 7 years

This period commences with a COMPREHENSIVE MIDDLE EAST PEACE TREATY.

[10]"*And he shall confirm the covenant with many for one week, and in the midst of the week he shall cause the sacrifice and the oblation to cease....*"

From this passage of prophecy, without becoming too involved, we learn the following.

"*He*" refers to a future world leader called 'Antichrist'.

"*Will confirm the covenant with many*" refers to the other Arab nations joining with the PLO, Egypt and Jordan, to sign for peace with Israel.

This means that Israel must give up the Golan Heights, then Syria and Lebanon can come in with the other Arab nations.

"*For one week*" – the word in Hebrew is 'heptad' and stands for a period of seven years.

It's so close – so very close.

Remember these important points.
a) The peace treaty we await will be all-embracing and comprehensive.
b) The treaty will be signed for an initial period of seven years. If it is not for seven years, it is not the one we are looking for.
c) It must be confirmed by a great world statesman called Antichrist.

Believers in Bible prophecy have waited and waited for this most important day, and lo and behold, it's almost here.

Watch carefully now, and positively identify the great world statesman who confirms this seven year treaty.

This man is Antichrist, the Beast, the Man of Sin, and the Son of Perdition. Read again a list of his qualifications in the chapter entitled "Who is he?" then look for a copy of our book 'Warning', penned in 1978 as this will add Scriptural veracity to the predictions.

What is a Christian's responsibility with regard to Israel?

1. According to Romans 11:25, God has put temporary blindness, **in part**, on Israel, until the last Gentile comes into the family of God.

2. If God put this blindness on, then only God can take this blindness off.

3. In the meantime, we are told by Jesus, in the book of Matthew 25 to bless Israel, and in doing so, we are doing it unto the Lord Jesus Christ Himself.

4. God will, at the right time, put His Spirit in them and they will live, according to the prophet Ezekiel 37:13-14:

*"And ye shall know that I am the Lord, when I have opened your graves, O My people, and brought you up out of your graves, And shall put my Spirit in you, **and ye shall live**..."*

To this point in history, we have taken fourteen tours to the Holy Land, and although we clearly reveal Christ as the Jewish Messiah, very little interest is shown by the local inhabitants. Some however do become believers. For these few, we praise God.

However, it is also a thrill every year to join with thousands of believers in our Lord Jesus Christ, who arrive in the land, regardless of the political and aggressive situation that exists, and show solidarity with the people of that land.

At the time of God's spiritual outpouring upon His ancient people, **He and the people of Israel will not forget** this support during this most difficult period in their history. Matthew 25:40 - "....Verily I say unto you, Inasmuch as ye have done it unto one of the least of these **My brethren**, ye have done it unto Me!"

Footnotes

1   Zechariah 12:3; The Holy Bible
2   Matthew 24:34; The Holy Bible
3   Luke 1:31; The Holy Bible
4   Luke 1:32-33; The Holy Bible
5   Micah 5:2; The Holy Bible

6   Jeremiah 31:31-34
7   Isaiah 9:6; The Holy Bible
8   Isaiah 53:6; The Holy Bible
9   Zechariah 4:4; The Holy Bible
10 Daniel 9:27; The Holy Bible

Prediction

We look forward to a comprehensive Middle East peace treaty which will be signed by a leading world statesman. This man will be a non-religious Jew and will confirm this treaty for a period of seven years.

Remember, Mr Netanyahu, as did Mr Rabin, will do exactly what he is told. The U.S. State Department makes all the decisions in Middle Eastern matters.

Before an election, you can stand tall, and promise what you like. Once you win the election, oftentimes your words and promises come back to haunt you.

As things stand at the time of printing this book, the sticking point in Israel is that the country is ungovernable. Coalition governments in Italy and soon in New Zealand, make this clear.

A military coup in Israel is a possibility as is another Arab invasion.

It is important also to watch Russia, the enemy from the north, with moderate Yeltzin a sick man. The man to watch for is a strong man who will take over the leadership of that country and fulfil the Ezekiel prophecy, by invading the Holy Land.

Possible coalitions later on may include Zhirinovsky and/or **Lebed**, but not necessarily.

Note that at this time in history (1996), it matters little as to how much land Israel relinquishes for peace, as **ultimately** they will take over all the land from the Nile River in Egypt to the Euphrates River in Iraq.

a) The Russians will ultimately invade Israel – Ezekiel 38 & 39.

b) Damascus in Syria will be utterly destroyed – Isaiah 17:1.

c) America will be so decimated, she will not be able to help Israel – Revelation 18.

Kissinger Speaks Out

An article in the New Zealand newspaper, 'Waikato Times', dated 10 July 1996, reads thus – "*Middle East Peace Urged*.

"*Former U.S. Secretary of State, Henry Kissinger, says furthering Middle-East Peace was necessary for Israel, and felt the Jewish state's new leader, Benjamin Netanyahu, would realise this.*

*Kissinger, speaking after visiting the grave of Yitzhak Rabin....said "What he (Rabin) has started, grew out of Israel's necessities, and I think any prime minister will come to conclusions that **the process has to be continued**...."*

*....**Israel and the United States have a common destiny** and their leaders have to come to express that common destiny," said Kissinger, whose fame, in part, was made by his diplomacy between Israel and Arab States in the 1970's."* End quote. (Emphasis added.)

(This author has waited 26 years for such information. See his original book "Warning".)

CHAPTER THIRTY

AN INTERESTING CALCULATION

An elderly man in the Island of Western Samoa taught me the following tidbit of history.

Adam – Abraham – 2000 years
Abraham – Christ – 2000 years
Christ – today – <u>1996 years</u>
<u>6000 years</u>
<u>- 5996 years</u> Adam – today

4 years left until 6000 years are complete.

Here is an interesting thought.....*"one day with the Lord is as a thousand years and a thousand years as one day"*. In other words, in the year 1996, we are presently four years (approximately) away from the end of God's sixth day since the creation of Adam.

However, those readers who have attended our meetings, may recall that we have clearly printed on our chart, that our Lord Jesus Christ, it is supposed, was actually born in the year 3 B.C.

"What is the meaning of this?" I hear you cry.

Therefore, we must go forward in our calculations from 1996 to 1999. This being the case, there is approximately one year left until the end of this millenium.

These points are not written in the form of conclusive proof, but are simply there for your consideration, as our dating systems are inconclusive.

No.6

In the art of Numerology, number 6 has always been applied to man. Man was created on the 6th day. The Antichrist's number is 666.

No.7

The number which applies to God Himself, or perfection, is 7. The prophecies talk about 7 vials, 7 angels, 7 churches, 7 trumpets, and God rests on the 7th day. Perfection you see.

No.8

Numerology equates number 8 with a new beginning. An octave

played on the piano leads us on again to number 8 – a new beginning. The Greek, Hebrew, and Latin languages have numerics built into their alphabets so that if you write the IESOUS ('Jesus' in Greek), its numerics add up to 888. **Jesus Christ the Lord is a new beginning. Fully God, and also fully man, and the only one who can save us from our sins with His precious blood.**

Before you read on at this point, I suggest to you that you will be grateful throughout all eternity for the information presented in chapter 32.

By the way, **you will not, and cannot forget what you have just read in the preceding chapters**. It will crop up everywhere now that you are aware of the plan.

Happy reading.

Clarification

We are not yet living in the days when the world will end.

We are living at the end of an era when Jesus Christ will return for those who have chosen Him as their Lord and Saviour.

Remember His words "this generation" can be anywhere between 1998-2007.

Even these are appoximations as there are different forms of dating systems.

Therefore, the key is "watch and be ready"!

CHAPTER THIRTY-ONE

HEALTH AND HEALING

Scenario no.1

If you were the owner of a large business, promoting a certain product, and the opposition down the road set up in business selling a superior product to yours and in doing so, destroyed your business, what would your feelings be towards the opposition?

Scenario no.2

If you were in the business of selling oil, gasoline, and its by-products, and some backyard inventor discovered a method of separating water into its two components of H2 and O, then built a special carburettor to run the engine of his car on hydrogen gas (H2), what would your feelings be towards the opposition?

Scenario no.3

If you were in the health business and connected with the pharmaceutical companies, possibly on occasions even having shares in these companies, and some private citizen with a brilliant mind, invented a simple method of dealing with disease, that excluded drugs and did not involve massive amounts of money, what would your feelings be towards the opposition?

Statement – Believe it or not!

Scenarios no's 2 & 3 – The majority of this earth's population would never have thought deeply enough to realise that the
a) oil
b) pharmaceutical companies
are making massive, massive, profits, and there is no way that they will be willing to give up these benefits, **unless the general public knows that there are alternatives and demand the right to choose**.

It is not the purpose of this book to go into much detail on the health and healing issue, as we are not medically trained.

However, we enjoy passing on good news.

Please feel free to read our books 'Final Notice' and 'P.S.' for a list of therapies that are of great benefit in promoting relief from many previously incurable ailments.

It is of note that organisers for the Olympic Games 2000 in Sydney are using ozone to purify their swimming pools in the place of chlorine. The reason for this is that many European swimmers object to the burning sensation of chlorine in their eyes.

Challenge

If ozone purifies water, what can it do to blood products?

Ozone treatment may be administered in different ways. Here is one of them:

Polyatomic Apheresis

An advertisement for this form of treatment says:

"The most advanced diseased cell treatment available anywhere in the world today!

It is the single greatest development and treatment for eradicating blood borne viruses invitro and invivo, in the history of contemporary medicine. Similar to dialysis, the patient's blood is removed from one arm, passed through a special mixing chamber where it is mixed with Polyatomic Oxygen, (a sophisticated form of ozone), and then purified and returned back to the patient's other arm. This continuous treatment of the blood....has demonstrated its incredible efficacy in numerous international studies.

Because of its amazing capabilities, it is considered the greatest development and treatment method in the history of medicine. This new technology, developed by Basil E. Wainwright, (Nobel nominee), is being sought after world-wide to establish clinics. Even more astounding is that Polyatomic Apheresis has the ability to purify the donated and stored blood products of the world.

There are now antibiotic resistant strains of tuberculosis running rampant in the hospitals, and viruses from the rainforest escaping and multiplying into the interactive web of international traffic; these include the MARBURG and EBOLI viruses, and the generative conditions like AIDS, that allow people to succumb to even illnesses as simple as pneumonia.

Since we are now on the threshold of a whole new set of challenges in medicine, Polyatomic Apheresis is now ready to combat and offset this deadly onslaught of diseases....

The political benefits and economical savings to countries using this technology are enormous." End quote.

Good News!

Patients from various parts of the world have been thrilled and relieved to hear that at last, along with the German clinics listed in the back of our fourth book, 'P.S.', who are all using oxygen therapies, a clinic has been set up in Kenya, and is treating many patients per day.

The Beyond 2000 Treatment Centre in Nairobi, Kenya, has been set aside for this most incredible treatment. Patients from as far afield as Canada, America, and Australia, are testifying of the remarkable results of this amazing treatment.

For further information, the telephone number is: Nairobi, Kenya, 254-2-219348 or 240763; Fax 254-2-330292.

Consult the Internet for further help with Oxygen Therapies or Ozone Therapy Clinics.

Recommended Reading

Suppressed Inventions by Dr Brian O'Leary, Christopher Bird, Jeane Manning, Barry Lynes, and others; edited by Jonatham Eisen; Auckland Institute of Technology Press, Private Bag 92006, Auckland, New Zealand.

Left For Dead by Dick Quinn; R.F. Quinn Publishing Co., Box 17100, Minneapolis, MN 55417, U.S.A. Ph: (800) 283 3998 – **Excellent information for heart patients.**

DISCLAIMER

The material listed in this chapter is given for information purposes only, and must in no way be seen as a recommendation

---

CHAPTER THIRTY-TWO

RELIGION VERSUS RELATIONSHIP

The words 'Novus Ordo Seclorum' that are found at the base of the pyramid on the reverse side of every US$1 bill, not only mean

a One World Government
a One World Money System
a One World Law System
but also a One World Religious System

I switched on my t.v. set one morning to listen to a programme of hymn-singing. To my astonishment, the hymn singing had given way to a very strange gathering which was described for us in a newspaper called the 'Paymeham Messenger', 14th April 1992. The heading read thus *"Religious Unity to Greet Dalai Lama.*

Unity of all religions will be the theme of an event organised to celebrate the arrival in Adelaide of his holiness, the 14th Dalai Lama of Tibet.

Aboriginal, Buddhist, Christian, Hindu, Muslim and Sikh leaders will share the dias with the Dalai Lama, and representatives from more than 100 local spiritual organisations are expected to attend this major event a St Francis Xavier Cathedral.

...The Aboriginal community has nominated a didgeridoo player to play for the event...." End quote.

WORLD GOVERNMENT SEAL ON REVERSE SIDE OF U.S. $1.00 BILL

Now, I was quite amazed to view this gathering as the commentator softly and reverently intoned that the didgeridoo player was invoking the presence of the Holy Spirit.

227

A careful reading of the Word of God – the Bible, informs us clearly of the Holy Spirit's tasks.

1. To convict peoples' consciences of sin, righteousness and judgement.
2. To come alongside as a comforter to the believer in the Lord Jesus Christ.
3. To glorify the Lord Jesus Christ as God's only answer to the 'sin problem'.

You ask, "What sin problem?"

Q. Well, **how many things do I need to steal to be a thief**?
A. Just one.
Q. **How many lies do I need to tell to be classed as a liar**?
A. Just one.
Q. **How many sins need I commit to be a sinner**?
A. Just one.

[1]God sums it up by stating *"For all have sinned and come short of the glory of God."*

I well remember an open air meeting we were conducting in Shortland St, off lower Queen St, Auckland, New Zealand. A man stepped forward and shouted that he was not a sinner, as he had never sinned.

The speaker for the evening replied "Could we see you for five minutes after the meeting sir. We wish to take your name and address, so that when you die, we can have you stuffed and put on display in the museum. Above your head we will have a placard placed with the words outlined "**The Only Man Who Never Sinned**".

Everybody else has. You sir, are absolutely remarkable."

Now, every honest person knows intuitively that there is some evil bias inside us that perpetually causes us to either think or act in the wrong way.

Let us not become religious about all this type of thinking but stay 'real' at all times.

God says that a long eternity in Hell is the reward for our sins.

[2]*"For the wages of sin is death."*

What a wonderful God. He sets the rules and then provides the answer to the problem.

[3]*"But the gift of God is eternal life, through Jesus Christ our Lord."*

You may have gathered that this writer is not interested in theories, but in facts. Time is too short to be concerned with irrelevant information so let's go to it.

[4]**FACT 1.** We are all sinners. *"If we say that we have no sin, we deceive ourselves and the truth is not in us."*

FACT 2. We all recognise that there is a God, in spite of a few who bluster on in a macho manner that there is no God.

a) Creation is so brilliantly designed that there must be a designer.

[5]*"For the invisible things of Him from the creation of the world are clearly seen, being understood by the things that are made, even His eternal power and Godhead, **so that they are without excuse**."*

Some years ago, we visited Stoke on Trent in Great Britain. Seeking for some green grass, we visited a little park, which also included a duck pond. As we sat on the park bench, a beautifully coloured duck landed on the water. So brilliant and precise were the coloured patterns on its feathers, I remarked that every would-be atheist or agnostic should be forced to study this phenomena and answer the obvious question.

How can this be? A man could paint that fantastic design on the duck's feathers, but only God could design each portion of the feather, matching on the two sides, mind you, so that the design is formed. How did each feather know what distance out it should grow to and then stop?

One duck therefore, exhibited on the day of judgement would adequately prove that men and women are **without excuse**.

Should a duck prove to be too simple an illustration, let us exercise our intellects to the extreme as we consider the tiny **bombadier beetle.**

In an article written by Eryl Cooke, a zoologist who holds a doctorate at Cardiff University, we share this amazing information.

"The Unexplainable

To the creationist the bombadier beetle is a marvellous little creature, but to the evolutionist it is a headache – Eryl Cooke.

Studying to be a zoologist was one of the great privileges that God gave me. I was introduced to a startling variety of animals and plants that were so beautifully and intricately made. The whole experience convinced me that there was a Creator par excellence behind every beauty of creation. This was no chance happening but a grand design. One of the smaller animals that popped up in our Arthropod course was Brachinus crepitans, otherwise known as the 'bombadier beetle'. To the creationist this is a marvellous little creature, but to the evolutionist it is a headache.

Beetle's Boiling Jet

This beetle has two chambers within the abdomen; one called the basal reservoir and the other the apical reservoir. The former is filled with a chemical mixture of quinones and hydrogen peroxide (used in hair perming) obtained from some gland cells. The two chambers are connected by a short tube, the opening of which is controlled by a contracting muscle. The apical reservoir has cells in its walls that secrete a variety of enzymes which are able to speed up reactions involving the quinones and peroxide. When the contractor muscle contracts and the quinones, peroxide and enzymes all react chemically, an amazing amount of heat is generated. Quinone at 100 degrees centigrade is sprayed at high pressure out of a nozzle type valve at the rear of the animal. The nozzle is capable of revolving a little like a tank turret. The jet of boiling chemical can therefore be directed at a potential attacker.

The problem for the evolutionist is:

1. If the quinones had merely remained in the body of the beetle, they would have eventually rotted the animal and accomplished nothing.
2. If the quinones had been reacted with the enzymes and peroxide the resulting explosion would have blown the beetle apart.
3. If the beetle was not fixed with a controllable muscle valve between the chambers, the moment of mixing could not be controlled.
4. If the beetle did not have a revolvable nozzle at the rear there would be no exit for the chemicals and no way of directing their flow.

The bombadier beetle had to be created with the **whole** system intact and operational, otherwise there would have been no beetles left to perpetuate the next generation. Evolutionists believe that systems like this one evolved slowly step by step, the changes being so gradual that it would take millions of years to develop a complicated defence mechanism like this one. From the above it is obvious that this just would not have worked with our explosive little friend!

Another striking example of the amazing hand of the Creator is the 'midwife toad'. Any child will tell you that, on the whole, frogs and toads lay their eggs in ponds. These hatch into tadpoles which become frogs. The midwife toad however, is an amazing exception to the rule. The female lays its eggs on **land**, these are collected by the male toad who uses his back legs to scoop them onto his back. For three weeks he carries them around, making sure that they remain damp, but not too wet, cool and not exposed to too much sunlight. At the end of the this period he takes the eggs, which have now developed young tadpoles within them, to a pond and releases them. The tadpoles chew their way out of the egg cases and continue developing in the pond.

Again the evolutionists are faced with a similar problem.

1. How did the female know not to put her eggs into the water?
2. How did the male know that he had a part to play in the egg protection (other males don't)?
3. How did the male know what to do with the eggs?
4. How did the male toad know when three weeks had elapsed and that then was the time to take them to water?

If any one of these stages had gone wrong the eggs would have failed to hatch. Absolutely none of these stages could have developed gradually. Each part of the life cycle had to have existed in the first pair of midwife toads. All the information necessary had to be genetically and physically in place right at the start.

Darwin is Downed

Charles Darwin wrote, "If it could be demonstrated that any complex organ existed which could not possibly have been formed by numerous successive slight modifications, my theory would absolutely break down." On the basis of what we have demonstrated with the bombadier beetle and the midwife toad, his theory breaks down." End quote. (Emphasis added).

b) God has revealed Himself to every person. It is for this reason that in a crisis, at some stage in their lives, all men and women cry out to God, sometimes even against their will.

As a young school-teacher in the South Pacific Islands of Samoa some years ago, a fellow-teacher involved in a staff-room discussion boasted about his being an atheist.

I replied "Ted, you are out at sea in a small boat. A storm is looming and you lose your oars. What is your next move? Be honest please."

He answered "I suppose I would pray, as a last resort!"

[6]*"Because that which may be known of God is manifest in them, for God hath shewed it unto them."*

c) Therefore, self-proclaimed atheists are **liars and fools** at the same time.

[7]*"Because that when they knew God, they glorified Him not as God, neither were thankful, but became vain in their imaginations and their foolish heart was darkened. Professing themselves to be wise, they became fools."*

<u>FACT 3.</u> Men do not normally seek after God, until a time of crisis.

Q. Why is this? It was true in my own case, and probably in yours also. Why?

A. One of the Devil's most clever lying tricks is to convince people he does not exist.

[8]*"But if our gospel be hid, it is hid to them that are lost. In whom the god of this world hath blinded the minds of them which believe not, lest the light of the glorious gospel of Christ who is the image of God, should shine unto them."*

A friend of mine was preaching in an open air meeting when an interjector shouted out "You're cracked", to which my friend replied, "Quite right sir, and it was through that crack that the light came in."

<u>FACT 4.</u> Religion has turned millions of people off, including this author.

A study of t.v. programmes always shows the preacher up in a bad light.

a) A gibbering idiot who bumbles his way through life.
b) A man with his collar back to front, giving the prizes out at the flower show, or drinking cups of tea with old ladies.
c) A madman, bellowing from the pulpit.
d) A sexual pervert.
e) A rip-off artist relieving people of their hard-earned money.
f) A lazy person who preaches once or twice on Sunday and then lives for himself.

[9]*"His watchmen are blind. They are all ignorant. They are all dumb dogs, they cannot bark, sleeping, lying down, loving to slumber. Yea, they are greedy dogs which can never have enough and they are shepherds that cannot understand, they all look to their own way, every one for his gain, from his quarter."*

FACT 5. **The true church started in Jerusalem – Relationship**.

A journey by boat from Caesarea took some of them to Rome, where pagan idols and systems of worship corrupted the good seed of the gospel. **Therefore the false church started in Rome – Religion**.

FACT 6. If I were God, I would hate <u>religion</u>, because it robs me of "relationship" with my children.

[10]*"For they being ignorant of God's righteousness and going about to establish their own righteousness, have not <u>submitted themselves</u> unto the righteousness of God."*

The sad part to this aspect is, that when men are invited to listen to **sense**, many times they refuse to come because they have been turned off through the **nonsense**.

An actor, one day remarked to a liberal religious minister. "You know Reverend, you and I are rather similar in a way!"

"How is that?" asked the minister.

"Well, I as an actor, take false things and make them real, while you, as a religious man, take real things and make them false."

FACT 7. Only a madman would actively seek opportunity to burn in Hell for ever and ever, yet it appears that the vast majority will choose this road.

[11]*"Enter ye in at the strait gate, for wide is the gate, and broad is the way that leadeth to destruction and <u>many</u> there be which go in thereat.*

Because strait is the gate and narrow is the way which leadeth unto life, and <u>few</u> there be that find it."

232

I heard my son Andrew, one day, make this very sensible statement. **"Whatever the cost, I'm going through that narrow gate."**

FACT 8. It is up to each individual. It is every man for himself.

A religious, theologically liberal Padre, was approached by a group of soldiers with the following question.

"Padre, do you believe there is a Hell?", to which he replied, "Of course not!"

The soldiers then said, "If that is the case, would you please resign."

"Why?" asked the startled minister.

The soldiers said, **"If there is no Hell, we don't need you, and if there is a Hell, we don't want to be deceived by you."**

[12]*"Ask and it shall be given you, seek and ye shall find, knock, and it shall be opened unto you."*

[13]*"The kingdom of heaven suffereth violence and the violent take it by force."*

Meaning – If you or I recognise that we are sinners lost forever under the awful judgement of God, we will do anything to find out God's truth.

[14]*"That they should seek the Lord, if haply they might feel after him and find him, though he be not far from every one of us."*

The old English words 'if haply' have been variously translated – if by any means, they might feel their way to Him (TCNT); if perhaps they could grope for Him (Weymouth); on the chance of finding Him, in their groping for Him (Moffat); and, it might be, touch and find Him (N.E.B.); in the hope that they might feel after Him and find Him (R.S.V.).

Meaning – You look for relationship with Him, and ignoring religion, you will find that He is very near at hand.

It is called being **born again**.

Never forget:

**The inoculation against the real thing – Religion = Hell forever
The real thing – Relationship = Heaven forever**

An Asian woman stands weeping beside a slow moving muddy river. She speaks a few words of prayer to her gods, then lifts her first born baby above her head. With a terrible cry, she throws it into the mouth of a waiting crocodile. With a swirl of water, the crocodile and baby disappear beneath the murky waters.

I approach the distraught woman and kindly ask her "Why did you do that?"

Her red-rimmed eyes, still gushing tears meet with mine for an instant as she tries to explain through her sobs.

"Don't you understand sir? I must appease the gods. Nothing must be withheld from them. I have always given my very best that my sins may be forgiven. I hope one day to leave this world of misery and shame and enjoy a place called Paradise."

I feel my heart break as I say "**Hasn't anybody ever been to your village to tell you that God has provided Himself a Lamb to atone for your sins**?"

"No sir", she replies. "Nobody has told me anything like that", and she moves on, her pathetic little figure shaking with grief.

The scene changes.

Further up the road, I meet with a man, his clothing torn, filthy, his bare hands and face cut, and bleeding. He throws himself forward on the dusty gravel and measures his length, picks himself up and then repeats the exercise over and over.

I am absolutely horrified at this exhibition of self-torture.

"Excuse me sir", I cry out. "Why are you doing this?"

"Oh", he replies, "I know that I have a soul in me that will never die, and because of my evil nature, I am punishing myself as I continue on this holy pilgrimage, in the hope of a better life after death."

I do not know exactly what to say in reply as I come from such a careless, indifferent society, that I feel almost like a hypocrite offering such a dedicated man such as this, my humble advice.

"**Hasn't anybody come to your area to tell you that God has provided Himself a Lamb to take care of the forgiveness of your sins**?"

He looks briefly at me for a moment through his hopeless, grey eyes, then ignores me and continues on with his pitiful journey to nowhere.

I return to my own country. It is 6 a.m. in the morning as a I see a smartly dressed businessman climb from his BMW and begin to enter a church with a steep spire.

"Excuse me sir", I say. "I am doing a survey on the subject of religion. Why do I find you here so early in the morning?"

He smilingly answers, "I have an immortal soul, you know. Before works starts each day, I come here, light a candle, pray to the saints to celebrate a mass with others of like mind, and then continue on with the day with a clear conscience. By the way, I also attend confession regularly and get rid of all my dirty laundry, as it were. Being a fairly well-off individual, I contribute quite a bit to religious causes, as you will understand I am sure, that the old heavenly scales tend to dip to my disadvantage from time to time. All these good deeds and religious acts are helping to restore the balance in my favour. Basically, I am working for 'merit'."

"Oh sir", I reply softly. "**God sees your endeavours I am sure, as it shows Him that you have a heart towards Him**. I would that others of my fellow countrymen felt after God as you do.

However, in all your long years, has anybody ever explained to you in simple language, that God has made provision for our sins? He has provided Himself a Lamb!"

He is quick to reply "I don't really need any religious advice. My grandfather and my father taught me that the church and religious acts are all I need. Have a good day!"

A clear understanding of what you are now about to read, can deliver you from the bondage of religion and place you in the enviable **position of relationship**.

Footnotes

1   Romans 3:23; The Holy Bible
2   Romans 6:23a; The Holy Bible
3   Romans 6:23b; The Holy Bible
4   1 John 1:8; The Holy Bible
5   Romans 1:20; The Holy Bible
6   Romans 1:19; The Holy Bible
7   Romans 1:21-22; The Holy Bible
8   II Corinthians 4:3-4; The Holy Bible
9   Isaiah 56:10-11; The Holy Bible
10 Romans 10:3; The Holy Bible
11 Matthew 7:13-14; The Holy Bible
12 Matthew 7:7; The Holy Bible
13 Matthew 11:12; The Holy Bible
14 Acts 17:27; The Holy Bible

Prediction

'Interfaith' and 'religious unity' will speed up as tolerance and harmonisation become the catchwords.

Born again Christians will continue to have laws issued against them through anti-discrimination groups.

A department of Religious Harmonisation (or something similar to that as is found already in Singapore) will be set up so that prison will be the punishment for proclaiming Jesus as the only way to God.

CHAPTER THIRTY-THREE

WAKE UP IN HEAVEN

'National' Newspaper, 3rd May 1994, Wewak, Papua New Guinea:
"***Evangelist stoned***.

International evangelist, Barry Smith, came under a barrage of stones last Saturday night as he was preaching to a capacity crowd at the Prince Charles Oval here.

*Pastor Smith said the incident occurred during the altar call when he urged the crowd to "**receive Christ**", probably because some of them had misinterpreted his message as being directed against their churches.*

"The stones sounded like guns going off when they landed on the roof", the pastor told the National, adding that some people "came at us with spears and knives", after the stone throwing incident.

Pastor Smith and his Samoan wife May, were escorted by police off the stage to a police car. Meanwhile, some rascals smashes (sic) the windows of a hire vehicle thinking the couple were riding in it. Nobody was hurt in the attack, and police have taken into custody some of the people involved.

On Sunday night, Pastor Smith preached again at the same venue, but he and his entourage travelled under police escort.

The group later travelled to Mt Hagen where they were invited to share a mumu with Prime Minister Paias Wingti at his home, before preaching there last night...." End quote.

By now, it should be becoming obvious to you, the reader, that we are on to something here which excites the people to such a degree that over the years, we have been physically attacked about half a dozen times.

Sometimes it is an attack with sticks and rocks and other times it is an occult attack; sometimes a martial arts attack; sometimes it is a physical attack as the result of pure anger but in this case, it was a religion versus relationship attack.

Listen, after wading through all this material, I suggest (humbly of course) that you read this particular chapter very, very, carefully.

The Divine Plan

We will call the **relationship folk "seeds"** and the **religious folk "weeds"**. Remember **the weeds hate the seeds**.

<u>FACT 1</u> – Almighty God, who created us is aware that we have a sin problem. As a result, He set the conditions in very clear [1]language. *"Without the shedding of blood, there is no remission...."*

Throughout the Old Testament, the priests therefore sacrificed the blood of bulls, goats, and even turtle doves. In heathen countries today, the people still offer blood sacrifice. **This animal and bird blood could never wash away sin on a permanent basis, but merely temporarily cover sin**.

God's plan was so ingenious that to fiddle with it and alter one point, would destroy the end result.

Example

Following the Jewish Midrashic pattern of the original event, then one which would follow the same basic plan later in history, God chose an old man called Abraham to take his son Isaac to [2]Mount Moriah to offer as a sacrifice to God. *"And they went, both of them together"* to Mt Moriah (the type or shadow).

Later, the same scene was re-enacted all over again. Same plan, different characters.

Reality

And they went both of them together to Mt Moriah, God and His Son, the Lord Jesus Christ (the reality).

Rules

1. God requires blood sacrifice.
2. **My blood cannot save you, and your blood cannot save me. Our blood is all sinful**.
3. God created a special sinless blood, in a very special and involved manner.

800 years before Christ, the Old Testament prophet Isaiah predicts Stage 1.

[3]*"Therefore the Lord Himself shall give you a sign. Behold a virgin shall conceive, and bear a son and shall call His name Immanuel."*

4. In the year 4 B.C. a girl aged about 14 years is visited by the angel Gabriel and is told that she is to be the blessed one.

[4]*"And the angel came into her and said, "Hail, thou that art highly favoured, the Lord is with thee, blessed art thou among women"."*

5. Mary was a young Jewish virgin, born of normal parents. There is nothing in the Bible to suggest she was born without sin.

In fact, we have two Biblical texts, establishing that she was a normal person, prone to sin, just as is everybody else.

[5]a) Her testimony – "*And Mary said, My soul doth magnify the Lord, and **my spirit hath rejoiced in God my Saviour**.*"

So, here is the world's most blessed woman telling us that the child to be borne by her for a period of 40 weeks, will one day become her Saviour.

In some of our meetings as Mary's words are read out, weed women take their weed husband's hands and march out in a great display of anger, not realising that in doing so, they are openly pronouncing that Mary, the world's most blessed woman, is prone to lying.

There is a psychological reason for this. The woman has often shared more intimacies with her confessor than with her husband and thus becomes subconsciously bound to the system. The husband, using his intellect, can often see through the lies and deceit but the woman, following only her emotions, gets angry and stalks out dragging her obedient husband after her.

We spoke on the subject in Dublin, Ireland, to a packed hall. The interest was intense, and at the end of the gathering, a lady said to me "Mr Smith, **I have found further Biblical proof that Mary was a normal, sinful, person**."

We now turn to the Old Testament and look at the rules provided for a Jewish lady after giving birth to a son or a daughter.

We will then check up to see whether Mary observed these rules or not.

[6]b) "*And when the days of her purifying are fulfilled for a son, or for a daughter, she shall bring a lamb of the first year for a burnt offering, and a young pigeon or a turtle dove **for a sin offering**....unto the priest.*"

We now go to the New Testament narrative to see whether Mary fulfilled this law, or was she excluded because of her so-called sinless nature.

[7]"*And when the days of her purification according to the law of Moses were accomplished, they brought Him (Jesus) to present Him to the Lord.*

As it is written in the law of the Lord; every male that openeth the womb shall be called holy to the Lord.

And to offer a sacrifice according to that which is said in the law of the Lord, a pair of turtledoves or two young pigeons."

This final argument settles it for the clear thinking non-

indoctrinated individual. Seeds can easily accept the pure Word. Weed folk unwisely put tradition ahead of God's Word and in doing so, damn themselves for ever.

Why is this section so important to understand?

The medical profession tells us that the mother's blood does not pass the placenta. This is just as well, for had Mary's sinful blood flowed in Jesus' veins, there would be no salvation.

It is important to note <u>Mary's true role</u> in the conception and subsequent birth of our Saviour.

She might be described as a chosen human vessel to incubate God's Son and to bring Him into the world.

With great care now, we quote again God's infallible Word. This is Jesus speaking prophetically.

[8]*"....a body has Thou prepared Me."*

It now becomes clear that the life principle which flowed in the veins of this child, was a special blood, having the following characteristics.

a) It was sinless blood.

b) It was human blood - as the life of heaven is not blood but the spirit.

c) His DNA was made up of the earthly chromosomes from His earthly mother and perfectly created chromosomes from His heavenly Father.

d) Thus our Lord Jesus Christ was fully human and yet fully divine. Throughout His life, He showed both sides.

Seated tired and thirsty, on the side of the well in Samaria – **that's man**.He told the woman all about herself – **that's God**. Lying sleeping in a fishing boat during the storm, **that's man**. Standing up and stilling the waves – **that's God**. Going for a rest in the hills about Capernaum - that's man. Feeding the five thousand - that's God.

As He walked the streets of Palestine in those days, His features would no doubt have been clearly Jewish (from Mary), yet hidden within would have been a distinctive glow of heaven reflected in His knowledge and use of the Scriptures (from God, His Father).

[9]*"It is evident that our Lord sprang out of Judah...."* Therefore, in His genes, the characteristics of both heaven and earth would make up His character and features.

It is also of note that the human side of Him was pronounced enough to be subject to disobedience, yet He was not disobedient.

[10]"*Though He were a Son, yet learned He obedience by the things which He suffered.*"

When He was young, Joseph and Mary must have given Him similar treatment to that which they gave to their other six or more children.

[11]Remember, temptation is not sin. He was "*...in all points tempted like as we are yet without sin.*"

These statements cause many thoroughly indoctrinated weeds to want to rush out of our meetings.

The Good News

The Old Testament Passover lamb, a type of Christ, was examined for 72 defects. The true Lamb of God, our **Lord Jesus Christ, was absolutely without fault also**.

[12]No wonder Pilate said to the chief priests and to the people "*I find no fault in this man*".

Our Saviour's full Name with titles is the

    Lord – the God part

    Jesus – the man part

    Christ – the anointed one – the promised Messiah

Q. **Was Mary therefore the Mother of God?**

A. **No. God was there before mothers were invented**.

She was the privileged, blessed woman who conceived of the Holy Ghost and gave birth to the **man part** of the Word of God.

That is why the angel spoke in the future tense and said [13]"*Thou shalt call His name Jesus.*" There was no Jesus in the Old Testament. Only God and His Word.

[14]At a certain time in history, "**And the Word was made flesh and dwelt among us and beheld His glory, the glory as of the only begotten of the Father, full of grace and truth.**"

MThus, at this particular time in history, God in His wisdom, placed a human body on His Word, placed special sinless blood in His veins, and then allowed a situation to develop on the cross when that special blood flowed out for us. He called His name **Jesus - Yeshua**, which in Hebrew means '**Saviour**'. Thus in God's divine plan, Jesus could not be poisoned to death or strangled.

Crucifixion was the most horrible, excruciating death a man could die, yet it perfectly fulfilled God's requirements.

  The blood was shed.

There is therefore now remission and forgiveness of sin for all, who apply in humility, repentance, and faith towards God.

Notice now.

[15]"*If we confess our sins, He is faithful and just to forgive us our sins and to cleanse us from all unrighteousness.*"

[16]And again "*If we walk in the light, as He is in the light, we have fellowship one with another, and the blood of Jesus Christ, His Son, cleanses from all sin.*"

Notice that it doesn't only cover up sin, it washes it away into the sea of God's forgetfulness.

Can you see now? **The weeds get angry when you try to explain this but the seeds are absolutely delighted**.

Religion versus relationship

Rome versus Jerusalem

Darkness versus Light

Hell versus Heaven

6. Initially Mary was engaged to Joseph.

[17]"*And in the sixth month, the angel Gabriel was sent from God unto a city of Galilee named Nazareth. To a virgin espoused to a man whose name was Joseph.*"

The word 'espoused' is similar to our word 'engaged', yet was viewed as more binding.

7. Once she had given birth to Jesus, Mary married Joseph.

[18]"*Then Joseph being raised from sleep, did as the angel of the Lord had bidden him and took unto him his **wife**.*"

[19]"*And Jacob begat Joseph, the **husband** of Mary....*"

The weed people begin to shuffle and glance nervously around at this point.

What do most couples do once they are married? They consummate the marriage physically.

8. Mary and Joseph came together physically in the marriage relationship.

[20]"*And **knew her not**, **till** she had brought forth her firstborn son and he called His name Jesus.*"

The term **knew her not till** is very clear. The old King James English is translated more clearly elsewhere. "***But he had no intercourse with her till** she had brought forth her first born son.*"

Please do not be shocked. The same term is used in Genesis where [21]it says "*And Adam knew Eve his wife and she conceived.*"

9. As a result of the union between Joseph and Mary, at least six other children were born to them.

When Joseph and Mary and Jesus arrived back in their small town of Nazareth, everybody knew who they were and everything about them.

Have you ever lived in a small town? There are no secrets there. If Mr Brown is assaulting Mrs Brown, the whole town knows. It is known by the term 'bush telegraph'.

If a fire engine goes up the road, everybody in town with red-blood flowing through their veins, would wish to follow it. Let's read on and see what the Nazareth townspeople said.

[22]*"Is not this the carpenter's son? Is not his mother called Mary? and his brethren **James**, and **Joses**, and **Simon**, and **Judas**?"* These are the names of Jesus' four half-brothers.

Now for the next verse - *"And **his sisters**, are they not all with us?"* This means, to this point, we have now discovered the four boys' names.

Q. Do we know of any of the girls' names?

A. Yes. Let us look at Mark's view of the crucifixion.

[23] *"There were also looking on afar off, among whom was Mary Magdalene and Mary the mother of **James the less**, and **of Joses**, and **of Salome**."* Here are two of the boys mentioned once again and one of the sisters.

Notice not only is the second Mary mentioned here the mother of Jesus Himself, but also of his half brothers James, Joses and his half sister Salome.

Therefore, when Mary called the children for dinner, she called their names – **"Yeshua, James, Joses, Simon, Judas, Salome, bring your sister and come for dinner**."

What are the repercussions of this information?

a) Some weed religious leaders have been withholding this information from their flocks.

b) **Great News** – At last some Catholic scholars are reading their Bibles.

Christchurch 'Press', 22 December 1995 - *"Jesus not Mary's only child say Catholic scholars.*

...It is a portrait rooted in Christian teachings going back to the late third century, and backed since by the Catholic Church, which has held fast to the ancient doctrine declaring Jesus' mother a lifelong virgin, despite more than a half dozen references in the New Testament to Jesus' brothers and sisters.

Some Catholic scholars are gingerly voicing the view** – long held by Protestants – **that Mary had other children besides Jesus.

...But Catholicism has long declared that when the Gospels described Jesus' siblings or the Apostle Paul mentioned the "brothers of the Lord", the words, translated from the Greek, really meant "cousins" or "relatives".

Then, four years ago, in his presidential address to the Catholic Biblical Association, Father John P. Meier, told a meeting at Loyola Marymount University, that on historical grounds, "the most probable opinion is that the brothers and sisters of Jesus were His true siblings.

...In books published this year, three more American Catholic Biblical specialists have voiced agreement that Jesus had brothers and sisters.

"No linguistic evidence warrants our interpreting Gospel passages about Jesus' brothers and sisters as His cousins writes Notre Dame scholar, Jerome Neyrey, in the Harper Collins Encyclopaedia of Catholicism.

Neyrey says the original Greek word could not be interpreted as "cousin".

Catholic scholar Pheme Perkins, of Boston College, contends that calling Jesus' brothers cousins "is plain ridiculous".

...the Gospel of Mark, the oldest Gospel generally considered to have been written about 40 years after Jesus' death – which names four brothers and an unstated number of sisters.

...Luke Timothy Johnson, another Catholic scholar, finds compensating value in the image of Jesus as one of many children. "Certainly, if Jesus had brothers and sisters then the humanity of Jesus, and the motherhood of Mary takes on a richer resonance..."

...For the most part, Jesus' siblings are given no good reputation in the New Testament writings.

They are portrayed as sceptical non-believers during Jesus' lifetime. ("For not even His brothers believed in Him," comments the Gospel of John.)

Johnson suggests..."To state that this is what the language says, does not mean one is undertaking a challenge to church doctrine. Nothing critical or essential to Christian faith rests on this point...." End quote. (Emphasis added.)

Actually, Mr Johnson is not strictly correct here. These facts undermine a basic doctrine that Mary is still a virgin. As she has given birth to at least seven children, let us not continue to stretch our faith beyond the point of common-sense.

We looked all this up from the original Greek text and found the following in literal translation.

"*To be being astonished them and to be saying which place to this one the wisdom this and the abilities no this is other of the artisan son not the mother of him is being said Mariam and the brothers of him Jacobus and Joseph and Simon and Judas and the sisters of him not all toward us*." End quote.

The word in Greek for brethren is "adelphos". The weed people need to take note that a key word derived from adelphos is that word '**delphus**' which means "**from the womb**".

Thus, the same womb that brought forth Jesus is the same womb which brought forth the other children named above.

Further proof please.

Even when Jesus was dead, buried and about to rise again on the third day, let's see what Mark tells us in his gospel. Notice, as Jesus has left the scene, His name is missing, but some of the other children are mentioned.

[24]"*And when the sabbath was past, Mary Magdalene and* **Mary the mother of James and Salome** *had bought sweet spices that they might come and anoint Him*."

What have we now learned?

Mary ceased to be a virgin after the birth of Jesus!

She then proceeded to bear at least six other children.

A lady seated on the floor during our Dublin meeting called out "**Mr Smith, if Mary is no longer a virgin, what about all these so-called appearances at such spots as Madjagore – Lourdes – Fatima** – etc etc?"

Get ready to run from the meeting non-thinking weed people.

a) **These are all demon spirits posing as a person who does not exist**. She only exists in the minds of the millions who have been deceived by Satan and his ministers of religion who should know better.

[25]"*And no marvel, for Satan himself is transformed into an angel of light.*

Therefore it is no great thing if his ministers also be transformed as ministers of righteousness, whose end shall be according to their works."

I speak gently to all religious weed people, who have to this point been thus deceived.

God loves you. Reserve your anger towards those who so cruelly hid this information from you.

[26]"*Vengeance is mine. I will repay saith the Lord.*"

I'm sorry, but that's not all.

Not once does the Bible record Jesus calling Mary 'mother'

Example 1 – Do you remember as Jesus and His family were returning from the feast in Jerusalem? He was 12 years of age, when He went missing for three days. Joseph and Mary were distraught. Who wouldn't be?

[27]She said "*Son, why hast thou thus dealt with us? Behold thy father and I have sought thee sorrowing.*"

Jesus' reply according to our way of thinking should have sounded like this. "*Mother*, I am very upset at the grief I have cause you both. Please accept my humble apologies and I assure you that this inconsiderate type of behaviour will never re-occur."

[28]Now – what did He actually say? "*How is it that you sought me? Wist ye not that I must be about my Father's business?*"

Meaning – "Why did you bother looking for me? I'm 12 years of age now. My Bar Mitzvah is coming up when I will then be recognised as having manly responsibilities. You've done your job well Mary but now leave me alone to fulfil my true mission to earth. You no longer have any part to play in that mission."

Example 2 – A wedding was held at Cana in Galilee. Jesus was there with Mary and His disciples. They ran out of wine, and made the mistake of going to Mary instead of Jesus for help.

[29]Mary went to Jesus and said "*They have no wine*".

Jesus' reply according to our way of thinking should have sounded like this – "Mother, you have come to the right person. Because I am the Word of God, veiled in human flesh, miracles such as this will prove to be no problem at all."

Now – what did He actually say?

[30]"*Woman, what have I to do with thee? Mine hour is not yet come.*"

Meaning – "Mary, what gives you any more right than anybody else to make such a request of me. The governor of the feast could just as well have asked me himself. Don't take it upon yourself to try and direct Me. It is not yet time for me to act publicly."

Example 3 – Jesus is speaking at a public meeting when He was told His mother and brethren were outside, apparently wishing to pass on an urgent message.

Jesus' reply, according to our way of thinking, should have been like this. "Excuse me ladies and gentlemen, an urgent personal matter has arisen. Song leader, would you please lead the folk in a few choruses until I return. I won't be a moment."

Now - what did He actually say?

[31]*"Who is my mother? and who are my brethren? And He stretched forth His hand toward His disciples, and said "Behold my mother and my brethren. For whosoever shall do the will of my Father which is in heaven, the same is my brother and sister and mother."*

If Mary didn't get the message at Cana, she certainly got it this time.

No favouritism. It was not a case of "who you know". There were no advantages at all for Mary, save the beautiful memory of the past blessings.

Jesus' blood saved Mary just as it saves others who put their trust in Him.

<u>Example 4</u> – Get excited everybody. Jesus is about to use the word mother at last, but not in the way we may suppose.

Here, we find our Saviour, the Lord Jesus, hanging on the cross, shedding His precious blood for our sins. He is obviously still very clear and lucid in His thinking.

What a wonderful opportunity to express His thanks to this woman who brought Him into the world.

According to our thinking, what should Jesus have said?

"<u>Mother</u>, as you can see, I have reached the culmination of my earthly mission. Before I die, however, I want to say a very heartfelt 'thank you' to you, my mother.

You carried me for nine months and put up with the discomfort of a pregnancy. Not only that but also the snide remarks of people who saw you as an unmarried mother. When I was a little baby, you cared for me, suckled me and loved me. During my schooldays, as a young lad, I would come home hurt and crying, and you were always there for me.

You cut my lunch and cooked lovely meals. As a family, we were blessed having a mother like you. Goodbye, my dear mother, and thank you again."

Now - what did He actually say?

[32]*"When Jesus therefore saw His mother, and the disciple standing by whom He loved (obviously John - the beloved disciple) He saith unto His mother "**Woman**, behold thy son."*

*Then saith He to the disciple, "Behold **thy mother**" and from that hour, that disciple took her unto his own home."*

When a person moves into a born-again relationship with Jesus, fellow believers often become more close to them than to non-born-again relatives. As Jesus' earthly family didn't believe in Him, He handed Mary over to John, His beloved disciple.

Meaning – "Mary, without being cruel or rude, I have tried to point out very clearly to you, that you were originally chosen by God to be the woman who would bring me into the world to fulfil my divine mission of salvation. **I am God's chosen Lamb Mary. You are not. I am God's way of salvation Mary. You are not**.

Even our former close relationship does not in any way give you any more clout or rights with my Father or myself than any other human being.

You've done your job. I didn't call you mother, so that you would understand clearly that you no longer have any part in God's plan of salvation.

Mary, the time will come, when wicked, religious men, will deceive their millions of followers and tell them that you have special favour with God. They will even pray to you and make statues to you, which they will kiss and venerate but **as they die, they will cry out in anguish knowing that at that point they have been taught a lie**.

In the last days, to keep the lie going, demons will appear in mystical form claiming to be the Blessed Virgin Mary.

As we both know Mary, and you do not need an obstetrician to understand this, that **once a woman has had a child, she is no longer a virgin**.

Now Mary, you have borne at least seven of us, and although you are still blessed of God with that lovely memory, my precious blood will ultimately take care of your sin problem.

Go home with John and be a real mother to him."

Ladies, be careful of deception.

Even when Jesus was on earth, there were mixed up women around, just like the ones who attend our meetings and lead their weak husbands out with a show of great indignation, just as we are explaining these important matters.

Some of these husbands would be well-advised to express their role as the head of the family and whisper "**Would you please sit down and listen to some Biblical common sense. We have been deceived long enough**."

[33]"*And it came to pass as He spoke these things, a certain woman of the company lifted up her voice and said unto Him, "Blessed is the womb that bore Thee and the paps which thou hast sucked.*"

These women were even around in the early days. Listen to Jesus' answer, which included a very gracious rebuke.

[34]"*Yea, rather blessed are they which hear the Word of God and keep it.*"

Many of the weed religious people today have never learned this fact, that, **the Bible – not tradition, is the authority**.

If you are prepared to trust your everlasting future to some tradition let it be clearly known that you are obviously not a clear thinker.

Wherein lies the final authority? Read slowly – don't skip over this statement.

[35]"*And if any man hear my words, and believe not, I judge him not, for I came not to judge the world, but to save the world.*
He that rejecteth Me, and receiveth not My words, hath One that judgeth him, the Word that I have spoken, the same shall judge him in the last day."

Good news – Jesus won't judge us.

Bad news – the Word of God (the Bible) will.

Not tradition then – the Word of God!
Read it. Do your soul a favour!

Footnotes

1   Hebrews 9:22b; The Holy Bible
2   Genesis 22:6; The Holy Bible
3   Isaiah 7:14; The Holy Bible
4   Luke 1:28; The Holy Bible
5   Luke 1:46-57; The Holy Bible
6   Leviticus 12:6; The Holy Bible
7   Luke 2:22-24; The Holy Bible
8   Hebrews 10:5: The Holy Bible
9   Hebrews 17:14; The Holy Bible
10 Hebrews 5:8; The Holy Bible
11 Hebrews 4:15; The Holy Bible
12 Luke 23:4; The Holy Bible
13 Luke 1:31; The Holy Bible
14 John 1:14; The Holy Bible
15 1 John 1:9; The Holy Bible
16 1 John 1:7; The Holy Bible
17 Luke 1:26-27a; The Holy Bible
18 Matthew 1:24; The Holy Bible
19 Matthew 1:16; The Holy Bible

20 Matthew 1:25; The Holy Bible
21 Genesis 4:1a; The Holy Bible
22 Matthew 13:55-56a; The Holy Bible
23 Mark 15:40; The Holy Bible
24 Mark 16:1
25 II Corinthians 11:14-15; The Holy Bible
26 Romans 12:19b; The Holy Bible
27 Luke 2:48b; The Holy Bible
28 Luke 2:49; The Holy Bible
29 John 2:26; The Holy Bible
30 John 2:4; The Holy Bible
31 Matthew 12:46-50; The Holy Bible
32 John 19:26-27; The Holy Bible
33 Luke 11:27; The Holy Bible
34 Luke 11:28; The Holy Bible
35 John 12:47-48; The Holy Bible

Predictions

As a result of reading this chapter, there will be a lot of angry words spoken and written. However, once the surgeon cuts the boil open, the poison and pus spew forth.

Many will ultimately give thanks and turn to our Lord Jesus Christ for His gift of full salvation.

CHAPTER THIRTY-FOUR

DEATH – THE ULTIMATE EXPERIENCE?

Why did we put a question mark at the end of this statement?

Answer – because **"salvation" through the precious blood of the Lord Jesus Christ is the ultimate experience!**

What thoughts go through the tortured mind of one about to die, without understanding all about what lies on the other side.

From the ledge of a tall sky-scraper;

From a hospital bed, with family all around;

Lying bleeding in an open field with shells flying overhead;

On the railing of a bridge;

Sitting petrified as your plane goes into a steep dive;

Sitting in the gas chamber of a U.S. prison;

Lying with your body broken, on a ledge in a forgotten ravine...

Here are some notable last words:

a) Voltaire – a godless philosopher who died in 1778 – *"In the name of God, let me die in peace."* He then looked at a lamp flaring up alongside him and exclaimed, *"The flames already"*.

b) Francis Newport – a militant atheist who died in 1692 – *"Oh, the insufferable pangs of hell and damnation"*.

c) William Pope – he led an atheistic cult, at whose meetings a Bible was ritually kicked around the floor. He died in 1797 -*"I have done the damnable deed. The horrible damnable deed. I cannot pray, God will have nothing to do with me. I will not have salvation at His hands. I long to be in the bottomless pit, the lake which burneth with fire and brimstone. I tell you I am damned. I will not have salvation. Nothing for me but hell. Come eternal torments. Oh God, do not hear my prayers for I will not be saved. I hate everything that God has made"*.

d) Thomas Scott (who died in 1887) talking to a priest – *"Begone, you and your trumpery. Until this moment, I believed there was neither a God or a hell. Now I know and feel that there are both and that I am doomed to perdition by the just judgement of the Almighty"*.

e) Tony Hancock – British comedian who over-dosed in 1968. In 1964, prior to his death, he did a t.v. monologue which later on

[1]could be called his obituary as the Bible says *"For out of the abundance of the heart, the mouth speaketh"* - *"What have you achieved? What have you achieved? You lost your chance me old son. You contributed absolutely nothing to this life. A waste of time you being here at all. No place for you in Westminster Abbey. The best you can expect is a few daffodils in a jam-jar, a rough hewn stone bearing the legend, "He came, and he went, and in between, nothing*.

Nobody will even notice you're not here. After about a year afterwards, somebody might say down at the pub, "Where's old Hancock? I haven't seen him around lately."

"Oh, he's dead you know".

"Oh, is he?.....Nobody will ever know I existed. Nothing to leave behind me. Nothing to pass on. Nobody to mourn me. That's the bitterest blow of all".

The Blood of Jesus makes the difference

Note the contrast!

f) Anthony N. Groves – a missionary who died in 1853. He wrote to his son – *"Now, my precious boy, I am dying. Be a comfort to your beloved mother, as you dear brothers Henry and Frank have been to me.*

And may the Lord Himself bless you and make you His own.

May the Lord give you the peace and joy in Himself that He has given me, for these are true riches.

What would thousands of gold and silver be to me now?

Now, I give you a father's blessing." (Emphasis added.)

g) James Kent – an American jurist who died in 1847 – *"Go, my children. My object in telling you this is that if anything happens to me, you might know, and perhaps it would console you to remember, that on this point my mind is clear.*

I rest my hopes of salvation on the Lord Jesus Christ".

Q. How can the reader know that we are speaking the truth?

A. You will. **The moment you breathe your last breath, you will know very clearly**.

You will see the Lord Jesus Christ portrayed as a Lamb.

[2]Remember, *"God will provide Himself a Lamb"*.

Hey, don't you dare die without this Lamb!

[3]*"For there is none other name under heaven given amongst men whereby we must be saved."*

251

Q. Which name?

A. **His Name is Jesus**!

The Death Experience

You give a little gasp and your spirit leaves the body on the breath. Nothing matters now.

Your managerial position - don't worry, someone else is already sitting in your seat.

The halls of Parliament, the millions of empty words and jibes; the cut and thrust of politics; the back stabbing, just to keep your job - your seat is already filled.

Your position at the university. No longer do you have to put up with that horrible little group of born again Christian students who keep asking those niggly questions that seem to turn your philosophic views into matters for ridicule.

The dark passage is silent now. You are lonely. No friends to encourage. No other sceptics like yourself to titter at your clever witticisms. Just you in this particular tunnel. It is, you will notice, all downhill.

But wait - who is that dark figure that comes alongside? What a horrible leering expression on his diabolical face. What's he saying? "Come with me to your final destiny – fool. You missed the Lamb and His blood."

Look up for a moment now, and observe with your own eyes what you have just missed. That place is called 'Paradise'.

[4]Remember what Jesus said – "*I go to prepare a place for you...*" but of course you knew best – fool.

Come, the fire is waiting.

Your excuse is that you didn't read the text book. Really? How sad! You can spend **forever** wondering why not.

The Scene Changes

The family gathers around his bed, as suddenly, against all odds, in his final moment, he sits up, a supernatural strength comes upon him, as his eyes light up. He exclaims, "They've come for me. The room is full of them, can't you see them?"

His wife quietly answers, "Who are you talking about my dear? Who is here?"

[5]"*The angels of course*". ("*Are they not all ministering spirits, sent forth to minister for them who shall be heirs of salvation.*")

He slips silently from his body, like a hand from a glove.

From a vantage point somewhere up by the ceiling, he looks down and sees the medical staff pull the sheet over that body that a few minutes ago had been his home for 75 years. He observes the family hugging, praying, some even singing a few words of an old familiar hymn – "*It is well with my soul*".

He moves now into the dark valley with a little trepidation. He has never been this way before. He feels somebody next to him in the darkness and upon reaching up and taking this Person's hand, he instinctively knows that all is going to be well from here on.

He then hears a familiar passage of Scripture being read, which now seems to make more sense than it ever has before.

[6]"*Yea, though I walk through the valley of the shadow of death, I will fear no evil: for thou art with me; thy rod and thy staff they comfort me.*"

At last, the two of them reach the end of the valley. There is a river flowing vast and wide. People, real people, dressed in white await him on the far shore. They beckon from their grassy vantage points as he looks up into the face of the most wonderful Person he has ever seen or ever hoped to see.

There are a number of unusual features about this man. He has wounds all over His body.

[7]"*And one shall say unto Him. What are these wounds in thine hands? Then He shall answer, Those with which I was wounded in the house of my friends.*"

"Who are you, Sir?"

"*Fear not. I am the first and the last. I am He that liveth and was dead and behold I am alive for evermore, Amen, and have the keys of hades and death.*" Look up my son!

Suddenly, the scene is so splendid and outstanding that all earthly memories pale into insignificance by comparison.

[9]"*...Eye hath not seen, nor ear heard, neither have entered into the heart of man, the things which God hath prepared for them that love Him.*"

This is reality.

What stops people being saved?

1. Crazy, godless parents with so little intellect still operating, they neglect to prepare themselves or their children for the future.

¹⁰"*And ye fathers, provoke not your children to wrath, but bring them up in the nurture and admonition of the Lord.*"

2. Someone who laughs or mocks at a child who is looking for God.

¹¹"*But whoso shall offend one of these little ones which believe in me, it were better for him that a millstone be hanged about his neck, and that he were drowned in the depths of the sea.*"

The Lord has ample millstones waiting, ready to use.

3. Fear of man.

¹²"*Who are thou, that thou shouldst be afraid of a man that shall die?*"

In simple English, the person that you are afraid will mock you if you give your life to the Lord Jesus Christ, will one day die. So will you.

Q. **Where will he/she finish up?**
    Where will you finish up?

4. Pride. Science tells us that each person's body is built of the fourteen elements found in the dust of the earth.

¹³"*Let not any man think more highly of himself than he ought*".

¹⁴"*God resisteth the proud but giveth grace to the humble.*"

Remember, anything that you are good at is a gift from God.

¹⁵"*For who maketh thee to differ from another and what hast thou that thou didst not receive?*"

Facts remain facts, and this life is obviously not the main act – it is only a dressing room for the next.

A little boy in the U.S.A. won a prize on a t.v. programme entitled, "Why I like your programme the best."

His entry read, "**I like your programme the best, because when it is finished, something better comes on.**"

Life's Purpose

In year 1995, we visited a number of African nations on a lecture tour.

One evening, some businessmen put on a dinner party to which members of the diplomatic corps and important businessmen were invited.

The President of Kenya, Daniel Arap Moi, sat on a raised platform with us, and after dinner, I spoke on these subjects to the gathered assembly.

Nearing the end of my talk, I asked a question which apparently too few ask before it is too late. "Why are we here? What is life's purpose? God alone knows the answer to this question and He puts it in a short, pithy, answer."

[16]*"Thou art worthy O Lord, to receive glory and honour and power. For thou hast created all things **and for thy pleasure, they are and were created**."*

You do not need to be a philosopher to discover the great joy and satisfaction genuine men and women derive from watching their children growing up, and learning the ways of life.

What a tragedy to go through life without having the pleasure of meeting on a very personal level, your Heavenly Father.

[17]No wonder Jesus said, "***You must be born again***." This is a spiritual birth.

A dear friend of mine put it like this – "**If you're born once, you'll die twice. If you are born twice, you'll die once**."

Think about it. God has no time for lukewarm attitudes. It is either **hot** or **cold**!

[18]*"I know thy works, that thou art neither cold nor hot. So then, because thou art lukewarm and neither cold nor hot, I will spue thee out of my mouth."*

A True Story

During the early 1990's, we conducted a speaking tour throughout the country of South Africa.

One night as we concluded the address, as is our custom, an invitation was given for folk to come to the front of the hall and publicly commit their lives to Jesus Christ, and make Him Lord and Saviour of their lives.

We have discovered that **this public stand is invaluable** as it makes clear to all that the person making the public confession of Christ means business.

Jesus put it this way –

[19]*"Whosoever therefore shall **confess me before men**, him will I confess also before my Father which is in heaven.*

*But whosoever shall **deny me before men**, him will I also deny before my Father which is in heaven."*

That night, in East London, around the coast from Durban, a young farming couple were in attendance. They had travelled over 100 miles to the meeting, and at the conclusion, climbed back into their car for their return home.

The story was narrated to us as follows.

Very little was spoken for the first part of the journey and then she said "I should have gone forward tonight and given my life publicly to Jesus." He replied, "So should I. When Mr Smith read the verse about being hot or cold, that spoke to me very strongly." She then told her husband that the very same Bible verses spoke to her.

[19a]"*So then because thou art **lukewarm**, and neither cold nor hot, I will spue thee out of my mouth.*"

Apparently, both of them were waiting for the other to make the first move.

Arriving home that night, absolutely worn out, she took a bath and called out to the kitchen for her husband to make her a hot drink of chocolate.

He put two cups on the bench, boiled the jug, made himself a cup of tea, and a cup of hot chocolate for his wife.

Upon handing it to her in the bath, she cried out "What an evil trick to play on me at this time of night. This chocolate is freezing cold!" Mystified, they felt both cups, which had been filled with hot water from the same jug, and came to the very quick realisation that Almighty God Himself had intervened in their lives, and that it was high time to make a firm decision for Jesus Christ.

They travelled all that way back the following night and when the invitation was given once again at the conclusion of the service to confess Jesus Christ as personal Lord and Saviour, **who do you think were two of the first to walk down the aisle hand in hand**?

The challenge is clear. If God in Heaven put so much value on human souls as to reveal Himself miraculously to the two people living in the back of beyond in South Africa, be sure He knows your address as well.

Your firm choice for or against Jesus Christ is what makes the difference.

Tell me! Are you seriously prepared to miss an eternity of joy, satisfaction, fellowship and communion with Almighty God and His Son, Jesus, for five cents worth of fame, fortune, and popularity, including eternity, forever and ever, in the lake of fire.

[20]"*For what shall it profit a man if he shall gain the whole world and lose his own soul*".

The Lord has far better plans for your life than you could ever dream up for yourself. He wants to make a new person of you.

Will you let Him?

If so, pray the prayer at the back of this book and begin a fantastic adventure which goes on forever.

[21]*"Therefore, if any man be in Christ, he is a new creature. Old things are passed away and behold all things are become new."*

Finally a little quote from Madam Guyon – "***Why do the old leaves fall off a tree? To make room for the new ones.***"

Footnotes

1	Matthew 12:34b; The Holy Bible
2	Genesis 22:8a; The Holy Bible
3	Acts 4:12b; The Holy Bible
4	John 14:2b; The Holy Bible
5	Hebrews 1:14; The Holy Bible
6	Psalm 23:4; The Holy Bible
7	Zechariah 13:6; The Holy Bible
8	Revelation 1:18; The Holy Bible
9	1 Corinthians 2:9; The Holy Bible
10	Ephesians 6:4; The Holy Bible
11	Matthew 18:3; The Holy Bible
12	Isaiah 51:12b; The Holy Bible
13	Romans 12:3b; The Holy Bible
14	James 4:6b; The Holy Bible
15	1 Corinthians 4:7a; The Holy Bible
16	Revelation 4:11; The Holy Bible
17	John 3:3; The Holy Bible
18	Revelation 3:15-16; The Holy Bible
19	Matthew 10:32-33; The Holy Bible
19a	Revelation 3:16
20	Mark 8:36; The Holy Bible
21	II Corinthians 5:17; The Holy Bible

Prediction

If the Lord gives you time to prepare for death, you will be so relieved that you made this most vital of all choices.

PERPETUAL SACRIFICE

CHAPTER THIRTY-FIVE

THE CROSS

We left the Upper Room and strolled down the dark alleyways in Old Jerusalem.

Ali, a young lad who was a member of our tour party, ran up to me and with great excitement, showed me about half a dozen crucifixes that he had bought from an Arab hawker.

"I'm taking these back to Australia to give to my friend, Uncle Barry", he explained.

"No, Ali", I replied gently. "Take them back to the man and ask for empty crosses. It is most important that you do what I say."

A few minutes later, he returned with the empty crosses and I marvelled that the Arab trader had been so obliging, and so quickly too.

Later, Ali's parents, our friends, Paul and Michelle Randall, told us with a smile how Ali had pulled the figures off each cross and thrown them away.

Some readers may find themselves horrified at this story, that they feel to stop reading at this point. Please don't. This is most important information.

Crucifixes or Crosses

Travelling the world, tends to broaden one's mind, and many questions are generated by continually observing new places and things.

My question was this. "Why do some churches insist on leaving a figure hanging on the cross?"

a) e.g. Orthodox Russian
   Orthodox Greek
   Orthodox Yugoslavian
   Roman Catholics
   High Anglican
   Lutheran (in some cases)

b) The majority of others seem quite satisfied with the religious symbol of an empty cross.

A Special Message For Crucifix People

Over 90% of people who attend these churches have never ever

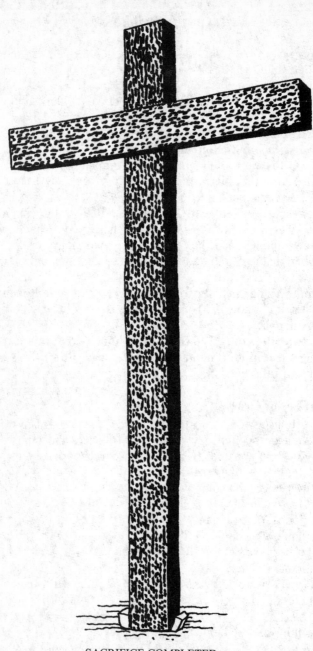

SACRIFICE COMPLETED

260

been told the reason that the figure of Christ's body remains nailed to the cross.

Some years ago, I wrote a book called 'Second Warning'. The quote of a statement made by the then Archbishop of Hartford will assist us with our understanding. We quote again herewith in part only.

1) *"Sacrifice is the very essence of religion...*
2) *It is only through sacrifice that union with the creator can be perfectly acquired....*
3) *It is only through perpetuation of that sacrifice that this union may be maintained...*
4) *Thus the Mass is the same as the sacrifice of the cross...*
5) *Christ is forever offering Himself in the Mass...."*

Shocked, surprised, disgusted, angry?

It makes no difference really.

That's what they believe, but rarely do they ever inform the people.

On and on, like lost sheep, the dear people pass these statues and **no-one ever seems to ask the question "Why is Jesus still hanging on the cross?"**

Some irate readers are by now getting ready to throw my book in the fire.

We received a letter from a man in Australia, who became so angry, he did just that, then in a fit of remorse, rescued the book, beat out the flames, continued reading, asked Jesus into his life, and got **out of religion, into relationship**.

"Do you have any further proof?" I hear you ask.

Yes indeed. From a recent book on doctrine entitled "**The Holy Sacrifice of the Mass**", we read:

a) Jesus is still with us in the Holy Eucharist
b) The Mass is the same sacrifice as the sacrifice of the cross
c) Jesus offers Himself again to His Heavenly Father, but in an unbloody way in the sacrifice of the Mass.

This makes me cry out in horror, shock and disbelief.

Thank the Lord. Praise Him for giving us His written Word. It is called 'The Bible'.

The Bible

This is the only Book in the world that answers these three questions **with authority**.

a) Where did we come from?

b) What are we doing here?

c) Where are we going to?

If any reader can point me to any other book with similar authority, please let me know. The future of my soul depends on my getting the foundation right.

Get Angry

After reading what you have just read, you have the Lord's permission to express some anger.

[1]*"Be ye angry and sin not"*.

If I had been brought up from my early childhood in a church with a crucifix not only prominently displayed, but on occasions, even kissed and reverenced, I would be excessively enraged at this point.

I would direct my rage on the leaders in my church who gave me this lying, weird, explanation of its true meaning.

a) Pick up your telephone, and make an appointment with your church leaders. **Go as a group**, as you are dealing with very skilled and clever people.

If you do not wish to talk to them, write a letter asking the following questions:

1) "Why are you playing games with my soul?

2) Do you have a Bible?

3) Do you speak and understand the English language?

4) Do you realise that Jesus made this statement? *"Let them [2]alone. They be blind leaders of the blind. And if the blind lead the blind, both shall fall into the ditch."*

5) I trusted you all these years to give me my spiritual instruction that would fit me for Heaven.

6) Instead, you have led me away from God's plan for my salvation and am preparing me for an eternity in Hell.

7) What is wrong with you? If you spent less time watching television, drinking and smoking and being "one of the boys", you may find an odd moment or two to **read the book of Hebrews, which is found in the Bible.** I suggest you arm yourself with a pen and underline the relevant passages.

8) If it weren't for the love and the grace of God in my heart, I would now be calling you unmentionable names – you religious fraud.

God's Beautiful Plan

My daughter, Becky, once asked me the question "**Dad, why was Jesus so hard on the religious leaders of His day?**"

I replied, "Becky, if you were God and had devised a fantastic plan to bring your created people to Heaven, wouldn't you become extremely angry and upset if some **upstart** came along and changed the plan? The thing which really upsets God is that His plan involved the death of His dear Son, and the shedding of His precious blood."

The story is told of a man who dreamed he was observing the horrors of Hell, sometimes called the Lake of Fire.

He saw another man searching the area at a frantic pace. He saw human beings rising and falling in the flames and this man picking the others up by the hair, turning their faces towards him, then with a cry of despair, dropping them back into the billows of the Lake of Fire.

He asked, "What are you looking for, Sir?"

The man replied, "**I am searching for the preacher who brought me to this dreadful place!**"

It is Finished

When Jesus said these words from the cross, He wasn't joking. He didn't mean that it was half-finished, but that the work to get us to heaven was fully completed.

Remember that Galatians 3:13 tells us, "Christ was made a curse for us." Anyone therefore, who worships a crucifix, worships a curse.

O.K. – Now for the book of Hebrews

Underline all these passages or circle them with a pen. (If you are using someone else's Bible, do not mark it.)

Hebrews 7:27 – "*Who needeth not daily as those high priests to offer up sacrifice, first for his own sins and then for the peoples, for this He did **once** when he offered up Himself.*"

Hebrews 9:12 – "***Neither by the blood of goats and calves, but by His own blood** He entered in **once** into the holy place, **having obtained eternal redemption for us**.*"

Hebrews 9:22 – "*And almost all things are by the law purged with blood; and **without shedding of blood is no remission**.*"

Hebrews 9:26 – "*For then must He often have suffered since the foundation of the world: but now **once** in the end of the world **hath He appeared to put away sin by the sacrifice of Himself**.*"

Hebrews 9:28 – "*So **Christ was once offered** to bear the sins of many; and unto them that look for Him shall He appear the second time without sin unto salvation.*"

Hebrews 10:10 – "*By the which will **we are sanctified through the offering of the body of Jesus Christ once** for al*l."

Hebrews 10:12 – "*But this Man, **after He had offered one sacrifice for sins for ever**, sat down on the right hand of God.*"

Hebrews 10:14 – "*For **by one offering** He hath perfected for ever them that are sanctified.*"

Here are 8 clear passages. Notice the very special blood comes into effect here and the key word is "**once**".

Why the Blood?

Often-times, we are asked this question and as I have just learned the answer, I will share it with you.

a) **The life of the flesh is in the blood**.
b) Our salvation relies on a **covenant, agreement, testament or will**, struck between God and the sinner. (In this case people like you and me.)
c) **A will is useless unless the person who made it dies**.
d) When Jesus died on the cross, and shed that very **special, precious, blood**, His testament or will came into operation from that very moment.

[3]No wonder, at the last supper He said, "***This cup is the new testament (will) in My blood which is shed for you.***"

[4]Now you can understand this – "*For where a testament (will) is, there must also **be the death of the testator**.*

For a testament (will) is of force, after men are dead, otherwise it is of no strength at all while the testator liveth."

This makes me very happy and secure. My soul is not saved through a lot of religious clap-trap, but there is a **divine covenant** in operation that requires only **that I**: trust – believe, adhere to, cling to, Christ and his finished work for me, and I am saved forever.

The Cross is now "empty"!
Look at it.

Billy Bray

Some years ago, we were holding lectures in Southern England. The area of Cornwall is very beautiful and one of the highlights of my experience was to be invited to speak in a little old church called the B.C.C. or Bible Christian Church.

I have in my library a book which was given to me from a friend in Truro, Cornwall, on the life of this outstanding preacher.

Originally, he was a hard-drinking, swearing, cursing, ruffian, who worked in the Cornish clay mines.

God's Choice

There must come a time in each person's life, when they sicken of their seemingly purposeless existence, and they hear a voice within say "**There has to be more to life than this**."

At such a stage in his life, Billy heard another converted man preach of a new life style, which was possible through personally understanding and accepting the **precious blood** of Christ, as his very own. For three days and nights, a terrible inward struggle took place and during that time, Billy wept and cried out that he was too much of a wretch to be saved.

On the fourth morning however, the realisation of true salvation hit him like a rock between the eyes.

He understood at last, because the Lord Himself gave him that understanding.

You, the reader, please find a quiet place. Just you alone with God. **Ask Him to show you the inward joy of saying goodbye to religion and hello to relationship**.

Pray like this.

Dear **Lord Jesus Christ**
   Please hear me as I:
a) **repent and turn away from all my past life.**
b) **I believe Lord Jesus that you are God's one and only Lamb.**
c) **Today, right now, I open the door to my life. I receive you now and will walk and talk with you until you call me home.**
   Thank you Jesus. I am Yours forever and You are mine.
   Amen.

[5]Read and understand this Bible promise. "*But as many as received Him, to them gave He power to become the sons of God, even to them that believe on His Name.*"

Billy Bray did just this, and became thoroughly born again.

If you are as sincere as he was, you will also, right at this moment, be thoroughly born again.

Billy Bray then became an enthusiastic disciple and preacher for our Lord Jesus Christ.

The book on his life is so exciting that you can feel the joy expressed as from then on, he became a real embarrassment to all the dry old religious people of his day.

Day and night as he travelled around England telling of this wonderful born again experience, it welled up within him, causing him to shout *"Hallelujah, praise the Lord – I'm saved through the precious blood of Jesus."*

When asked on occasions to be more subdued he would reply ***"I am so full of joy, you can lock me in a barrel to quieten me down, but I will shout 'Praise the Lord' through the bung-hole."***

Footnotes

1   Ephesians 4:26a; The Holy Bible
2   Matthew 15:14; The Holy Bible
3   Luke 22:20
4   Hebrews 9:16-17; The Holy Bible
5   John 1:12; The Holy Bible

Please write to us and tell us of your clear decision for Jesus Christ. Address your letters to:

Barry Smith
International Support Ministries – Pacific
Pelorus Bridge
Rai Valley
Marlborough
NEW ZEALAND

God bless you. We'll meet in Heaven.
Your friend
Barry R. Smith

Ph: (03) 571 6134
Fax: (03) 571 6135

To help you understand the main subjects in this book, we include herewith a glossary and explanation of helpful words and phrases.

GLOSSARY

Illuminati – The Enlightened Ones. A Luciferian cult with connections to top degrees in esoteric Freemasonry. Commenced in Bavaria in the year 1776.

The Rothschilds – The House of the Red Shield. A fabulously wealthy family with links to both Europe and the U.S.A.

Freemasonry – A men's fraternal society with religious overtones. The vast majority of its members are sincere persons who are completely unaware of its links with the occult world, and Luciferianism.

The U.S. Federal Reserve – A group of European and U.S. bankers who cleverly misled the citizens of the U.S. into handing over their monetary power, including the issuing of all U.S. currency, under the guise of being the official U.S. government agency.

Skull & Bones – A secret club of men, connected with Yale University. It has German origins and thus follows the ideas of German philosopher - Hegel.

The Order – Connected to the Skull and Bones Society. These men, upon leaving Yale University, continue on in the background of world affairs in the setting up of a Luciferian-led One World Government or a 'Global Village'.

The Council on Foreign Relations – A group of advisers to the President of the United States. Many of them are dedicated to the formation of a global government.

The Bilderbergers – The European counterpart of the CFR, many of whose members attend their annual meetings held under strict and tight security. The media and photographers are excluded.

The Tri-lateral Commission – A group set up by David Rockefeller and others to link Japan and Europe to the U.S.

The Club of Rome – A group who present massive problems to the world's people. These problems can only be solved through a united response.

The New World Order – Code for a world dictatorship where everything is controlled by Luciferian Illuminists who have the secret knowledge and know what is best for us all.

Internationalism – The gradual organised decay of 'independence' and 'sovereignty' making way for 'interdependence'.

United Nations – A formerly weak, laughable, group who meet regularly on Rockefeller donated land in New York. They have cleverly gained massive power over the nations by sending out many treaties and conventions to countries world-wide. Naive, unthinking politicians sign these documents and gradually yield power and sovereignty.

The U.S. Constitution – A document written with great care by America's Founding Fathers, to prevent this present scenario that is taking place in the U.S. at this very time.

Militia – A loosely knit group of patriotic Americans who understand much of what is taking place, and have armed themselves to take whatever steps are necessary to protect the U.S. Constitution.

Internet – An invisible monster that is taking over the world. This giant computer is not owned by any single organisation. A computer and a telephone make up a super highway which will ultimately be commandeered by the New World Order leaders.

Gun Laws (Control) – NRA – The National Rifle Association is fully aware of the treasonous efforts being undertaken to undermine the Right to Bear Arms Clause of the U.S. Constitution. This high profile group present a valid and viable voice in protecting the citizens' rights.

Their key argument is very clear and succinct i.e. "Is the "individual" or the "government" to be trusted more?" 'N.R.A. Journal', 23-27 April 1993.

BATF (Bureau of Alcohol, Tobacco & Firearms) – The U.S. Federal Agency that is purportedly there to see that the U.S. Constitution is upheld in regard to each of the areas listed. These people made up a large part of the group who attacked David Koresh and his group at Waco, Texas.

Luciferian – Satanic and evil. Its connections with the occult are numerous. Lucifer, a created being, who was expelled from heaven, now seeks readmission. He is now the god of this world – Satan/the devil. He will burn in hell forever!

Globalism – A term coined by advocates of a One World Government, ruling everybody's lives from the cradle to the grave.

National Sovereignty – A thing of the past as nations privatise, sell out assets to overseas buyers. Independence of course, goes out with the asset sales, and each nation becomes interdependent upon the other nations.

For a catalogue of other books and videos by Barry Smith, please write to:

International Support Ministries
Pelorus Bridge
Rai Valley 7156
NEW ZEALAND

Telephone: 64 (03) 571 6046
Facsimile: 64 (03) 571 6135